Formal Ethics

Harry J. Gensler

London and New York

First published 1996
by Routledge
11 New Fetter Lane, London EC4P 4EE

Simultaneously published in the USA and Canada
by Routledge
29 West 35th Street, New York, NY 10001

© 1996 Harry J. Gensler

Typeset in Times by the author
Printed and bound in Great Britain by
Clays Ltd, St Ives PLC.

British Library Cataloguing in Publication Data
A catalogue record for this book
is available from the British Library.

Library of Congress Cataloging in Publication Data
Gensler, Harry J., 1945–
Formal ethics/Harry J. Gensler
224 p. cm.
Includes bibliographical references and index.
1. Ethics. 2. Social ethics. I. Title.
BJ1012.G44 1996   95–38892
170–dc20 CIP

ISBN: 0–415–13065–4 (hbk)
ISBN: 0–415–13066–2 (pbk)

Contents

Preface   vii

1   What Is Formal Ethics?   1
   1.1   Formal Logical Principles   1
   1.2   Formal Ethical Principles   5
   1.3   The Plan of This Book   13

2   Logicality   15
   2.1   Conflicting Beliefs   15
   2.2   Consequences of Beliefs   17
   2.3   Qualified Consistency   19
   2.4   Conjunctivity   23
   2.5   Logicality Questions   25
   2.6   Why Be Consistent?   29
   2.7   Logic Bashing   35

3   Conscientiousness   40
   3.1   Accepting an Imperative   40
   3.2   A Rationality Axiom   44
   3.3   Ends and Means   46
   3.4   Ends–Means Questions   49
   3.5   Follow Your Conscience   52
   3.6   Conscientious Pacifism   55
   3.7   Why Be Conscientious?   56
   3.8   Conscientiousness Examples   60

4   Impartiality   69
   4.1   Universalizability   69
   4.2   Is Universalizability Useful?   71
   4.3   Why Be Impartial?   84
   4.4   Impartiality Examples   88

5   The Golden Rule   93

    5.1   A GR Theorem   93
    5.2   GR Misformulations   95
    5.3   GR Variations   101
    5.4   GR Questions   104

6   Universal Law   121

    6.1   Concern for Self and Future   121
    6.2   UL Theorems   123
    6.3   GR and UL Analogues   125
    6.4   Why Follow GR and UL?   131
    6.5   Universal Prescriptivism   134
    6.6   GR and UL Examples   143

7   Moral Rationality   149

    7.1   Rationality Conditions   149
    7.2   Rationality by Recursion   155
    7.3   Racism and Rationality   158
    7.4   Teaching Moral Rationality   165
    7.5   Aiding Other Theories   167
    7.6   Concluding Questions   171

8   Symbolic Logic   181

    8.1   Imperative Logic   181
    8.2   Deontic Logic   186
    8.3   Belief Logic   189
    8.4   Symbolizing Formal Ethics   190

Bibliography   198

Index   209

Preface

Formal ethics deals, not with tuxedos, but with formal ethical principles. More broadly, it studies rational patterns in our ethical thinking. Formal ethics was modeled on formal logic and inspired by the ethical theories of Richard Hare and Immanuel Kant.

The most important formal ethical principle, and perhaps the most important rule of life, is the golden rule: "Treat others as you want to be treated." The golden rule has wide support among the different cultures and religions of the world; but philosophers tend to neglect it. This book will give the rule the attention that it deserves.

The golden rule is part of a family of related formal principles. Here are some other family members:

- Be logically consistent in your beliefs.
- If you want to achieve an end, then carry out the necessary means.
- Follow your conscience.
- Practice what you preach.
- Make similar evaluations about similar cases.
- Don't act in a way that you'll later regret.
- Act only on a maxim that you could will to be a universal law.

These principles are important and useful. But we'll see that each one leads to absurdities if taken literally. Formal ethics will try to formulate these principles more clearly and adequately, organize them into a defensible system, and show how they can help us to think more rationally about morality.

Formal principles have a special role in morality – supplementing, rather than replacing, traditional ethical theories. I stay neutral on foundational questions. I don't claim that my formal principles are self-evident truths, empirical truths, or social conventions, nor that they only express feelings, imperatives, or a commitment to a way of life. Rather, I try to show how they can be defended from practically any foundational view. So I often relate them to traditional ethical theories and issues.

Since I pattern formal ethics after formal logic, I often appeal to logic. But I keep the technical parts isolated, so that the general reader can understand the main points.[1] My parallel between logic and ethics raises questions; logic seems hard (precise and uncontroversial) while ethics seems soft (vague and controversial). But I aim to show that the *formal* part of ethics is as hard as logic – and that formal ethical principles deserve the same wide acceptance that formal logical principles enjoy.

So my goal is to explain and defend some formal tools of moral reasoning (especially the golden rule) that can supplement and enhance virtually any approach to ethics.

Some thanks are in order. Richard Hare, Tom Carson, and Jeff Wattles read the manuscript and made good suggestions. Jeff also lent me his insightful manuscript on the golden rule (Wattles 1996); his historical-religious slant complements my logical-rational approach and helped to deepen my thinking. And the Quebec Nordik Express cargo ship (that I took for four days as part of a 4000-km bicycle trip) provided the solitude that inspired the concept of formal ethics.[2]

Harry J. Gensler
University of Scranton
Scranton, PA 18510 USA

[1] Those who want to read only parts of the book can find suggestions at the end of Chapter 1.

[2] *Formal Ethics* has a home page on the World Wide Web, featuring downloadable software and exercise modules to accompany the book; for information, see http://www.routledge.com/rcenters/philres/fe_main.html.

Chapter 1

What Is Formal Ethics?

The goal of moral philosophy is to help us to think better about morality. In pursuit of this goal, philosophers sometimes appeal to *formal* principles like "Follow your conscience," "Evaluate similar cases similarly," and "Treat others as you want to be treated." This book is about such principles.

Formal ethics is the study of formal ethical principles. It tries to formulate such principles clearly (and without absurd implications), organize them into a defensible system, and show how they can help us to think more rationally about morality.

Our first task is to clarify the distinction between ethical principles that are *formal* (like "Follow your conscience") and ones that are *material* (like "Don't steal"). Is there a clear distinction here? How can we draw the distinction? To answer these questions, I'll first explain the notion of a formal logical principle; then, by analogy, I'll explain the notion of a formal ethical principle.

1.1 Formal Logical Principles

Formal logic is the study of formal logical principles.

Philosophers have disputed this argument for many centuries:

> If God doesn't want to prevent evil, then he isn't all good.
> If God isn't able to prevent evil, then he isn't all powerful.
> Either God doesn't want to prevent evil, or he isn't able to.
> ∴ Either God isn't all good, or he isn't all powerful.

Practically every aspect of this argument is controversial: the plausibility and truth of each premise, the interpretation of key terms, the usefulness of arguing such matters, and so forth.

As far as I know, there's been no dispute over whether the conclusion follows from the premises, that is, whether the argument is *valid*. Rather, the dispute has focused on the premises. The validity is clear. If we had doubts about this, we could work it out (using the logical machinery from any logic text) – as we work out a multiplication problem to check the answer.

Our argument is valid because its *form* is correct. We can express its form by using variables, which are letters that abbreviate phrases. Here's the form in English and in symbols:

$$\begin{array}{ll}
\text{If W, then G.} & (W \supset G) \\
\text{If A, then P.} & (A \supset P) \\
\text{Either W or A.} & (W \vee A) \\
\therefore\ \text{Either G or P.} & \therefore\ (G \vee P)
\end{array}$$

These use statement variables (like "W" for "God doesn't want to prevent evil") and logical terms (like "if–then"). The result is a *formal logical principle* – a principle of inference expressible using only variables and logical terms. Formal logic studies such principles.

The variables and the logical terms change between systems. In propositional logic, the variables stand for statements and the logical terms are "if–then," "and," "or," "if and only if," and "not." With syllogisms, the letters stand for general terms and the logical terms are "all," "no," "some," "is," and "not." Quantificational, modal, and deontic logic bring more changes.

Formal logical principles are correct (valid) or incorrect (invalid). Most beginners at logic are poor at distinguishing the two;[1] but the experts largely agree. We can generally show incorrect principles to have clearly absurd instances. Consider the fallacy of affirming the consequent (on the left):

$$\begin{array}{ll}
\text{If A then B.} & \text{If I'm in Texas, then I'm in the US.} \\
\text{B.} & \text{I'm in the US.} \\
\therefore\ \text{A.} & \therefore\ \text{I'm in Texas.}
\end{array}$$

This principle is wrong, since it lets us infer false conclusions from true premises – as on the right. Here both premises are true; but the conclusion is false, since I'm in Chicago. So we reject the fallacy as leading to absurdities.[2]

---

[1] I give a logic pretest on the first day of my introductory logic course. The problems are easy, but my students get almost half wrong. The pretest is in my introductory logic textbook (Gensler 1989: 2–5).

[2] The fallacy also lets us prove self-contradictions from true premises:

If 2=2 and 2≠2, then 2=2. (A truth of logic.)

2=2. (A truth of logic.)

∴ 2=2 and 2≠2. (This follows using the fallacious principle.)

The appeal to concrete instances generally shows whether a logical principle is correct. We test a principle by trying to demolish it, and reject it if we find absurd instances. We accept it (at first tentatively) if we look hard and find only acceptable instances. We may later develop further methods to check validity.

Philosophers of virtually all viewpoints accept roughly the same principles of logic.[1] These philosophers may use wildly different premises and conclusions; but disputes over validity – whether the conclusion follows from the premises – are rare.

A few logical principles are disputed. Logicians differ, for example, on the validity of this inference:

> It's possible that it's possible that A. $\Diamond\Diamond A$
> ∴ It's possible that A. ∴ $\Diamond A$

Other logical disputes deal with the law of the excluded middle; classical logic versus intuitionist and multi-value logic; standard quantification versus free logic; conflicting modal systems (especially T, B, S4, and S5); and the Barcan modal formulas.

These disputes have little impact on philosophical arguments. I counted 178 such arguments (most from actual philosophers) in my *Symbolic Logic* textbook (Gensler 1990). Only five of them (3 per cent of the total) depend for their validity on controversial principles.[2] Disputes over logic seldom make a difference to the validity of our arguments.

---

[1] Occasionally you find exceptions – people who deny the law of noncontradiction, for example. I suspect that such people don't understand the principles that they're denying (see Section 2.3), and that they accept in their lives what they deny in their theories (see Section 2.7).

[2] I counted 74 propositional, 49 quantificational, and 55 modal arguments. My sample isn't random, since when I wrote *Symbolic Logic* I consciously searched for arguments whose validity is disputed.

One disputed argument, by Kant on the ontological argument (*Symbolic Logic*, #12 on page 111), presumes that "all A is B" entails "some As exist" (accepted in traditional logic but usually rejected today). The other disputed arguments were modal – ontological arguments by Hartshorne and Plantinga (#0 on page 172 and #14 on page 181) and attacks on reductive views of modality (#4 and #5 on page 173). In this book, I won't use disputed modal principles but only ones that are common to the major systems (T, B, S4, and S5). There also are disputes about intuitionist logic that relate to realism (see Williamson 1982) and disputes about dialethic logic that relate to the liar paradox (see Smiley and Priest 1993).

Many of these disputes may be resolvable, since different logical rules may fit different senses of terms. For example, "all A is B" entails "some As exist" if we take the former to mean "$((x)(Ax \supset Bx) \cdot (\exists x)Ax)$" instead of "$(x)(Ax \supset Bx)$." A person's argument should be taken to be sound if it's sound on the most favorable way of taking the terms.

Disagreements intensify when we ask about the meaning and justification of logical principles:

- Is logic about sentences or about abstract entities like propositions? What kinds of things are true or false? What is truth?
- What does *valid* mean? Does it mean that it's logically impossible for the premises to be true while the conclusion is false? Does logical impossibility make sense?
- What is the scope of logic? Does logic include set theory? Is there a "logic" of imperatives only in an extended sense?
- How are the basic principles of logic to be justified? Do they express metaphysical truths about reality? Or language conventions? Or self-evident *a priori* truths? Or empirical truths?

Such issues fall, not under logic, but under philosophy of logic.

The ultimate basis of anything – even logic – is controversial. What is the meaning and justification of my claim that this is a pencil? That there are other conscious beings? That there's a God? That Hitler acted wrongly? That 5+7=12? That our basic logical principles are valid? Such questions raise endless battles. Even logic isn't exempt from disputes over foundations.

"Foundations" suggests the image of a basement that needs to be built before the rest of the building. Until we build the foundation, we can't do logic or ethics (or math, or science, or religion). A different image is that we already live in the building, find it secure, and needn't worry about what supports it. Foundational questions are unhelpful speculations.

Both images are misleading. Foundational questions influence practice and are important in their own right (since the unexamined life isn't worth living), but they're highly speculative. We can do logic or ethics without resolving the foundational issues; but we could probably do them better if we resolved the issues.

To sum up:

- Formal logical principles are largely uncontroversial. We can test such principles by searching for absurd instances.
- We have to fudge the previous statement somewhat, since there are genuine disputes over formal logical principles. But these disputes touch few of the arguments that we use.
- The philosophy of logic (about the meaning and justification of formal logical principles) is very controversial.

1.2 Formal Ethical Principles

Formal ethics is modeled after formal logic. Formal logic studies formal logical principles – principles of inference expressible using only variables and logical terms – like *modus tollens*:

Correct	Incorrect
If A then B. Not-B. ∴ Not-A.	If A then B. Not-A. ∴ Not-B.

Similarly, formal ethics studies formal ethical principles – expressible using only variables and constants[1] – where the constants can include logical terms, terms for general psychological attitudes (like *believe*, *desire*, and *act*), and other fairly abstract notions (like *ought* and *ends–means*). We can express our earlier examples using only variables and constants:

Follow your conscience.	If you believe that you ought to do A, then do A.
Make similar evaluations about similar cases.	If you believe that X ought to do A in situation S, then believe that anyone else ought to do A in situation S.
Treat others as you want to be treated.	If you want X to do A to you, then do A to X.

Material ethical principles (like "Don't steal") can't be analyzed this way, since they contain concrete terms (like "steal"). Here are some further formal ethical principles:

Be logically consistent in your beliefs.	If A and B are inconsistent and you accept A, then don't accept B.
If you want to achieve an end, then carry out the necessary means.	If you want to do E and believe that doing M is necessary to do E, then do M.
Act only on a maxim that you could will to be a universal law.	If you aren't willing that everyone do A, then don't do A yourself.

---

[1] Chapter 8 gives symbols for the variables and constants that I use. We might define a formal ethical principle as one that is expressible using this symbolism.

These variable–constant formulas are crude and lead to absurdities if taken literally. We'll refine the formulas later.

If my analogy with formal logic works, we'll find that:

- Formal ethical principles are largely uncontroversial. We can test such principles by searching for absurd instances.
- We may have to fudge the previous statement somewhat.
- Metaethical issues about the meaning and justification of formal ethical principles are very controversial.

Is formal ethics, conceived in this way, possible? I think that the answer is yes. Developing formal ethics is the task of this book. I'll now consider some questions about the project.

> (Q1) You plan to test formal ethical principles by searching for absurd consequences. But absurd to whom? Ethical intuitions vary greatly and won't give us uncontroversial principles.

This objection may be correct for material ethical principles. The case is different with *formal* principles of ethics or logic; here the incorrect forms, if expressed clearly, generally lead to clear-cut absurdities and contradictions.

Consider this "Practice what you preach" formal principle:

PP   If you believe that everyone ought to do A, then you ought to do A yourself.

PP[1] can entail absurdities – for example, that a madman ought to commit mass murder. Suppose that the madman believes that *everyone* ought to commit mass murder. Then *he* ought to do this himself. But this is absurd.

My argument appeals to a moral intuition; but such appeals often seem weak. Suppose I point out an "absurd" consequence of your ethical principle. You might not find my consequence "absurd" at all. And you might claim that moral intuitions come from upbringing and social background, and aren't a solid basis for arguing about ethical theories.

My argument is different. I'm appealing to a very widely shared intuition; virtually anyone would find "The madman ought to commit mass murder" absurd. But if you don't share this intuition, that's fine; we can use another example. As long as you have *some*

---

[1] I'll use a sans serif font (as in "PP") for global variables that refer to the same principle throughout the book – and a regular serif font (as in "P") for local variables that have a temporary reference.

clear moral beliefs, we can find an implication of PP that strikes you as clearly absurd. Our attack on PP will work regardless of what specific intuitions you have – even if you were taught PP and have a strong intuitive sense that it's correct. So the appeal to intuitions is stronger when we attack a *formal* ethical principle.

Formal principles that yield absurdities usually yield contradictions. Some people may be more impressed by the latter. So when I derive an absurdity, I'll also try to derive a contradiction.

Here's a case where PP yields contradictions. Ima Absolutist believes that everyone ought to do everything without exception that they promised; so *he* ought to do everything without exception that *he* promised. But he promised (to the judge) to tell the truth; so he *ought* to tell the truth. And he promised (to the defendant) not to tell the truth; so he *ought not* to tell the truth. So facts plus PP can entail contradictions.

The problem isn't that Ima would be led to conflicting conclusions about his duties; this is understandable, since his principle can lead to such conflicts. The problem rather is that PP forces *us* into conflicting conclusions about Ima's duties – it forces *us* to assert contradictions. So PP is wrong.

"Practice what you preach" is an important principle. But it needs a better formulation than PP.

> (Q2) Are there any formal ethical principles that now have the wide acceptance that you hope that your principles will have?

Yes, the universalizability principle has this wide acceptance. Here's a crude formulation of this principle:

U   If it's all right for you do A, then it's all right for anyone else in similar circumstances to do A.

I once read all the discussions of U that I could find. I found 111 people explicitly accepting universalizability, and no one explicitly rejecting it. (I didn't include a few people who reject formulations that I also reject.) So the consensus in favor of U was 111 to 0. This is impressive – especially since philosophers tend to disagree about almost everything.

Philosophers debate, not the truth of universalizability, but its usefulness and justification. They raise questions like:

- Is U a useful tool in ethical reasoning? Or is it trivial and useless?

- Is U analytic (true by virtue of the meaning of "all right" and other deontic terms)? Or is it an empirical truth, based on naturalistic definitions of ethical terms? Or is it a self-evident truth?

U resembles the principles of logic: people agree on the principle and yet disagree on the theory behind it. This is the kind of agreement that I foresee formal ethical principles as having.

> (Q3) I'm suspicious of your analogy between logic and ethics. Logical principles are analytic (true by virtue of the meaning of the concepts); ethical principles aren't. So the two are very different.

The logic side is messier than this. Quine 1986 rejects the analytic-synthetic distinction and modal terms like "necessary" or "impossible." He explains logic without these. For Quine, an argument is *valid* if it has a form whose instances always have true conclusions when they have true premises.[1] For many other logicians, an argument is *valid* if it would be logically impossible for the premises to be true but the conclusion false.

Suppose that we claim that a formal logical principle, which we represent as "$\alpha \therefore \beta$," is *valid*. This claim could be taken in various ways. Many logicians would take it to mean this:

LG1 It's logically impossible for α to be true while β is false.

Quine would interpret it this way:

LG2 Whenever an instance of α is true, the corresponding instance of β is also true.

Another logician may see it as a pragmatic or empirical claim:

LG3 In our experience, we've found it useful to conclude β whenever we've established α.

For others, it describes how people think:

LG4 People who believe α always believe β.

LG5 Intellectually mature people who believe α always believe β.

For others, it's metaphysical, conventional, or normative:

LG6 Necessarily, if a state of affairs α is actual then the state of affairs β is actual.

LG7 According to our language conventions, one who asserts α is committed to asserting β.

LG8 One ought not to accept α without also accepting β.

---

[1] Quine 1986 doesn't define *valid argument*. My definition is based on how he defines *logical truth* plus a familiar definition of *valid* in terms of this (roughly: "A $\therefore$ B" is *valid* =df "If A then B" is a *logical truth*).

We could imagine eight logicians who accept the same logical principle but differ on its meaning and justification.[1]

Formal ethical principles work similarly. Suppose we find an adequate version of "You ought to practice what you preach":

PP You ought to....

Philosophers might agree on PP but explain it differently. Some might take it to be an analytic principle about what is required to follow an ideal of moral consistency:

PP1 If you want to be morally consistent, then you ought to....

Others could interpret it as expressing feelings:

PP2 Hurrah for....

For others, it may express the will of God, or of society, or of an ideal observer:

PP3 God commands that you....

PP4 Society demands that you....

PP5 An ideal observer would desire that you....

For others, it's a categorical imperative based on reason:

PP6 You categorically ought to....

So philosophers might accept the same formal ethical principle and yet disagree on its meaning and justification.

(Q4) You sound like a relativist on metaethics.

No, not at all. I have definite views on metaethics; I'm planning another book on the moral realism issue. But this current project is quite different – and less speculative. It presents some formal tools of moral reasoning that can supplement and enhance practically any approach to ethics.

(Q5) Is formal ethics normative or metaethical?

We could take either approach. PP2 to PP6 see formal ethical principles as normative judgments. But PP1 takes them to analyze *moral consistency*; this makes them analytic and metaethical.

Formal ethical principles, however we interpret them, differ methodologically from the material ethical principles that norma-

---

[1] My LG-formulas are rough versions of historical positions. Mill and Dewey saw logic as empirical (like LG3). Husserl at first took logic psychologistically (like LG4 or perhaps LG5); after criticisms by Frege, he came to see logic as expressing necessary *a priori* truths. Aristotle and Aquinas took the law of non-contradiction and other logical principles metaphysically (like LG6). Wittgenstein saw logic as conventional (like LG7). Ramsey took logic normatively (like LG8).

tive ethics focuses on. So it's better to take formal ethics as a *third* area of ethical philosophy. In this book, I'll distinguish between *normative ethics* (about material ethical principles), *formal ethics* (about formal ethical principles), and *metaethics* (about the meaning and justification of all ethical principles).

(Q6) How does formal ethics relate to deontic logic? Are the two the same thing?

No, the two are different. Formal ethics is part of ethics. It studies formal ethical principles – principles like:

PP   If you believe that everyone ought to do A, then you ought to do A yourself.

Deontic logic is part of logic. It focuses on the validity of arguments using "ought" or "right" – arguments like:

$$\begin{array}{ll} \text{You ought not to do A.} & \text{O}{\sim}\underline{A} \\ \therefore \text{ You ought not to combine} & \therefore \text{ O}{\sim}(\underline{A} \cdot \underline{B}) \\ \text{doing A with doing B.} & \end{array}$$

The two studies, while different, are natural partners. We'll often use deontic logic in developing formal ethical principles.

People sometimes use "logic" in an extended sense that isn't about the validity of arguments. Formal ethics may be about "the logic of ethics" in some such extended sense.

(Q7) Do people ever use the word "formal" in a sense different from yours?

Yes. We use "formal" in various ways. For example, we speak of "formal dress" and "formal agreements"; here "formal" means "following official standards strictly" and is opposed to being loose or casual. Or we speak of the "A-B-B-A form" of a painting or song; here "form" is about structure or arrangement, and is opposed to matter or content. This is closer to my meaning. Even closer is a written "form," which is a document with blanks to be filled in. But my central notion of "form" is borrowed from logic.

I defined a "formal ethical principle" to be an ethical principle expressible using only variables and constants – where the constants can include logical terms, terms for general psychological attitudes (like *believe*, *desire*, and *act*), and other fairly abstract notions (like *ought* and *ends–means*). Derivatively, "formal ethics" is the study of formal ethical principles. These define "formal ethical principle" and "formal ethics." They don't give any sense to phrases like "formal action" and "formal property" – which I avoid. Some philosophers use the term "formal ethical principle" more broadly, to cover methodological principles like "Be factually informed" and "Develop your imagination." I call such principles "semiformal" and deal with them in Chapter 7.[1]

(Q8) Is formal ethics a new area of study?

Yes; formal ethics, as I conceive it, is a new area. While the formal principles themselves are common enough, the systematic study of the principles as a group is new. My exact formulations are also new; the usual formulations lead to absurdities.

Previous philosophers – especially Immanuel Kant (1785) and Richard Hare (1963) – have investigated the formal aspects of morality. Their project differs from mine. They give a comprehensive view of the nature of morality, while I keep neutral on this. So I'm not concerned with whether "ought" or "morality" are to be defined using formal features like universalizability. My project, rather, is to develop a system of formal ethical principles.

I see formal principles as having a special role in moral thinking. They give clear-cut consistency constraints and a practical way to understand the golden rule. They don't presuppose or replace traditional normative or metaethical theories; instead, they supplement such theories. Many ethicians already see formal principles as playing this role; my task is to sharpen and refine the principles so that they can play the role even better.

(Q9) Tell me more about how formal ethics can help normative and metaethical theories.

Let me give some examples. These two views emphasize the role of intuitions and feelings in making ethical judgments:

- Intuitionism: there are objective irreducible ethical truths that are known through our individual intuitions or feelings.
- Emotivism: ethical judgments simply express feelings ("X is good" means "Hurrah for X!"); there are no ethical truths.

[1] Kant and Hare sometimes use "formal" in senses different from mine (even though their principles are also "formal" in my sense). Kant 1787 (387) calls a principle "formal" if it deals with objects of every sort; he says that ethical principles aren't formal in this sense (since they must deal with actions). Later he calls a practical principle "formal" if it abstracts from all subjective ends (ibid., 427); such imperatives have the "form of universality" (ibid., 431). Hare 1981 (4–5, 62–4) calls a claim about morality "formal" if it has to do with the meaning or logical properties of the moral words. None of these is what I mean by "formal."

Suppose that Ima Racist was taught by his society to have racist intuitions and feelings. Do we want Ima to just follow these intuitions and feelings? Surely not! Instead, we'd want Ima to subject them to the kind of critical framework that formal ethics provides. The principles of formal ethics might themselves be justified by further (and more basic) intuitions and feelings.

My second example is the ideal observer theory. This bases ethics on what would be desired by a hypothetical person who was ideal in certain qualities – such as being informed, consistent, and impartial. But what do the qualities mean? And why pick these qualities and not others? Formal ethics can help here. It can transform vague ideas like consistency and impartiality into clear and workable principles – and systematize these under a few axioms. A proponent of the ideal observer theory might use ideas from formal ethics in working out the definition of an ideal observer.

My third example is supernaturalism. This sees ethics as based on God's will, perhaps as revealed in the Bible. The Bible emphasizes love of God and neighbor – and following the golden rule. But how can we understand these ideals? Without clarification, the ideals risk becoming vague or sentimentalized. Formal ethics can clarify the golden rule, show its usefulness, and fit it into a wider framework. It accords nicely with biblical ethics – and can provide a common ground for dialogue with those who don't accept religion. The principles of formal ethics might themselves be justified by their accord with God's will.

My last example is utilitarianism. One form of this view bases our duties on what would maximize pleasure (and minimize pain) for humanity. But it's difficult to apply this theory directly to concrete actions. So practical utilitarians (like Mill 1861: 22) suggest that we apply subsidiary principles – like impartiality and the golden rule – in order to maximize pleasure. Formal ethics can clarify and systematize such principles.

Toward the end of the book (in Section 7.5), we'll again consider how formal ethics can aid other theories.

(Q10) Which is your most important principle?

The golden rule (GR – "Treat others as you want to be treated") is the most important principle of formal ethics, the central jewel of the theory. GR is important in all the great world religions; Jesus, Hillel, and Confucius used it to summarize their teachings.

And GR is influential among conscientious people in our own time. I've recently read articles endorsing GR for areas such as nursing, business, government, wilderness backpacking, and using the internet – as well as for life in general. GR is often claimed to be at the root of our moral thinking.

On the other hand, it's far from clear what the golden rule means and how to apply it. Consider this literal formulation:

G1a If you want X to do A to you, then do A to X.

This leads to absurdities. Imagine that you're a patient who wants the doctor to remove your appendix. Then you are to remove the doctor's appendix. This is an absurd conclusion.

Here's a case where **G1a** yields contradictions. You want Alice and Betty to do whatever you ask; so you are to do whatever *they* ask. Alice asks you to do A, and so you are to do A. Betty asks you *not* to do A, and so you are *not* to do A. So facts plus **G1a** can entail contradictions.

The golden rule is important, and it deserves a better formulation than **G1a**. While we might tinker with the wording to avoid counterexamples, understanding is better than tinkering. So we'll begin by investigating the larger family of formal ethical principles (of which GR is a member). Once we see how other formal ethical principles work, formulating GR will be easy and natural.

1.3 The Plan of This Book

Formal ethics is the study of formal ethical principles. It formulates these principles in a clear way that avoids absurdities. It also systematizes them under a few basic axioms and defends them from various perspectives.

Chapters 2–6 develop the core principles of formal ethics: logicality, conscientiousness, impartiality, the golden rule, and the formula of universal law. These chapters gradually go from bones (theoretical framework) to meat (important principles for ethical reasoning – especially the golden rule).

Chapter 7 builds a richer theory of moral rationality, by adding *semiformal* principles like "Be factually informed" and "Develop your imagination." These supplement the formal principles and are important for applying the golden rule.

Chapter **8** is an optional chapter on symbolic logic. It begins with sections on imperative and deontic logic; you might look at these as you read earlier chapters. Then it shows how to symbolize our formal ethical principles.

If you don't have time to read the whole book, you might just focus on the essential parts. These sections are less technical:

- Essential parts: Preface, 1.1–1.3, 2.1–2.2, 2.7, 3.1–3.3, 3.5–3.6, 4.1–4.2, 5.1–5.4, 6.1–6.3, 7.1–7.4, 7.6.
- Justifications: 2.6, 3.7, 4.3, 6.4.
- Examples of theorems: 4.4, 6.6.
- Aiding other theories: 7.5.

Even if you keep to just these sections, Chapter 2 and 3 can be difficult; but they provide a framework that's important for further chapters. The following sections are somewhat technical:

- Technical details: 2.3–2.5, 3.4.
- Examples of theorems: 3.8.
- Universal prescriptivism: 6.5.
- Symbolic logic: 8.1–8.4.

If you skip nonessential parts, you may miss some references; but you should be able to follow the main drift.[1]

---

[1] This book builds on some of my previous works. See especially Gensler 1985, 1986b, and (for a technical formalization) 1990 (216–74).

Chapter 2

Logicality

Logicality is the requirement that we be logically consistent in our beliefs. By logicality, we are not to accept incompatible beliefs – and we are not to accept a belief without also accepting its logical consequences. The idea is important, and useful in disputes. It seems straightforward; but we'll have to work hard to formulate it adequately. Our work will pay off, since the ideas we develop here will be useful for principles like the golden rule.

2.1 Conflicting Beliefs

Ima Student begins her philosophy paper like this:

> Since right and wrong are relative to culture, there's no duty that binds universally. What's wrong in one culture is right in another; universal obligations are a myth. Relativism should fill us with toleration toward other cultures. We can't say that we're right and they're wrong. So everyone ought to respect the values of others.

Here Ima's first statement is incompatible with her last:

P   There's no duty that binds universally.

Q   Everyone ought to respect the values of others.

If everyone ought to respect the values of others, then some duties bind universally. Conversely, if no duty binds universally, then neither does the duty to respect others. And if right and wrong are relative to culture, then intolerance is right in a culture that approves of it. P and Q are clearly inconsistent.

This inconsistency isn't trivial; it cuts deeply. Our unexamined views are often incoherent. Socrates showed how difficult it is to have consistent beliefs on the deeper issues of life.[1]

---

[1] D.M. Johnson 1987 (323) states: "The most fundamental way of characteriz-ing the general achievement of the Greeks ... is to say that they introduced a new ideal of thought – viz., that of complete mental consistency, necessitating a forced

As we tell Ima that P and Q are inconsistent, we might say:

- "You can't accept both at the same time."
- "If you accept one, then you can't accept the other."

This suggests two principles that sound almost the same:

L1 (correct)	L1a (incorrect)
If A and B are inconsistent, then you ought not to combine accepting A with accepting B.	If A and B are inconsistent, then if you accept A then you ought not to accept B.

L1 is the better formulation. I'll give two objections to L1a.

First, L1a can have bizarre implications. Ima holds P and also Q. Since she holds P, and P is inconsistent with Q, she ought not to accept Q. And since she holds Q, and Q is inconsistent with P, she ought not to accept P. So L1a absurdly tells her to give up *both* beliefs! L1 just tells her not to combine the two. Equivalently, she ought to give up at least one of them. L1 doesn't say which belief to give up; that depends on further factors.

My second objection is that L1a entails that people who believe a self-contradiction ought then to believe *nothing*. Suppose that Ima believes a self-contradiction P.[1] Then, for any Q we pick, P is inconsistent with Q.[2] Since Ima holds P, and P is inconsistent with Q, she ought not to accept Q. Thus, for any Q we pick, Ima ought not to believe Q. So Ima ought to believe nothing – thus becoming a complete skeptic! Again, this is absurd. More plausibly, L1 entails that one shouldn't accept P if it's self-contradictory.[3]

The difference between L1 and L1a is subtle but important. If A and B are inconsistent, then the principles tell us:

---

choice among incompatible alternatives." Compare Plato with Genesis on the role of literalness and consistency.

[1] People sometimes believe self-contradictions. The logician Frege believed his axiom 5; Russell's paradox later showed it to be self-contradictory. The barber paradox is a simpler example. Tell your friends that there's a town with a barber who shaves all and only those in the town who don't shave themselves. Many will believe your statement; but it entails the self-contradiction that this barber shaves himself if and only if he doesn't.

Do people ever *knowingly* believe self-contradictory statements? Maybe abnormal people do – I'm not sure. Normal people tend to give up self-contradictory beliefs once they see them to be self-contradictory.

[2] A self-contradiction is inconsistent with anything: $\sim\!\Diamond P \therefore \sim\!\Diamond(P \cdot Q)$.

[3] If P is self-contradictory, then P is inconsistent with P. So you ought not to combine accepting P and accepting P. Simplifying this, you ought not to accept P: $O\sim\!(\underline{A} \cdot \underline{A}) \therefore O\sim\!\underline{A}$.

- You ought not to combine accepting A with accepting B. **(L1)**
- If you accept A, then you ought not to accept B. **(L1a)**

The *don't-combine* form is better; it forbids inconsistencies but doesn't tell us what to believe. Most formal consistency principles lead to absurdities when we use the *if–then* form.[1]

L1 isn't perfect yet. It requires further refinements and qualifications, but we needn't worry about these just yet.

2.2 Consequences of Beliefs

Logicality also requires that we accept the logical consequences of our beliefs. This leads to a familiar form of argument. You accept a principle P; but we point out P's implausible consequences. Do you accept these? If not, then you're inconsistent and have to either give up P or else accept P's consequences. It's wrong to say that we can't dispute first principles. We often dispute first principles by appealing to logical consequences and consistency.

Ima Racist tells us, "We ought to treat blacks poorly – because they're inferior." While we could attack his factual premise, I'm more interested in his implicit principle: "All who are inferior ought to be treated poorly." To criticize this, we must first clarify its meaning. Suppose that Ima by "inferior" means "of IQ less than 80"; then his principle means:

P   All who have an IQ of less than 80 ought to be treated poorly.

But every race clearly has some members of IQ less than 80 and some of IQ greater than 80. So we should remind Ima that his principle P has this consequence about whites:

C   All *whites* with an IQ of less than 80 ought to be treated poorly.

Ima's principle commits him to thinking that he ought to treat many whites poorly (as he treats blacks). As a racist, he won't accept this.[2] But then he's accepting a principle and yet refusing to

---

[1] The *don't-combine* form forbids us to accept incompatible judgments at the same time. We could take the *if–then* form in two ways:

(1)   If you accept A *now*, then you ought not to accept B *in the immediate future*.

(2)   If you accept A *at time t*, then you ought not to be accepting B *at time t*.

I usually take the *if–then* to say (1); but my objections also hold against (2).

[2] If Ima says that we ought to treat these whites poorly (as he treats blacks),

accept its logical consequences. His views are incoherent. To bring his beliefs into harmony with each other, he must either give up principle P or else come to accept consequence C.

The appeal to consistency isn't always useful in ethical disputes and won't help if both sides are already consistent; then we need other methods. But inconsistency is common, since we often don't think through our beliefs. One beauty of the appeal to consistency is that it doesn't presume material ethical premises – premises that another party may reject – but just points out problems in one's belief system.

Ima violates these two consistency principles:

L2 (correct)	L2a (incorrect)
If A entails B, then you ought not to combine (1) accepting A with (2) not accepting B.	If A entails B, then if you accept A then you ought to accept B.

L2 is the better formulation. L2a means that you ought to believe the consequences of your beliefs regardless of how implausible these are. I'll give two objections to L2a.

First, L2a can have bizarre implications. Suppose that Ima affirms P but denies its consequence C. Since he holds P, and P entails C, he ought to accept C. But since he holds not-C, and not-C entails not-P,[1] he ought to accept not-P. So L2a absurdly tells him to accept the opposite of both his beliefs!

L2 just forbids a certain inconsistent combination: believing something but not believing its logical consequence. If Ima violates this, then he has to change something; but L2 doesn't tell him what to change. Should he give up his principle or should he come to accept its consequence? It depends on how solid the principle is, and how obnoxious the consequence is.[2]

Another objection is that L2a entails that people who believe a self-contradiction ought then to believe *everything*. Suppose that Ima believes a self-contradiction P. Then, for any Q we pick, P

---

then he's given up racism in favor of elitism. If he's a genuine racist, he'll reject both this and the IQ principle that leads to it – and perhaps try another defense of racism. Section 7.3 will discuss racism further.

[1] If P entails C, then not-C entails not-P: $\Box(P \supset C) \therefore \Box(\sim C \supset \sim P)$.

[2] L2a suggests a "Cartesian" approach to ethics, where the first principles are firm and need only to be applied. L2 suggests a "reflective equilibrium" approach (see Rawls 1971: 20, 577–9), where we adjust both our theories and our concrete beliefs so that the two fit together coherently.

entails Q.[1] Since Ima holds P, and P entails Q, he ought to accept Q. Thus, for any Q we pick, Ima ought to believe Q. So Ima ought to believe every proposition (including every self-contradiction). Again, **L2a** leads to absurdities.[2]

The *don't-combine* formulation **L2** is better. It tells us not to believe something without believing its logical consequence. It doesn't tell us what beliefs to change if we're inconsistent.

2.3 Qualified Consistency

L1 and **L2** say that we ought not to accept incompatible beliefs, and that we ought not to accept a belief without accepting its logical consequences. These need to be qualified; most of my formal principles will need a similar qualification. (At this point, things start getting rather technical; go directly to Section 2.6 if you want to skip the details.)

As we saw in Section 2.1, **L1** entails that you ought not to accept a self-contradiction. But this has exceptions. Maybe a statement P is in fact a self-contradiction; but you don't know this – and indeed you have strong evidence that P is true. (Your truth table for P keeps coming out *always true*, since you keep making the same mistake.) Then it seems that you should accept P, even though it is in fact a self-contradiction.[3] To avoid this problem, we can qualify **L1** so it applies only when the person is (or should be) aware of the logical relationships.

L2 also needs qualifications. It requires that I believe all the logical consequences of my beliefs, but this is humanly impossible, since every belief has an infinity of complex consequences. For example, my belief that it's snowing entails:

> It's snowing and I'm at a ski resort and I'm wearing gloves, or it's snowing and I'm not at a ski resort and I'm wearing gloves, or it's snowing and I'm at a ski resort and I'm not wearing gloves, or it's snowing and I'm not at a ski resort and I'm not wearing gloves.[4]

---

[1] A self-contradiction entails anything: $\sim\!\Diamond P \therefore \Box(P \supset Q)$.

[2] If we combined **L1a** with **L2a**, we'd get a self-contradictory result – that Ima ought to believe *nothing* (by **L1a**) and *everything* (by **L2a**).

[3] Plantinga 1974 (4) used a similar example to show that broadly-logical necessity is distinct from what cannot be rationally rejected; see also Plantinga 1993a (91) and 1993b (43, 174–5).

[4] "S" entails "$(S \cdot R \cdot G) \vee (S \cdot \sim\!R \cdot G) \vee (S \cdot R \cdot \sim\!G) \vee (S \cdot \sim\!R \cdot \sim\!G)$." Introductory logic students can show this using an 8-row truth table.

I clearly can't believe all the consequences of my beliefs. Since "ought" implies "can," it follows that I don't have an obligation to do this. Again, we can qualify L2 so it applies only when the person is (or should be) aware of the logical relationships.

Even when the logic is clear to us, we might be unable to be consistent because of psychological defects or strong emotions. I might know that my daughter is blown apart by an explosion, and that anyone so blown apart is dead. But I might now be psychologically unable to accept the conclusion that my daughter is dead. I can't have an obligation to be consistent if I'm incapable of this. So the duty to be consistent applies only when we're capable of such consistency.

Consistency is a prima facie duty and can be overridden by other considerations. Perhaps if you're consistent then Dr Evil will destroy the world – or you'll get painful headaches. Or it might be very difficult to find and eliminate certain inconsistencies.

In addition, L2 would clutter our minds with trivialities – things that neither interest us nor should interest us (see Harman 1986: 11–20, 55–63). Since I believe that I'm under 100 years old, I'd have to believe that I'm under 101, that I'm under 102, and so on. Also, I couldn't forget an intermediate implication that has relevance only as part of a longer proof. Harman suggests that the duty about the inferred belief holds only if we have (or ought to have) some interest (at least a trivial whim) in whether the belief is true. We can add a proviso like this to L2.

Our principles apply only to *persons* (in the sense of beings capable of beliefs). Rocks can't have inconsistent beliefs and can't violate the consistency duties. In this sense, consistency duties wouldn't apply to rocks.

So L1 and L2 hold subject to an implicit "provided that QF" qualifier, where QF goes roughly like this:

QF   You're a person who is (or should be) aware of the logical relationships involved, you have (or should have) at least some interest in the inferred belief (if there is one), you're able to act in the manner specified, and there are no offsetting reasons why you shouldn't do so.

We normally satisfy QF when we appeal to consistency. We make the person aware of the inconsistency, the person is able to avoid it, and Dr Evil isn't threatening to destroy the world. In practice, the QF proviso isn't too important.

The qualifications show that our principles aren't entirely neat and clean. They also suggest a dissimilarity between formal ethics and formal logic. Formal ethical principles require qualifications – but formal logical principles seem to hold without qualifications. Isn't this an important difference?

The difference is only apparent. Logical principles need qualifications too. Neither area is entirely neat and clean – although both are neater and cleaner than most other areas. Consider this classic statement of the law of noncontradiction:

"The same thing cannot at the same time both belong and not belong to the same object and in the same respect"; and all other specifications that might be made, let them be added to meet logical objections.

(Aristotle, *Metaphysics*, Γ, 1005b)

Note the open-ended qualifications.[1] Modern logicians prefer a more succinct formula:

"It is not the case that (P and not-P)."   ~(P · ~P)

This can't mean that every sentence of the form "P and not-P" is false. People would raise "logical objections." Consider:

It rained, and it didn't rain. Then the sun came out.

The first part has the forbidden "P and not-P" form. But it can be true if it means "It rained, and *then later* it didn't rain." We shift the temporal reference. Here's another example:

We are free and not free.

This is true if it means "We are free to choose between a range of alternatives, but not free to choose everything." The meaning of "free" shifts. We suspect a shift in meaning when someone asserts "P and not-P." We assume that there's no such shift in a logical formula. We interpret the law of noncontradiction as follows:

Any sentence of the form "P and not-P" is false – provided that the meaning and reference (including temporal and other qualifications) of "P" is the same in both instances.

So "~(P · ~P)" requires qualifications.

The law of the excluded middle also needs qualifications:

---

[1] Aristotle saw this as the most certain principle; but he wasn't sure what qualifications it needed. In many ways, the law of noncontradiction is like the golden rule and the other principles of formal ethics. The basic truth is there intuitively, but it's difficult to formulate it in a clear way that withstands logical objections. We can't be completely confident of our qualifications; we can be more confident that *some* suitably qualified formulation is correct.

"P or not-P."   (P ∨ ~P)

This says that P is either true or false. But "My shirt is white" might be too vague to be either true or false in a given situation. This quantified formula has a similar problem:

"For any x, either x is F or x isn't F."   (x)(Fx ∨ ~Fx)

Logic assumes that "F" stands for a predicate that produces a definite truth or falsehood for all the entities in the universe of discourse. We can't satisfy this with empirical predicates like "white," all of which are somewhat vague. So these formulas are idealized and ignore vagueness.

Some solid logical principles fail in idiomatic English. These English arguments are invalid but the symbolic forms are valid:

I don't have no money.	Not-not-A.
∴ I do have money.	∴ A.
You do that, and I'll quit.	A and B.
∴ I'll quit.	∴ B.
If I have money, then I couldn't be broke.	If A then not-B.
I could be broke.	B.
∴ I don't have money.	∴ Not-A.

In each case, the first English premise is an *illogical idiom*: the logical meaning of the whole isn't a normal function of the parts. Due to irregularities in English, "not-not" can mean "not," "and" can mean "if–then," and "couldn't" in the consequent can claim that the whole conditional is necessary.

Quantificational theses are subject to two further provisos:

■ At least one entity must exist in the domain of objects. In most systems, "(∃x)(Fx ∨ ~Fx)" is a logical truth; but it really isn't a logical truth that something exists.

■ Our individual constants (like "a" in "((x)Fx ⊃ Fa)") must refer to existing entities. English can use names (like "Santa Clause") that don't refer to existing entities.

We could avoid both problems at the cost of added complexity. Most logicians prefer simpler systems with implicit provisos.

To avoid these problems, we can take each quantificational thesis (and English instance) to have an implicit "provided that QL" qualifier that goes roughly as follows:

QL   Each term has a constant meaning and reference (including temporal qualifications) in all its occurrences, each statement is clear enough to be definitely true or false, each predicate produces definite truths or falsehoods for all the entities in the universe of discourse, the statements aren't illogical idioms, at least one entity exists in the domain of objects, and the individual constants refer to existing entities.

So formal ethics and formal logic *both* need qualifiers.

Life is richer than formulas. Our theories are idealized and oversimplified. In relatively precise areas, like formal logic and formal ethics, the simplifications cause few practical problems and can safely be kept in the back of our minds. But we shouldn't forget them entirely.

While life is richer than formulas, it's also true that life needs formulas. A good formula is a powerful thing. Life would be impoverished if we had no formulas.

2.4 Conjunctivity

L1 and L2 cover inconsistencies with two beliefs. The following principles cover more complex cases:

L3   If A_1, ..., A_n ($n \geq 1$) form an inconsistent set, then you ought not to combine accepting A_1, ..., and accepting A_n.

L4   If A_1, ..., A_n ($n \geq 1$) entail B, then you ought not to combine accepting A_1, ..., accepting A_n, and not accepting B.

Equivalently, we could add *conjunctivity* principle L5, which demands that we not accept A and accept B without also accepting their conjunction (A & B):

L5   You ought not to combine accepting A, accepting B, and not accepting (A & B).

The set {L1, L2, L5} is logically equivalent to {L3, L4}; I'll skip the proof for this. L5 is easier to understand, but harder to use in deriving theorems.

This extension brings us to a complicated controversy and perhaps a further proviso. You can skip to the next section if you want to avoid the technical details.

I'll assume that belief doesn't come in degrees. Your belief may be more or less firm; but the notion itself is binary: you believe A or you don't.[1] On the other hand, *probability* and *degree of confi-*

---

[1] Derksen 1978 defends the binary nature of our ordinary notion of belief. See

dence come in degrees and can sometimes be expressed in numbers. If you're throwing a fair six-sided die, it's 67 per cent (2/3) probable that it will be at least a three. You might also have a 67 per cent confidence in this happening.

Perhaps numerical probability (relative to our total evidence) determines what we *ought* to believe. Here's a simple formula that incorporates this idea:

PB   If the probability of A is greater than 50 per cent, then you
        ought to believe A; otherwise, you ought not to believe A.[1]

PB can disrupt conjunctivity. Suppose that you throw a pair of dice. Let A = your first die will be at least a three, and B = your second die will be at least a three. By PB, you should accept A and you should accept B – since each is 67 per cent (2/3) probable; but you shouldn't accept (A & B) since it's only 44 per cent (4/9) probable. So you should combine accepting A, accepting B, and not accepting (A & B). This violates conjunctivity principle L5. But we could avoid the conflict by adding a restriction to L5:

L5*   You ought not to combine accepting A, accepting B, and not
        accepting (A & B) unless this happens: the probability of A
        is greater than 50 per cent, the probability of B is greater
        than 50 per cent, and the probability of (A & B) is 50 per
        cent or less.

PB would require similar restrictions for L3 and L4.

Consider the lottery paradox. Suppose that you believe that person-1 won't win the lottery, believe that person-2 won't win, ..., and believe that person-n won't win. Yet you believe that someone from 1 to n will win. You believe an inconsistent set of statements and so violate unqualified conjunctivity. But PB says that you're reasonable – since each statement believed is over 50 per cent probable. If we think that you're reasonable, then we'll be inclined toward rejecting unqualified conjunctivity and perhaps accepting something like PB and L5*. My intuitions are unclear.[2]

also Foley 1992, Harman 1986 (21–7), and Plantinga 1993a (118–19).

[1] We might use a number higher than 50 per cent – or speak vaguely of a "high" probability. Or we might specify a high number for a belief to be *required* and a low one for it to be *permitted*; Kitcher 1990 argues that this is better, since it lets people disagree if the evidence is ambiguous. PB entails L1 and L2 (I'll spare you the proof); some variations on PB might not do this. Changing PB would require changing the qualification that I later suggest for L5*.

[2] Derksen 1978; Foley 1979, 1992; Plantinga 1993a (145), 1993b (43); and J. Williams 1981 reject or qualify conjunctivity. Dudman 1992; Harman 1986 (21–7, 70–2); and Kaplan 1981 keep conjunctivity but reject principles like PB. Kaplan

PB can have strange consequences. Suppose that the Cubs have two games left in the baseball season. They win the division if and only if they win both games. Each victory is 60 per cent probable, but a string of two victories is only 36 per cent (60 per cent • 60 per cent) probable. With PB, I'd have to believe the following about the Cubs:

> I believe they'll win the first game and I believe they'll win the second game. But I believe that they won't win *both* games. And so I believe that they won't win the division.

It's hard to imagine even a Cubs fan saying such a thing. PB, which requires such beliefs, thus seems implausible.

PB fragments our beliefs. We accept an individual belief if it's over 50 per cent probable, and don't care if our beliefs fit together into a coherent system. If we believe A and believe B, we needn't believe their conjunction (A & B). We might even believe (A & B) to be false.

PB has another problem. Does *every* belief have a numerical probability? Perhaps numerical probabilities only make sense in a few special cases.

If we do need a proviso on conjunctivity, however, let's consider it to be built into QF and assumed implicitly. The proviso wouldn't make much difference for our system. Of the numbered theorems that follow, only three (E1, G7, and G8) presume conjunctivity (and they could be reworded to avoid this); and these theorems don't raise lottery-paradox problems.

2.5 Logicality Questions

(Q1) Your consistency principles are *ought* judgments. Could they be expressed in other ways?

Yes. We could talk about the virtue of consistency – or give descriptions, imperatives, or hypothetical imperatives about consistency. Here are five formats for L1 (for the first blank put "A and B are inconsistent" and for the second put "combine accepting A with accepting B"):

claims that it's reasonable to believe a complex theory even though we know that the probability of its complete truth is very low. Dudman claims that it's reasonable to withhold assent from "I won't win the lottery" even though its probability is very high. If both claims are correct, then there's no simple relationship between the probability of a statement and the reasonableness of holding it.

Lo1 Ought (same as **L1**): If ..., then you ought not to ....

Lv1 Virtue: Consistency is a virtue – and involves being disposed that if ... then you not ....

Ld1 Description: If ..., then it isn't consistent for you to ....

Li1 Imperative: If ..., then don't ....

Lh1 Hypothetical imperative: If you want to be consistent, then if ... then you ought not to ....

Various approaches to ethics may see one format as more basic:

Ethics of	*Ethics is about*
duty	how we ought to live
virtue	good and bad character traits
description	describing behavior
imperatives	choosing action guides
hypothetical imperatives	how to achieve our goals

Formal ethics could adapt to these – for example, to the hypothetical-imperative ethics of Harsanyi 1958 (who even suggests axiomatizing formal requirements as hypothetical imperatives).

Zimmerman 1962 wants to eliminate ethical terms. This is partly compatible with formal ethics. We could express logicality using descriptions, imperatives, or hypothetical imperatives (**Ld1**, **Li1**, or **Lh1**). We could do the same with our other principles (except conscientiousness and impartiality).

I see the five formats as complementary. The description format gives a useful analysis of consistency; but it doesn't say how we are to live. The imperative is a guide to action; but it needs to be based on what's right or good. The hypothetical imperative is correct as far as it goes; but consistency isn't just an optional goal. So I'd stress the *ought* and the *virtue* formats – which I see as different sides of the same ethical coin (see Frankena 1973: 61–71).

A virtue is a good habit – a disposition to act in certain ways and to have (or cultivate) the corresponding feelings. Virtues need principles (*oughts*) for their content; an *honest* person, for example, is one whose life reflects the principle, "You *ought* to tell the truth and not cheat or steal." But principles also need virtues. A principle is just empty words until we internalize it into a good habit – a virtue. A principle achieves its purpose when it's so built into our practice that we hardly think of it. A good person often acts instinctively (without thinking of the golden rule or other principles), just as a good logician often reasons instinctively (without thinking of logical principles). We call principles to mind mainly to train and criticize our habits – and to reflect philosophically on the kind of lives that we lead.

Formal ethics deals with areas like logical consistency, conscientiousness, and impartiality. These fit well into a virtue approach, since they deal with personal integration and what kind of persons we ought to be – instead of prescribing specific actions. While I generally use *ought* principles, I could equally well speak of character traits like consistency and impartiality.[1] This would change the language but not the substance of formal ethics – which is as much about formal ethical virtues as formal ethical duties.[2]

> (Q2) Your principles say that we *ought not* to have inconsistent belief combinations. Do these principles imply that we can *choose* what to believe?

They imply that we have *some* choice in the matter. Choosing what to believe isn't like choosing to move your finger. It's more like choosing to lose weight – we work at it indirectly.

We resolve inconsistencies through a combination of reason, feeling, and choice. We examine how beliefs connect with other beliefs and attitudes; and we consider the evidence. We may feel drawn toward a resolution. Or we may feel confusion and anguish – and hear the voice of Sartre 1957 (28) saying, "You're free, choose, that is, invent!"

> (Q3) What does "believe" ("accept") mean in your principles? Is a belief a mental state or disposition, a complex of behavioral dispositions, a complex of brain states, or some combination of these?

[1] My alternative derivations of the golden rule and formula of universal law (Sections 5.1 and 6.2) follow the virtue approach and are based on the idea of a person who is impartial and conscientious. This virtue approach is less technical and perhaps a better way to present formal ethics to many people.

[2] If we follow the Aristotelian division, we'd classify some of these formal virtues (like logical consistency) as intellectual and others (perhaps conscientiousness) as moral. "Formal Ethics" (like "Nicomachean Ethics") uses "ethics" broadly, to cover both intellectual and moral virtues (and duties).

There are two virtues for each principle – an idealized virtue and a real-world virtue. Being logically consistent in an idealized (and unrealizable) sense requires having a perfectly consistent set of belief attitudes. Being logically consistent in a real-world sense involves achieving consistency as far as we practically can (subject to human limitations and the qualification QF).

Philosophers take a bewildering variety of approaches to belief and desire; for example, see Fodor 1984 and J.L. Cohen 1989. I'm neutral here. I presume that any adequate approach can make sense of consistency norms. But it's important that believing is some kind of disposition; I am presently conscious of relatively few of the many things that I believe.

(Q4) Does "ought" in your consistency principles mean "morally ought" – or something else?

Philosophers tend to use "morally ought" in two main senses (see Mackie 1977: 106 and Frankena 1966, 1973: 61–70). The broad sense means "ought, all-things-being-considered"; this gives an evaluation based on the whole picture (all the facts). The narrow sense means "ought, insofar as responsibilities toward others go"; this partial "ought" may be overridden in the larger picture by responsibilities toward yourself. I'll generally use "ought" and "morally ought" in the broad sense because of the sort of issues that I want to discuss.

My formal ethical principles express moral duties in the broad (all-things-being-considered) sense when qualification **QF** is fulfilled. Some of the principles, like the golden rule, also give moral duties in the narrow (responsibilities-toward-others) sense. Each also expresses an intellectual duty about consistency and is useful in reasoning about duties in various senses.

(Q5) Section 1.2 Q3 sketched eight ways to understand logical validity. Are these compatible with your approach to formal ethics?

Roughly yes, but with some qualifications. You can skip to the next section if you want to avoid the technical details.

Five of the views are entirely compatible. These take a valid argument to express an *a priori* relationship between propositions (**LG1**), a reasoning pattern useful in our experience (**LG3**) or used by intellectually mature people (**LG5**), inclusion relationships between states of affairs (**LG6**), or language conventions about logical terms (**LG7**). The other three views would demand some changes in our approach.

Quine 1986 (**LG2**) accepts only a narrowly logical notion of necessary truths, limited to statements provable in standard systems of formal logic. He rejects as unclear the broadly logical

notion of necessary truths, which also covers examples like these
(see Plantinga 1974: 1–9):

- "All bachelors are unmarried."
- "2 + 2 = 4."
- "If this is entirely green, then this isn't entirely red."

He similarly rejects the broadly logical notions of validity, entailment, and consistency that I use. If I accepted Quine's approach,
then I'd avoid modal logic and I wouldn't say "If A entails B, then
…." Rather I'd say "If B is derivable in quantificational logic from
A, then …." While our principles would be weaker, we could still
do formal ethics from a Quinean perspective.

The two remaining views are very implausible. Psychologism
(**LG4**) says that logic describes how we think. We might then
rephrase our principles to express truths of formal psychology:
that people never accept incompatible beliefs and never accept a
belief without also accepting its logical consequences. If we have
a duty to be consistent, it's a duty that we always satisfy.

Normativism (**LG8**) says that logic states how we *ought* to
think. "A entails B" means "You ought not to accept A without
accepting B." Our logicality principles then become true by definition – thus making the next section unnecessary.

2.6 Why Be Consistent?

We need to face the issue of justification. Why should we be
consistent? How can we justify the logicality requirement?

A prior question is: "How do we justify an action or an ethical
belief?" Do we show that the action is a means to promoting
something that we desire? Do we appeal to antecedent normative
principles? Do we deduce an *ought* from an *is* – using an *is–ought*
definition? Or do we appeal to actual or ideal ethical intuitions,
feelings, or desires?

Instead of taking a stand on these issues, I'll try to show how
one might defend logicality from various points of view. Ideally,
I'd like to give conclusive justifications of my formal ethical
principles from every conceivable approach to ethics. But I can't
do this, since my university doesn't grant 50-year sabbaticals.
More practically, I sketch plausible defenses from the ten typical
(but simplified) approaches in the boxes on the right:

Promoting our desires	Idealistic desires Self-interest desires
Normative principles	Utilitarianism Prima facie duties
Is–ought definitions	Cultural relativism Ideal observer theory Supernaturalism
Actual or ideal intuitions, feelings, or desires	Nonnaturalism Emotivism Prescriptivism

Readers can adapt my suggestions to their particular theories.

The first justification strategy involves showing that an action is a means to promoting our desires:

> You want B.
> Doing A is a (necessary, sufficient, useful, …) means to B.
> ∴ Doing A is a (necessary, sufficient, useful, …) means to something that you want.

Here I'll consider only two extreme kinds of desires: idealistic and self-interested ones. My later remarks may appeal to those with other desires – for example, to follow society or God's will.

Let's suppose first that you have idealistic desires. Accordingly, you want to be rational, and hence consistent, so you don't want to have incompatible beliefs. And you don't want to believe something without believing its logical consequences. Then consistency is a necessary means to promote your goals.

To take a more challenging case, let's now suppose that you only want to promote your self-interest in some narrow sense. It's plausible to think that consistency will do this.

To see the harm of inconsistency, imagine that you wake up with *contradictitis* – a dreaded condition that makes you believe not-A whenever you believe A. As you get up, you say, "I have to go to work today" – and also "I don't have to go." As you make breakfast, you think that orange juice won't poison you (and also that it will). As you drive to work, you think you should turn left (and also that you shouldn't). Contradictitis would be a living hell. You'd be completely confused on what to think and how to act. Human relationships would be destroyed. You'd probably be locked up and regarded as insane – if you didn't crash in traffic first. So contradictitis would have harmful consequences.

In addition, inconsistency is inherently distressing and unpleasant. When Ima Student discovers the inconsistency in her philosophy paper (see Section 2.1), she'll probably feel bad and be motivated to readjust her beliefs. Psychologists call this phenomenon "cognitive dissonance." The pioneer in this area writes:

> Dissonance ... is a motivating factor in its own right.... Cognitive dissonance ... leads to activity oriented toward dissonance reduction just as hunger leads to activity oriented toward hunger reduction. It is a very different motivation from what psychologists are used to dealing with but, as we shall see, nonetheless powerful.[1]
>
> (Festinger 1957: 3)

Since inconsistency has harmful consequences and is inherently distressing, a tolerable life requires a large degree of consistency. Since consistency is sometimes beyond our ability or conflicts with other values, Section 2.3 admitted exceptions to the requirement. But inconsistency would hurt the quality of our lives in most cases, so self-interest can justify consistency fairly well.

This defense of consistency doesn't presume any ethical stance. Section 2.5 (Q1) sketched nonethical formats for consistency principles – as descriptions, imperatives, and hypothetical imperatives. You could accept these even if you rejected ethical judgments.

A second justification strategy derives an ethical judgment from a more basic normative principle:

> Any act that's F ought to be done.
> Act A is F.
> ∴ Act A ought to be done.

Here I'll consider appeals to utilitarianism and to Ross's theory.

Utilitarians say that we have one basic duty – to bring about the greatest total balance of good over harm (considering everyone). Utilitarians could oppose inconsistency because it harms the individual (as our contradictitis example shows) and also harms society. Consistency is important for the social good; widespread contradictitis would destroy social communication and cooperation and lead to the collapse of society.

Ross's theory claims that we have several basic prima facie duties. These are duties that hold other things being equal, but can be overridden in special circumstances. This view could see incon-

---

[1] See also Aronson 1969. Cognitive dissonance probably has social and evolutionary explanations. Since consistency is important for survival, societies would train their members to be consistent – and evolution would program our minds to avoid inconsistencies (as it programmed our bodies to spit out many poisons).

sistency as an inherently bad cognitive state that have a prima
facie duty to avoid. (Or it might appeal to prima facie duties to
seek truth and avoid error.)

A third justification strategy tries to deduce an *ought* from an *is*
by appealing to an *is–ought* definition:

"Act A *ought* to be done" means "Act A is F."
This act is F.
∴ This act ought to be done.

The definition may analyze current usage, stipulate the author's
meaning, or propose an improved meaning. Here I'll consider
three approaches that might use this definitional strategy: cultural
relativism, the ideal observer theory, and supernaturalism. I'll only
consider forms of these that give *is–ought* definitions.

Cultural relativism says that "We ought to do A" means "Our
society demands that we do A." It's plausible to hold that our
society demands consistency (often discrediting and ridiculing
people who are inconsistent); it's hard to imagine a society surviv-
ing without a norm against inconsistency. So cultural relativism
could accept our consistency principles.

The ideal observer theory says that "We ought to do A" means
"An ideal observer (person who was ideally consistent, informed,
impartial, etc.) would desire that we do A." It's plausible to hold
that ideal observers would desire that we be consistent, since this
would promote our well-being and make us more rational in our
beliefs (and more like ideal observers). So the ideal observer
theory could accept our consistency principles.

Supernaturalism[1] says that "We ought to do A" means "God
desires that we do A." We might know God's will from the Bible,
the church, individual conscience, or reason (or from some combination of these). These sources seem to support consistency. In the
Bible, Jesus often appeals to consistency; in Luke 13:14–17, for
example, he condemns as hypocrites Pharisees who criticized
others on the basis of principles (like Sabbath duties) that they
didn't hold consistently themselves. The church also denounces
inconsistencies. Conscience would likely support consistency,
since it tries to form consistent moral beliefs. Appealing to reason

---

[1] This view (also called the "divine command theory") is a minority view
among religious thinkers (most of whom link ethics closely to religion but don't
define ethical terms using religious ones). I'll use Christian examples in discussing
supernaturalism; readers of other religions may substitute their own examples.

might involve speculating on what an all-loving God would desire; this is like applying the ideal observer theory (except that God is viewed as an existing being of complete moral wisdom, and not a hypothetical construct). It's plausible to think that God would desire that we be consistent – since this is inherently rational, promotes our well-being, and makes us more like God (whom we'd never imagine to contradict himself).

A fourth justification strategy appeals to actual or ideal intuitions, feelings, or desires:

> An ethical belief is reasonable (warranted, justified) if and only
> if (or to the extent that) it accords with F (the person's actual
> or ideal intuitions, feelings, or desires).
> Your ethical belief accords with F.
> ∴ Your ethical belief is reasonable.

I'll consider three approaches that might use this strategy: nonnaturalism, emotivism, and prescriptivism.

Nonnaturalism posits objective irreducible ethical truths that we can know through our intuitions, feelings, or desires. It typically appeals to intuitions, viewing these as somewhat like either sense perceptions or mathematical convictions. Some nonnaturalists base our ethical knowledge on a direct grasp of self-evident truths that leaves no room for argument:

> Extreme nonnaturalism: Your basic ethical beliefs are reasonable
> if and only if they appear intuitively evident to you.

Others think that a principle that initially *seems* evident might be rejected for having nonintuitive implications; we look for the most coherent system that harmonizes with our considered beliefs:

> Moderate nonnaturalism: Your basic ethical beliefs are reasonable
> if and only if they're part of a body of consistent and reflective
> beliefs that are intuitively evident to you.

Others include all the features of an ideal ethical judge:

> Ideal nonnaturalism: Your ethical beliefs are reasonable if and
> only if you're consistent, informed, impartial, etc. about them.

Nonnaturalists could accept our consistency norm as an objective ethical truth. They might see it as self-evident, or as derived from another self-evident norm, or as coherent with our ethical intuitions, or as something that ideal moral thinking leads us to. Moderate and ideal nonnaturalism have a special commitment to consistency, as a condition of moral reasonableness.[1]

[1] Daniels 1979 distinguishes "narrow" from "wide" reflective equilibrium. The

Emotivism says that an ethical judgment is an expression of feeling (like "Boo on X!") – not a judgment that's factually true or false. Some emotivists think that ethical rationality requires ethical truths and ethical knowledge, and so deny the rationality of ethics:

Extreme emotivism: All ethical beliefs are equally reasonable.

Other emotivists look at ethical rationality in terms of personal competency; ethical judgments and feelings can be "flawed" or "unreasonable" if they're inconsistent or based on falsehoods:

Moderate emotivism: Your ethical beliefs are reasonable if and only if you're informed and consistent about them.

Others incorporate all the features of an ideal ethical judge:

Ideal emotivism: Your ethical beliefs are reasonable if and only if you're consistent, informed, impartial, etc. about them.

Emotivists are generally against inconsistency (especially in view of its harmful effects), and thus say "Boo!" to it. Moderate and ideal emotivism have a special commitment to consistency, as a condition of moral reasonableness.[1]

Prescriptivism sees ethical judgments as like imperatives ("Do A") in that they prescribe actions and aren't factually true or false. While we could distinguish extreme, moderate, and ideal forms, I'm only concerned with Hare's universal prescriptivism. This is an "ideal" form that emphasizes consistency (see Hare 1963). Prescriptivists could accept consistency norms as imperatives to which they give their assent – thus signaling their commitment to a way of life that values consistency.

These three views – nonnaturalism, emotivism, and prescriptivism – differ on what morality is about. Nonnaturalism is a moral realism, positing independent moral facts; the other two views reject this. Yet there are deep similarities on how the three views defend ethical beliefs: the *extreme* forms are somewhat alike – as are the *moderate* and the *ideal* forms. In terms of reasoning about morality, the extreme-moderate-ideal distinction is more important than the emotivism-prescriptivism-nonnaturalism distinction.

---

former (moderate) approach just systematizes intuitions. The latter (ideal) approach, brings in other factors – including an impartial and informed choice from the original position; see Brink 1989 (100–43) and Boyd 1988. Rawls 1980, while not a moral realist, offers a similar methodology.

[1] Frankena 1973 (105–14) has a good treatment of the three forms of emotivism. All these *ideal* views, of course, cry out for some higher-order principle to specify what factors ideal moral thinking requires.

Another strategy says that the consistency norm is inherently correct and justified and can't be defended without circularity. Suppose that I give you an argument that you ought to be consistent. If you don't already care about consistency, why shouldn't you accept my premises and yet reject my conclusion? This would be inconsistent – but you don't care! If you don't value consistency, then I'm wasting my time when I try to reason with you. The consistency norm, like basic logical principles, has to be assumed from the start. We can't rationally reject such principles (Lewis 1957: 100); we all recognize them in how we live.

A final strategy says that consistency is justified because at least one of the justifications for it must work. This defense rests on a range of theories, rather than on one particular theory.

Let me summarize. We might see our formal ethical principles as truths that are *a priori* (intuitionist nonnaturalism), empirical (cultural relativism and ideal observer theory), or based on experience in a broader way (supernaturalism and nonintuitionist nonnaturalism). Or we might see them as practices that promote our goals or are reasonable from a certain perspective. Or we might derive them from our other normative views. Or we might just accept them and not worry about their justification.

2.7 Logic Bashing

Some writers look with disfavor on consistency, logic, and the application of logic to ethics. I'll now consider some typical criticisms and show how they're based on misconceptions.

> (Q1) A wise man once wrote that a foolish consistency is the hobgoblin of little minds. How does it feel to have a little mind?

How does it feel to misinterpret Emerson? He truly was a wise man, and he did write the following:

> Suppose you should contradict yourself; what then? ... A foolish consistency is the hobgoblin of little minds, adored by little statesmen and philosophers and divines. With consistency a great soul has simply nothing to do.
>
> (Emerson 1841: 33)

Emerson is using *consistency* in a different sense, as "a reverence for our past act or word, because the eyes of others have no other data for computing our orbit than our past acts, and we are loath to disappoint them." Roughly, *consistency* is an undue hesitancy to change your mind in public. Emerson tells us to "speak what you think now in hard words, and to-morrow speak what to-morrow thinks in hard words again, though it contradict every thing you said to-day." In other words, it's all right to change your mind. Emerson isn't saying that it's all right to hold incompatible beliefs at the same time. He isn't objecting to our consistency norms.

Bertrand Russell illustrates the two senses of *consistency*. He changed his mind a lot. Tradition has it that he held every possible view at some time or other. But at any given moment his beliefs were consistent. Emerson would praise Russell as *inconsistent* (he changed his mind a lot). Formal ethics would praise him as *consistent* (he didn't hold incompatible beliefs at the same time). Only little minds confuse the two senses.

(Q2) How do you respond to someone who denies the law of noncontradiction?

Some logicians suggest hitting the person with a stick. A better idea (especially if the person is bigger than you) is to pretend to agree. Whenever you assert something, also assert the opposite. (See Aristotle's *Metaphysics*, Γ, 1006a.) Soon your opponent will want to hit you with a stick!

It's difficult to deny the law of noncontradiction. Consider this dialogue between two Hegelians:

A: ·Are you still a follower of Hegel?

B: Of course! I believe everything that he wrote. Since he denied the law of noncontradiction, I deny this too. On my view, P is entirely compatible with not-P.

A: I'm a fan of Hegel myself. But he *didn't* deny the law of noncontradiction! You read the wrong commentators!

B: You're wrong, he *did* deny this! Let me get my copy of *The Science of Logic*.

A: Don't get so upset! You said that he *did* deny the law, and I said that he *didn't*. Aren't these compatible on your view? After all, you think that P is compatible with not-P.

B: Yes, I guess they're compatible.

A: No they aren't!

B: Yes they are!

A: Don't get so upset! You said that they *are* compatible, and I said that they *aren't*. Aren't these two compatible on your view? Recall that you think that P is compatible with not-P.

B: Yes, I guess they're compatible. I'm getting confused.

A: And you're also *not* getting confused! Right?

Some people *say* that they deny the law of noncontradiction. But they accept it in the way they live.[1]

(Q3) Logic has little to do with ethics. We seldom, if ever, give watertight deductive arguments in ethics. So how can logic be useful for ethics?

Logic can help us to clarify, understand, and evaluate moral reasoning. Many moral arguments apply a principle:

Every action that's F ought to be done.
Act A is an action that's F.
∴ Act A ought to be done.

This presumes that we're appealing to an allegedly exceptionless principle (for example, that *every* act that maximizes pleasure ought to be done). If we instead use a prima facie principle (for example, that we ought other things being equal to keep promises), then we need a premise about counterbalancing reasons:

Any action that's F ought to be done unless there are special counterbalancing reasons against it.
Act A is an action that's F.
There are no special counterbalancing reasons against A.
∴ Act A ought to be done.

Another form argues from pros and cons:

The reasons for act A are $P_1, P_2, ..., P_n$.
The reasons against act A are $C_1, C_2, ..., C_n$.
Reasons $P_1, P_2, ..., P_n$ outweigh reasons $C_1, C_2, ..., C_n$.
If the reasons for act A outweigh the reasons against act A, then act A ought to be done.
∴ Act A ought to be done.

[1] There's a problem with claiming that even *one* self-contradiction is true. This traditional argument shows that from a single self-contradiction we can prove any arbitrary statement Q:

P is true and P isn't true. (Hypothesis – a self-contradiction.)
∴ P is true.
∴ P isn't true.
∴ At least one of these two is true: P or Q. {From the second step.}
∴ Q is true. {From the last two steps.}

This argument presumes that words like "and" are used in their normal sense and that different occurrences of variables "P" and "Q" have the same meaning. Given this, it's hard to deny any of the steps.

We may need additional forms for other moral arguments.

Logic can help us to understand our moral reasoning – how we go from premises to a conclusion. It can force us to clarify and spell out our presuppositions, to understand conflicting points of view, and to identify weak points in our reasoning. Logic is a useful discipline to sharpen our ethical thinking.

Arguments about morality (or other areas) are seldom watertight. Often the validity is clear but the premises are controversial. We often reason from probable premises – or hunches – or personal commitments. We reason whenever we apply a principle. Reasoning isn't always strict proof and doesn't have to have indisputable premises to be useful.

Formal ethics emphasizes a second role of logic – to help test consistency. Section 2.2 talked about Ima Racist, who argued for racist views. We didn't say: "Ima rejects our premises, and we reject his; so the dispute is a stalemate!" Instead, we appealed to consistency and easily demolished his argument.

Consistency often comes up in moral discussions. Smith makes a moral judgment and defends it by a moral principle. Jones then points out an implausible consequence of the principle. Smith, to be consistent, has to accept the consequence – or reject the principle – or modify the principle to avoid the consequence. This is a common pattern. It rests on logic and consistency.

> (Q4) Some people are mostly logical in their orientation, while others are mostly emotional. Formal ethics says that we should all be logical – we should all develop our reasoning at the expense of our emotions. Isn't this too limiting?

It's too limiting to think that emotion and logic are opposites and that we have to choose between the two. This is totally false. Consider these two classes of people:

- *emotional* people (those who have deep feelings);
- *reasoners* (those who reason a lot).

The two classes overlap. There are many (1) emotional reasoners,[1] (2) emotional nonreasoners, (3) unemotional reasoners, and (4)

---

[1] These *emotional reasoners* include my excitable teacher Hector-Neri Castañeda (from whom I learned deontic and imperative logic) and Quine (who in a two-page stretch [1986: 66–7] used 25 emotional or prescriptive terms – including "undesirable," "seduced," "despair," and [his favorite] "deplore").

unemotional nonreasoners. There's no neat dichotomy between *emotional* and *logical* orientations. The world isn't that simple.

The question suggests that logicality tells us to reason a lot. It doesn't; it just tells us to avoid inconsistencies. An emotional person who reasons little might still be consistent; and an unemotional person who reasons a lot might be inconsistent. Logicality tells us to be consistent; but it doesn't tell us to reason a lot – or to develop our reasoning at the expense of our emotions.

> (Q5) The problem with you logicians is that you think that everything is provable. Some things you just feel – but you can't prove them.

I've never met a logician who claimed that everything is provable. Aristotle, the first logician, pointed out that this idea leads to an infinite regress.[1] Every argument appeals to premises – and we can't prove these premises by further premises endlessly. So every argument eventually appeals to premises that we accept without further argument.

Yes, some things you just *feel* (or intuit, or know, or see). But suppose that our opponent just *feels* the truth of some preposterous racist principle. What do we do then? We appeal to logic and consistency. That's what formal ethics is all about.

---

[1] "A demonstration of everything is impossible; for the process would go on to infinity, so that even in this manner there would be no demonstration." (*Metaphysics*, Γ, 1006a.) Aristotle later mentions a "demonstration by refutation," which is like our appeal to consistency.

Chapter 3

Conscientiousness

W e can violate consistency in various ways. We might be
logically inconsistent in our beliefs – thus violating
logicality. Or we might have inconsistency of will. Perhaps our
desires, resolutions, and actions conflict with each other. Perhaps
our means don't accord with our ends. Or perhaps (violating conscientiousness) we don't live in harmony with our moral beliefs.

3.1 Accepting an Imperative

Suppose that I solemnly resolve to eat no ice cream. Yet I see ice
cream, and (as usual) I eat it. I'm inconsistent. A consistency
axiom should forbid this, and generate principles like:

> You ought not to combine
> being resolved to eat no ice cream
> with acting to eat this ice cream.

How can we generate such principles?

The simplest approach is to broaden our consistency requirements. These deal with believing (accepting a statement). We can
analogously look at willing as accepting an imperative.[1] We can
phrase our consistency axiom in terms of *accepting* (which covers
statements or imperatives). Then we can give this derivation
(which uses the abbreviations in the box):

> 1 = "Eat no ice cream."
> 2 = "Eat this ice cream now."

[1] Formal ethics needn't in principle use this analysis of *willing*; Section 5.1
gives a derivation of the golden rule that avoids it. However, this analysis makes it
easier to develop formal ethics as a unified system with a few basic axioms –
rather than as a mixed assortment of various principles.

    1 is inconsistent with 2.

∴ You ought not to combine accepting 1 with accepting 2. {By
    some broader axiom.}

∴ You ought not to combine being resolved to eat no ice cream
    with acting to eat this ice cream. {Rephrasing previous step.}

We derive the last step using these equivalences:

- To be resolved to eat no ice cream is to accept 1.
- To act to eat this ice cream is to accept 2.

As I break my resolution, we can imagine one part of me saying
"Eat no ice cream" while another part says "Eat this ice cream
now." (See Plato's *Republic*, IV, 436–45.)

My equivalences require poetic license. I can resolve to eat no
ice cream without verbalizing an "Eat no ice cream" imperative.
An act of will needn't be expressed in an imperative. But it could
be, and it's helpful to imagine it being done. So we'll imagine that
actors on the stage of formal ethics verbalize their acts of will in
imperative soliloquies. Displaying the content of acts of will as
imperatives helps us to formulate and prove principles about
consistency of will.

But there's a problem here. To express acts of will, we need
imperatives for each person and tense. English imperatives are
mostly limited to second-person present and future ("Do this
now"[1] and "Do this tomorrow" – with "you" understood). We also
need forms for the first and third person, and for the past.

Hare's approach (1952: 187–90; 1989c) is to invent a wider
imperative form. Hare politely suggests using "***, please" –
where we can fill in "***" to refer to *any* action of any person or
tense. So "Shutting of the door by you last night, please" is a past-
tense imperative; it expresses a wish (or preference) that you had
shut the door last night.

While Hare's approach works, I prefer to stretch our ordinary
English forms. I'd express Hare's example as "Would that you had
shut the door last night." I'll call this an "imperative," even though
it stretches the term (see Ibberson 1979 and Hare 1979a); we
might instead invent a term (like "volitive") for this stretched
sense. I'll also take these to be imperatives:

---

[1] Strictly speaking, "Do this now" means "Do this in the immediate future" –
and so is future tense (see Hare 1952: 17). The closest we can get to a genuinely
present-tense second-person imperative is "Would that you were doing this now"
and this is an "imperative" only in a stretched sense.

- "He is to do A," "Would that he do A."
- "Everyone is to do A," "Let everyone do A."
- "Act A is to be done," "Let A be done."

I'll also include imperatives that you address to yourself, like "Turn left at the next block" or "Let me turn now."

This wide notion of "imperative" is a theoretical construct. It's designed to help us represent the content of acts of will linguistically. It isn't derived solely from existing speech acts, and it isn't limited to sentences that tell someone else what to do.

Consider this ice cream imperative, which is intended to cover all persons and tenses:

IC   Would that no one in any situation at any time eat ice cream.

Suppose that (quite out of character) I accept this principle and intend it to be overriding. And suppose that it's fully integrated into my character, into my motivational system.[1] Then it would reflect my *will* – my actions, intentions, desires, regrets, and so on.

IC entails "Don't eat ice cream now" (addressed to myself). To accept this is to *act* on it: to try to conduct my actions accordingly – to act with the intention of not eating ice cream. Intentionally eating ice cream clashes with my acceptance of IC. But eating it by mistake (thinking that it was something else) needn't involve inconsistency of will. I distinguish these forms:

- I act (in order) to do A.
- I do A.

The first is about what I intend to do – what I'm trying to do. The second is about what I actually do. If I try to kick a goal, but I fail, then only the first form is true. If I fall down accidentally, then only the second is true. Consistency of will requires the first form – that I act with the intention of doing the thing.

IC entails "Don't eat ice cream in the future" (addressed to myself). To accept this is to *intend* to follow it – to *be resolved* not to eat ice cream in the future. Equivalently, it is to *desire* or *want* not to do it, using these terms to mean *intend* (instead of *feel like*).[2]

---

[1] This phrasing is from Audi 1989 (22). My motivational system may be largely a matter of habit; I might have a firm disposition to shun ice cream that I seldom think about or am consciously aware of.

[2] As I walk to the dentist's office, I *want* to go in the sense that I *intend* to go. But I don't *feel like* going (there's no "felt desire") – and in that sense I don't *want* to go. The *intending* sense is relevant here. So I take *wanting to do* as (roughly) a disposition or commitment to act, not a disposition to have positive feelings. I also

IC entails "Would that no one else eat ice cream." To accept this is to *desire* or *want* others not to eat ice cream.

IC also entails "Would that no one in the past had eaten ice cream." We don't use such forms much; but we do say "Would that I hadn't eaten so much yesterday!" To accept such imperatives (or wishes) about the past is to *regret* (or to *be glad*) that the action was (or wasn't) done. "Regret" here is a *wish* or *preference* that I had acted otherwise. There needn't be guilt, remorse, or blame (although these are sometimes appropriate).

So to *accept* an imperative is to *will* (in a generic sense) the corresponding actions to be done – to endorse the actions in a way appropriate to their person and tense. I act, am resolved to act, want others to act, regret the act, or am glad the act took place:

	My act	*Another's act*
Present	I act in order to do it	I want the person
Future	I am resolved to do it	to do it
Past	I regret it wasn't done or am glad it was done	

I'll often use these equivalences in deriving theorems.

The phrase "accepting an imperative" doesn't have a clear use in ordinary speech. I set it up as a technical phrase, to help us derive consistency theorems about willing. If these theorems are fine (see Sections 3.3 to 3.8), then I got my equivalences right.

I'll sometimes use the *permissive* form: "You *may* do A." I intend this to be a weaker member of the imperative family.[1] It expresses our *consent* to the act, but not necessarily our desire that the act take place. We can consistently consent both to the act and to its omission – saying "You may do A and you may omit A."

If I accept "Anyone in any situation at any time *may* eat ice cream" then I *consent* to the idea of anyone eating ice cream in any situation. We also can use words like *approve, allow, agree to, condone, tolerate,* or *am willing that*.[2] Consenting here is an inner attitude, the opposite of inwardly condemning (objecting to,

take "want" as "want on the whole" ("want on balance," "want more than any competing want") – not as "want to some degree." And I take it as "want for its own sake or for the sense of something else" – not as "want for its own sake."

[1] People sometimes use "You *may* do A" to express ethical permissibility – to mean "It's *all right* for you to do A." I won't use "may" in this sense.

[2] Words like "approve" can have other senses. For example, approving can be a bureaucratic action (as when you officially approve a student's thesis by signing a form). I have in mind rather an inner attitude.

disapproving, forbidding, protesting, prohibiting, repudiating) the act. Consenting is a minimal attitude and needn't involve favoring or advocating the act.

3.2 A Rationality Axiom

We now introduce our broader consistency axiom – applicable to statements and imperatives alike. I call it the *rationality* axiom.[1] Here's a rough formulation:

R   One ought to think and live consistently with logic and the
      other axioms of formal ethics.

This is like Lewis 1946 (481): "Be consistent in valuation and in thought and action." The precise version has two parts:

> R   If A_1, ..., A_n ($n \geq 1$), either by themselves or
>   conjoined with other axioms of formal ethics,
>   form an inconsistent set, then you ought not to
>   combine accepting A_1, ..., and accepting A_n.
>
>   If A_1, ..., A_n ($n \geq 1$), either by themselves or
>   conjoined with other axioms of formal ethics,
>   entail B, then you ought not to combine accepting
> A_1, ..., accepting A_n, and not accepting B.

Here A_1, ..., A_n and B can stand for statements, imperatives, or permissives. I modeled axiom R after {L3, L4}; all our L-principles are theorems derivable from R. Instances of axiom R have a *don't-combine* form. The "provided that QF" qualification is implicit in axiom R and any theorem derived from it.

The second part of R has "entail." What does it mean to say that one imperative *entails* another? And what does it mean to call an imperative argument "valid"? Consider this imperative argument:

> When the cocoa is boiling, remove it from the heat.
> The cocoa is boiling now.
> ∴ Remove it from the heat now.

This is intuitively valid – but not in the usual sense of "valid":

> A *valid* argument is one in which it would be contradictory for the premises to be true but the conclusion false.

---

[1] I call R the *rationality* axiom because one core sense of this ambiguous term (see Sapontzis 1979) is about avoiding inconsistencies. I don't claim that my axiom exhausts rationality. So I don't support what Darwall 1983 (49–50) attacks as *coherentism*: "that reason's only role with respect to conduct is to achieve a coherence with intentions, beliefs, desires and/or preferences."

This doesn't apply, since imperatives aren't true or false. So for imperative arguments we'll shift to this broader definition of "valid" that avoids "true" and "false":

A *valid* argument is one in which the conjunction of the premises with the contradictory of the conclusion is inconsistent.

Then to say that our cocoa argument is "valid" means that this combination is inconsistent:

When the cocoa is boiling, remove it from the heat. The cocoa is boiling now. But don't remove it from the heat now.

Since this is inconsistent, our cocoa argument is *valid* in the new sense. And we can use axiom R on it to derive a theorem:

You ought not to combine (1) accepting "When the cocoa is boiling remove it from the heat," (2) accepting "The cocoa is boiling now," and (3) not accepting "Remove it from the heat now."

This rephrasing uses the equivalences of the last section:

You ought to combine (1) wanting to remove the cocoa from the heat when it's boiling, (2) believing that the cocoa is boiling now, and (3) not acting to remove it from the heat.

We'll add three further axioms to help us generate consistency principles about ends–means, conscientiousness, and impartiality. Our system has this axiomatic structure:

- Four axioms (PURE): Prescriptivity, Universalizability, Rationality, Ends-means. These are used to derive theorems.

- Five groups of theorems (LOGIC): Logicality, Omni-perspective (Universal Law), Golden Rule, Impartiality, Conscientiousness.

- Theorems are labeled by one of these nine letters followed by a number. So L1 is a theorem about logicality.

- Nontheorems are labeled like theorems, except that they end in a small letter. So L1a is a nontheorem about logicality.

Just remember: formal ethics is based on PURE LOGIC.[1]

Section 2.5 (Q1) distinguished five formats for our principles. We'll accept these formats for axiom R (for the first blank put "$A_1, ..., A_n$ ($n \geq 1$), either by themselves or conjoined with other

---

[1] Other people may want to add axioms – perhaps to incorporate things like decision theory, supererogatory actions, or evaluative terms besides "ought" and "all right." Formal ethics is meant to be an open system.

There's irony in my "PURE LOGIC" acronym. Many would agree with B. Cohen 1977 (78), who says: "The aim of establishing systems of ethics on the basis of logic has long been abandoned as a project for moral philosophy." And while Plato (*Republic*, VI, 509–11) and others talk about axiomatic systems in ethics, I'm one of the few who actually gives one.

axioms of formal ethics, form an inconsistent set" – and for the second put "combine accepting A_1, ..., and accepting A_n"):[1]

Ro   Ought (same as R): If ..., then you ought not to ....

Rv   Virtue: Consistency is a virtue – and involves being disposed that if ... then you not ....

Rd   Description: If ..., then it isn't consistent for you to ....

Ri   Imperative: If ..., then don't ....

Rh   Hypothetical imperative: If you want to be consistent, then if ... then you ought not to ....

Rv, Rd, and Rh take *consistency* in a wide sense, to include logical consistency in believing and willing, ends–means consistency, conscientiousness, and impartiality. Ro equivalently claims that we *ought* to be consistent in this wide sense.

3.3 Ends and Means

Our *ends–means* axiom goes this way:[2]

> E   "Do end E" entails "If your doing means M is causally necessary for you to do end E, then do means M."

Here's an example:

> "Save the file" entails "If your clicking the SAVE button is causally necessary for you to save the file, then click the SAVE button."

The end and the means must be actions. So a computer can't literally be an end – but buying (borrowing, renting) one can be.

Suppose that you're a lawyer and want to defend your client competently. You realize that this requires that you investigate the case. So you investigate. This practical syllogism expresses your reasoning:

> Defend this client competently.
> Your investigating the case is causally necessary for you to defend this client competently.
> ∴ Investigate the case. {By E.}

---

[1] The second part of each axiom would be similar. I use an "o," "v," "d," "i," or "h" to show the format: *ought*, *virtue*, *description*, *imperative*, or *hypothetical imperative*. I'll sometimes use these letters with theorems.

[2] The words "end" and "means" in E are part of the variables and can be omitted. By our definition of "valid," E claims that this combination is inconsistent: "Do E. Your doing M is causally necessary for you to do E. But don't do M."

The premises express your desire and your belief. An imperative conclusion follows. Accepting this involves intending to act.

Our axiom speaks of the means being causally *necessary*. A causally *sufficient* means isn't enough. This is invalid:

> Quench your thirst.
> Your having a Coke is causally sufficient in order for you to quench your thirst.
> ∴ Have a Coke. {This *doesn't* follow using E.}

We might consistently affirm the premises and yet have water instead. However, we can validly derive a disjunctive conclusion telling us to pick from the possible thirst quenchers:

> Quench your thirst.
> Your having water or a Coke or orange juice or … is causally necessary for you to quench your thirst.
> ∴ Have water or a Coke or orange juice or …. {By E.}

We'd then need to decide between thirst quenchers. Typically we'd narrow the list using other principles (like "Don't have a drink with sugar") and then just pick one of the remaining choices.

Axiom E leads to this ends–means consistency theorem:

> E1 You ought not to combine (1) wanting to do E, (2) believing that your doing M now is causally necessary for you to do E, and (3) not acting to do M.

I violate E1 if I (1) have an end, (2) believe that the means are necessary to fulfill the end, and (3) don't carry through on the means. To avoid the inconsistency, I have to change my end, my belief, or my failure to act; any of the three may be defective.

To derive E1, we first note that axiom E makes this valid:

> Do E.
> Your doing M now is causally necessary for you to do E.
> ∴ Do M now.

So by R you ought not to combine accepting the premises with not accepting the conclusion. To accept these is to want, believe, and act; so we get E1 by substituting equivalents.

By E1, our lawyer ought not to combine (1) wanting to defend this client competently, (2) believing that investigating now is causally necessary to defend this client competently, and (3) not acting to investigate. This forbids an inconsistent combination but doesn't say what specifically to do. The lawyer might reject both the end and the means – deciding not to take the case because the means are too troublesome.

We shouldn't confuse **E1** with this *if–then* nontheorem:

> **E1a** If you want to do E and believe that your doing M is causally
> necessary for you to do E, then you ought to do M.

Instances of **E1a** are called *hypothetical imperatives* and are popular among philosophers. The popularity is undeserved. **E1a** can imply absurdities – for example, that a madman ought to blow up an H-bomb. Suppose that the madman wants to destroy Chicago and believes that blowing up this H-bomb is causally necessary to do this. Then he ought to blow up the H-bomb. But this is absurd.[1]

E1 just tells the madman not to combine (1) wanting to destroy Chicago, (2) believing that blowing up this H-bomb now is necessary to do this, and (3) not acting to blow up this H-bomb. The combination is defective both *logically* (because it's inconsistent) and *ethically* (because the first element is defective).

E1a also can have self-contradictory implications. Suppose that Ima Lazy combines these four:

> W1   wanting to become a doctor,
> B1   believing that studying is necessary to become a doctor,
> W2   wanting to party all the time, and
> B2   believing that not-studying is necessary to party all the time.

E1a then entails that she *ought* to study – and *ought not* to study. Facts plus **E1a** can entail contradictions. So **E1a** would force *us* (and not just Ima) to accept contradictions.

On my approach, Ima's combination of desires and beliefs is inconsistent – and so she has to change something. If the two beliefs are firm, she has to decide between wanting to become a doctor and wanting to party all the time.

Consider this Humean *rational action* formula:

> **E1b** If you want to do E and believe that your doing M is causally
> necessary for you to do E, then *reason* directs that you do M.

This leads to absurdities, since then reason tells the madman to blow up the H-bomb and tells Ima Lazy to do incompatible things (studying and not studying). It's better to see ends–means rationality (using **E1**) as a species of consistency.[2]

---

[1] Here's another problem. Suppose that you believe that doing A is always causally necessary (in a trivial way) for you to do A. From this and **E1a** we can derive: "If you want to do A (lie, cheat, steal, ...), then you ought to do A."

[2] **E1a** and **E1b** suggest a "foundationalist" approach to practical reason, where

A *corollary* is a theorem derivable from a single previous axiom or theorem. An important corollary of E is Kant's Law, that *ought* implies *can*. In the words of Kant 1787 (A548 B57): "The action to which the '*ought*' applies must indeed be possible under natural conditions." Here's our formulation:

E2   "You ought to do A" entails "It's causally possible for you to do A."

It's significant that axiom E leads both to ends–means theorem E1 and to Kant's Law E2. The proof of E2 is technical; I'll give it in a footnote in the following optional (and technical) section.[1]

3.4 Ends–Means Questions

(Q1) Are there ethical ends–means theorems?

Yes. These corollaries let us go from the obligatoriness of the end to the obligatoriness of the necessary means – and from the wrongness of the necessary means to the wrongness of the end:

E3   "You ought to do E" entails "If your doing M is causally necessary for you to do E, then you ought to do M."

E4   "You ought not to do M" entails "If your doing M is causally necessary for you to do E, then you ought not to do E."

We need to harmonize our evaluations of ends and means.[2]

ends are given and we can deliberate about means but not ends (so Aristotle's doctor in *Nicomachean Ethics* 1112b can't deliberate about whether to heal). E1 suggests a "coherence" approach, where we adjust ends and means to fit together.

Despite my objections to the traditional hypothetical-imperative form, I'll sometimes use it. It would be more technically correct to avoid it entirely in favor of *don't-combine* formulas.

[1] Kant's Law has trivial exceptions. We say, "I *ought* to call her – but I *can't*." But we really mean, "If I could call her (which I can't do), then I'd have a duty to do so." As we did with double-negation (Section 2.3), we'll accept Kant's Law with the proviso that it doesn't cover such idiomatic cases.

[2] Non-logicians may want to skip these proofs, while logicians my want to look at Chapter 8 to pick up my symbolism. E3 follows from E:

$\square(\underline{E} \supset (\boxdot(\sim M \supset \sim E) \supset \underline{M}))$ {Axiom E.}

∴ $\square(O\underline{E} \supset O(\boxdot(\sim M \supset \sim E) \supset \underline{M}))$ {By $\square(\underline{A} \supset \underline{B})$ ∴ $\square(O\underline{A} \supset O\underline{B})$.}

∴ $\square(O\underline{E} \supset (\boxdot(\sim M \supset \sim E) \supset O\underline{M}))$ {By $\square O(A \supset \underline{B})$ ∴ $\square(A \supset O\underline{B})$.}

E4 also follows from E:

$\square(\underline{E} \supset (\boxdot(\sim M \supset \sim E) \supset \underline{M}))$ {Axiom E.}

∴ $\square(\sim\underline{M} \supset (\boxdot(\sim M \supset \sim E) \supset \sim\underline{E}))$ {Rearrange the previous step.}

∴ $\square(O\sim\underline{M} \supset O(\boxdot(\sim M \supset \sim E) \supset \sim\underline{E}))$ {By $\square(\underline{A} \supset \underline{B})$ ∴ $\square(O\underline{A} \supset O\underline{B})$.}

∴ $\square(O\sim\underline{M} \supset (\boxdot(\sim M \supset \sim E) \supset O\sim\underline{E}))$ {By $\square O(A \supset \underline{B})$ ∴ $\square(A \supset O\underline{B})$.}

Are "O$\underline{A}$" and "R$\underline{A}$" true if act A is necessary? The yes answer, which I and most

(Q2) Are there further analogues of Kant's Law?

Yes. Here are two:

E5   "Do A" entails "It's causally possible for you to do A."

E6   "It's all right for you to do A" entails "It's causally possible for you to do A."

It's convenient to derive these and *ought*-implies-*can* theorem E2 together. All are derivable from axiom E.[1]

These are corollaries about nonduties:

E7   "You can't do A" entails "You don't have a duty to do A."

E8   "You can't combine doing A and doing B" entails "Either you don't have a duty to do A, or you don't have a duty to do B."

By E7, Ima has no duty to become a doctor if she's incapable of this. By E8, I don't have simultaneous duties to take care of my sick brother and drive you to the airport if I can't combine both actions. These ideas are useful when people make impossible demands on us.[2]

Here's another corollary:

E9   "You ought to do either A or B – but you can't do A" entails "You ought to do B."

---

deontic logicians give, is harmless and simplifies things. Some give a no answer, insisting that "O$\underline{A}$" and "R$\underline{A}$" entail or presuppose that act A is contingent. With this view, we'd have to add occasional provisos that a given act isn't necessary.

[1] Our proof goes as follows:

   $\Box(\underline{E} \supset (\boxdot(\sim M \supset \sim E) \supset \underline{M}))$ {Axiom E.}

∴ $\Box(\underline{A} \supset (\boxdot(\sim\sim A \supset \sim A) \supset \sim\underline{A}))$ {Put "A" for "E" and "~A" for "M."}

∴ $\Box((\underline{A} \cdot \underline{A}) \supset \sim\boxdot(\sim\sim A \supset \sim A))$ {Rearrange the previous step.}

∴ $\Box(\underline{A} \supset \Diamond A)$ {Substitute equivalents; this formula is theorem E5.}

∴ $\Box(\sim\Diamond A \supset \sim\underline{A})$ {Contrapositive.}

∴ $\Box(\sim\Diamond A \supset O\sim\underline{A})$ {By $\Box(P \supset Q) \therefore \Box(P \supset OQ)$.}

∴ $\Box(\sim O\sim\underline{A} \supset \Diamond A)$ {Contrapositive.}

∴ $\Box(R\underline{A} \supset \Diamond A)$ {Substitute equivalents; this is theorem E6.}

   $\Box(O\underline{A} \supset R\underline{A})$ {Law of deontic logic.}

∴ $\Box(O\underline{A} \supset \Diamond A)$ {From the last two steps; this is theorem E2.}

[2] It's important that E7 and E8 (and our other theorems) are about overriding (non-prima-facie) duties. Their derivations go as follows:

   $\Box(O\underline{A} \supset \Diamond A)$ {Theorem E2.}

∴ $\Box(\sim\Diamond A \supset \sim O\underline{A})$ {Contrapositive; this is theorem E7.}

∴ $\Box(\sim\Diamond(A \cdot B) \supset \sim O(\underline{A} \cdot \underline{B}))$ {Substitute "(A · B)" for "A."}

   $\Box((O\underline{A} \cdot O\underline{B}) \supset O(\underline{A} \cdot \underline{B}))$ {Deontic law; this fails for prima facie duties.}

∴ $\Box(\sim\Diamond(A \cdot B) \supset \sim(O\underline{A} \cdot O\underline{B}))$ {From the two previous steps.}

∴ $\Box(\sim\Diamond(A \cdot B) \supset (\sim O\underline{A} \lor \sim O\underline{B}))$ {From the previous step; this is E8.}

B. Williams 1965 and Donagan 1984 discuss E8.

So if I ought to either follow Red Canyon downstream or climb out the side drainage, but I can't do the former (because of a big drop that I can't get around), then I ought to do the latter.[1]

All these corollaries have corresponding *don't-combine* consistency theorems – like this one based on E5:

E10 You ought not to combine (1) believing that it's causally impossible for you to do A with (2) wanting to do A.

By E10, Ima Lazy ought not to combine (1) believing that she's incapable of being a doctor with (2) wanting to be a doctor. (Recall that we are using *wanting* in the sense of *intending*.)

(Q3) What does "can" mean in Kant's Law?

Indeterminists can take "It's causally possible for you to do A" ("◇A") to mean "Your-doing-A isn't precluded by the laws of nature plus the state of the world prior to the action"; with trivial premises, Kant's Law then entails the falsity of determinism.[2] To avoid this, determinists could take it instead to mean "Your-doing-A isn't *known* (prior to the action) to be precluded by the laws of nature plus the state of the world prior to the action." What would nullify a moral judgment (and make choosing redundant) would then be not just that our choice is determined but that we know beforehand what choice we were determined to make.

(Q4) What does "It's causally necessary that if you don't do M then you won't do E" mean?

---

[1] E9 follows from E6:

$\square(R\underline{A} \supset \Diamond A)$ {Theorem E6.}

$\square((O(\underline{A} \vee \underline{B}) \cdot \sim R\underline{A}) \supset O\underline{B})$ {Theorem of deontic logic.}

∴ $\square((O(\underline{A} \vee \underline{B}) \cdot \sim\Diamond A) \supset O\underline{B})$ {From the last two steps.}

We can't use E2 (*ought* implies *can*) in the first step, because then the second step would have to be "$\square((O(\underline{A} \vee \underline{B}) \cdot \sim O\underline{A}) \supset O\underline{B})$" – which isn't a deontic truth. E6 (*all right* implies *can*) is stronger than E2 (*ought* implies *can*).

[2] The anti-determinist argument goes this way (where A is some act that you ought to have done but didn't do):

Act A wasn't done. {Premise.}

Act A ought to have been done. {Premise.}

∴ It was causally possible to have done A. {From the previous step by Kant's Law.}

∴ Act A wasn't precluded by the laws of nature plus the state of the world prior to the action. {By the indeterminist reading of "causally possible."}

If determinism is true and act A wasn't done, then act A was precluded by the laws of nature plus the state of the world prior to the action. {By the definition of determinism.}

∴ Determinism is false. {By the two previous steps and the first step.}

Indeterminists can take it (and "$\boxdot(\sim M \supset \sim E)$") to mean "The laws of nature plus the state of the world prior to the action necessitate that if you don't do M then you won't do E." The determinist version (based on the Q3 answer and "$\boxdot A \leftrightarrow \sim \diamond \sim A$") would be "It's *known* (prior to the action) that the laws of nature plus the state of the world prior to the action necessitate that if you don't do M then you won't do E."

> (Q5) Could one accept *ought*-implies-*can* but take "implies" as weaker than logical entailment?

Yes. Here are some other possibilities:

> "*Ought* implies *can*" need not be construed as asserting a strict logical implication. It may plausibly be understood as saying: (a) moral judgments "presuppose" ... or "pragmatically imply" that the agent is able to act ...; or (b) the *point of uttering* moral judgments disappears if the agents involved are not able to act ...; or (c) it would be morally wrong to insist that an agent ought to do a certain action, if he is or is thought to be unable to do it.
>
> (Frankena 1954: 60)

If we wanted to weaken Kant's Law, we'd have to weaken axiom E (which entails Kant's Law). We could instead use a plain if–then (nonentailment) form of E6 as our axiom; this would let us prove plain if–then forms of all the E-principles. The practical difference to our system would be slight. I take *ought*-implies-*can* to express an entailment because this logically follows from the entailment form of axiom E – which in turn seems correct.

3.5 Follow Your Conscience

Conscientiousness requires that we keep our actions, resolutions, and desires in harmony with our ethical beliefs. We'll generate conscientiousness duties using *weak prescriptivity* axiom P:

P	If you ought to do A, then do A.
	If it's all right for you to do A, then you may do A.

Adding axiom P is equivalent to adding that we *ought* to be conscientious. We also could phrase the axiom as: "Would that everyone do what they ought to do; and anyone may do what is all right"; this expresses a practical commitment to morality – just as our ice cream imperative in Section 3.1 expressed a practical commitment to not eating ice cream. Our axiom applies to all persons and tenses, and to counterfactual judgments as well as to actual ones; starting it with "In every actual or hypothetical case" would make the second point explicit. "Ought" and "all right" here are to be taken in their all-things-being-considered evaluative sense. P doesn't say that an *ought* judgment logically entails an imperative; but it might be defended using such a principle.

This important theorem (expressed in precise and intuitive ways) requires that I act on my ethical beliefs:

> C1 Don't combine (1) believing that you ought
> to do A now with (2) not acting to do A.
> = Don't believe that something is your duty
> without acting to do it.

If I believe that I ought to do A but don't act with the intention of doing it, then I violate C1. Since my beliefs clash with my actions, I must change one or the other; either may be defective.

Our derivation of C1 uses the abbreviations in the box:

> 1 = "You ought to do A now."
> 2 = "Do A now."

1 with axiom P logically entails 2.
∴ You ought not to combine accepting 1 with not accepting 2. {By axiom R.}
∴ You ought not to combine believing that you ought to do A now with not acting to do A. {Rephrasing previous step.}
∴ Don't combine believing that you ought to do A now with not acting to do A. {By axiom P – which lets us go from "You ought not to...." to the more concise "Don't...."}

C1 just forbids inconsistent combinations. Even when we add further facts, C1 doesn't tell us specifically what to believe or do.

This *if–then* form of "Follow your conscience" is a nontheorem:

C1a If you believe that you ought to do A, then you ought to do A.

This can imply absurdities. Suppose that Ima *believes* that he ought to commit mass murder. Then he *ought* to do it. C1a tells us, implausibly, that whatever we take to be our duty actually is our duty – we can't be in error about what we ought to do.[1]

---

[1] The distinction between C1 and C1a makes precise Whately's 1857 (29) point: "While ... you take care, on the one hand, not to do anything that your

The example of Huckleberry Finn (Twain 1884: 124–8) brings out further problems with **C1a**. Huck helped his friend to escape from slavery – even though he believed that he ought to have turned him in. His actions clashed with his beliefs; but his beliefs were defective, not his actions. **C1a** says otherwise; since Huck *believed* that he ought to have turned in the slave, he thus *ought* to have done this.

Here's a case where **C1a** has self-contradictory implications. Ima Absolutist *believes* that he ought to do everything that he promised; so he *ought* to do everything that he promised. But he promised the judge to tell the truth; so he *ought* to tell the truth. And he promised the defendant not to tell the truth; so he *ought not* to tell the truth. So facts plus **C1a** can entail contradictions.

Other conscientiousness principles are somewhat like **C1**. This theorem forbids us to do what we think is wrong:

C2 Don't combine (1) believing that it's wrong for you to do A now with (2) acting to do A.

If you combine the two, then either your belief or your action is defective.[1] Here are three further theorems:

C3 Don't combine (1) believing that act A is all right with (2) not consenting to the idea of A being done.

C4 Don't combine (1) believing that everyone ought to do A with (2) not acting to do A yourself.

C5 Don't combine (1) believing that everyone ought to do A with (2) not willing that everyone do A.

Theorem **C3** covers *permissibility* judgments. **C4** expresses "Practice what you preach" (see Section 1.2 Q3). And **C5** requires

---

conscience tells you is wrong, you must beware, on the other, of concluding that your conduct is necessarily right because your conscience approves of it." Ewing 1965 (144–5) defends **C1a** by distinguishing different senses of *ought*. My *don't-combine* solution is better, since it has wider application (to consistent believing, ends–means rationality, the golden rule, and so forth) and doesn't multiply senses. See also Dancy 1977, Govier 1972, and Jennings 1974.

[1] The proof of **C2** is somewhat like that of **C1**. Let 1 = "It's wrong for you to do A now" and 2 = "Do A now." The proof then goes this way:

    1 with axiom **P** is inconsistent with 2. {Since 1 means "You ought not to do A" – which with **P** entails "Don't do A."}

∴ You ought not to combine accepting 1 with accepting 2. {By **R**.}

∴ You ought not to combine believing that it's wrong for you to do A now with acting to do A. {Rephrasing previous step.}

∴ Don't combine believing that it's wrong for you to do A now with acting to do A. {By axiom **P**.}

that we will our *ought* principles as universal laws (intending to follow them and wanting others to follow them too).

Many of our theorems will use this corollary of P:

P1   "Do A" with axiom P entails "It's all right for you to do A."

By our Section 3.2 definition of "entails," this means:

"Do A" with axiom P is inconsistent with "It's not all right for you to do A."

This holds because "It's not all right for you to do A" entails "You ought not to do A" – which by axiom P gives us "Don't do A."

P1 doesn't say that if you do A then your act is all right – or that "It's all right to do A" follows from the truth or endorsement of "Do A." Instead, P1's main implication is that acting to do A (accepting "Do A now") commits us to believing "It's all right to do A now" (see Gensler 1983):

C6   Don't combine (1) acting to do A with (2) not believing that it's all right for you to do A now.

(Since believing is a disposition, we needn't *consciously* judge that our act is permissible – see Section 2.5 Q3.) So our theorems require both that we act on our ethical beliefs and that we form ethical beliefs about our actions.

3.6 Conscientious Pacifism

Jim was a pacifist friend of mine during the Vietnam War. His example may help us to understand conscientiousness better.

Jim held that one ought in no conceivable case to kill a human being. He tried to be conscientious. He was concerned that his ethical principles be, not just words, but in harmony with his life – how he acted and resolved to act, and how he wanted others to act. One challenge was difficult. Jim imagined coming home and finding a madman about to kill his wife and family – and the only way to stop it was by killing him. By Jim's pacifist principle, this was wrong; so he'd have to resolve not to kill. After a struggle, he concluded, "Yes, I firmly resolve and intend and hope never to kill – even in a situation where if I don't kill then my family will die."

The relevant consistency principle here goes like this:

C7   Don't combine (1) believing that one ought in no conceivable case to do A with (2) not being resolved to refrain from doing A if situation S took place.

Jim satisfied the theorem. He believed that one ought in no conceivable case to kill a human being; and he was resolved to refrain from killing – even if killing a madman were needed to save his family. If Jim had violated the theorem, then he'd have a duty to get his ethical beliefs and resolutions into harmony with each other; he could then either give up his pacifism or else resolve to follow it in this situation.

The important question for Jim's case is this:

Q1   Do you resolve that if killing a madman were needed to save your family then you refrain from killing?

This is about his *present attitude* toward a hypothetical situation. To be consistent *now*, Jim has to be able to answer yes. But his draft board asked him something else:

Q2   If killing were needed to save your family, would you refrain from killing?

The second question is about what he'd do if the situation came about – whether he'd *then* be consistent. This has nothing to do with whether he's consistent *now*. Jim responded well:

I don't know. I might lose control and kill; it's hard to predict what you'll do in a panic situation. But I *now* firmly hope and resolve that I not kill in such a situation.

This brings out an important distinction. Our theorems prescribe that we be consistent *now*. They deal with our *present* attitudes, including those toward hypothetical situations. They don't deal with how we would act or what attitudes we would have under different conditions. Q1 is the correct question to test Jim's present consistency.

3.7 Why Be Conscientious?

Since discussing "Why be consistent?" in Section 2.6, we added three axioms. Two of these – rationality and ends–means – can be defended in roughly the same ways as before. To see the parallel, imagine that you have volitional contradictitis: every time you desire to do A, you also desire *not* to do A. This too would be a living hell. As Blackburn 1993 (190) put it, "Incompatible and therefore unrealizable goals are bad in a way quite analogous to the way in which inconsistent beliefs are bad."

Our *weak prescriptivity* axiom presents a new problem:

P   If you ought to do A, then do A.
    If it's all right for you to do A, then you may do A.

P generates *conscientiousness* duties: that we ought to keep our actions, resolutions, and desires in harmony with our ethical beliefs. P is equivalent to adding that we *ought* to be conscientious. How can we justify axiom P? Why be conscientious?

Our answer depends on how we view *strong prescriptivity* – logical-entailment principle SP:

SP   "You ought to do A" entails "Do A."
     "It's all right for you to do A" entails "You may do A."

Let's suppose for the moment that SP is true. This would solve the problem of justifying P and conscientiousness. For then P would be derivable from the true logical-entailment principle SP. And violations of conscientiousness would be violations of logical consistency (which we have already shown how to defend).

SP relates ethical judgments closely to imperatives and actions. An ordinary statement like "This man is bleeding" doesn't by itself entail an imperative to do any specific thing. And if I believe that this man is bleeding, that doesn't commit me, under pain of inconsistency, to any specific act; the way I live can't be inconsistent with this belief (taken by itself). But "I *ought* to call the doctor" *does* entail a specific imperative ("Call the doctor"). And if I believe that I *ought* to call the doctor, then that commits me, under pain of inconsistency, to action; if I don't act, then the way I live is inconsistent with my belief.

We need some cautions here. First, SP presupposes that we're using an all-things-being-considered evaluative sense of *ought* (or *all right*). This combination is inconsistent: "All things being considered, you *ought* to do A; but *don't* do A." But there needn't be any inconsistency if we use a weaker sense of *ought*:

- You ought (according to company policy) to do this – but don't!
- You ought (other things being equal) to keep this promise. But other factors override the obligation. So don't keep the promise.
- You ought (insofar as your duties to others go) to volunteer. But you need to think of yourself too. So don't volunteer.

Our discussion here presumes that *ought* and *all right* have an all-things-being-considered evaluative sense.

Also, SP doesn't entail that we in fact always act to do what we think we ought. Rather, it entails that we're logically inconsistent when we don't do this.[1]

Nonnaturalists and Kantians could accept SP. Both groups are sometimes criticized for making these two claims but not explaining how they're possible on their theory:

- Moral judgments have a rational authority over us.
- Normal people are motivated to follow their moral beliefs.

Using SP, they could explain that an *ought* judgment is authoritative because it's a truth that logically entails an imperative. If we accept the *ought* but don't act on it, then we're inconsistent (and violate reason). Normal people are motivated to be consistent, and thus to follow their moral beliefs.

Emotivists could accept SP – and say that *ought* judgments have imperative force in addition to emotive force. Ayer 1946 (108) states, "The sentence 'You ought to tell the truth' also involves the command 'Tell the truth.'"

SP is a standard part of prescriptivism, which sees *ought* and *all right* judgments as prescriptions that entail imperatives and permissives. Hare 1952 (161–72) makes it true by definition that an *ought* judgment isn't *evaluative* unless it entails an imperative and thus commits one to action.

SP is less plausible on views like cultural relativism, the ideal observer theory, and supernaturalism. These see moral judgments as ordinary descriptive judgments – which don't seem to entail imperatives or logically commit us to action.

Let's now assume that SP is false[2] – and see how to defend P and conscientiousness on this basis. If SP is false, then P and conscientiousness have no special logical credentials. There's no logical inconsistency in saying: "All things being considered, you

---

[1] *Internalism* is a family of views about moral beliefs and motivation (see Frankena 1954 and Dreier 1990). Internalists hold that it's logically (or causally) necessary that one who has a moral belief always (or typically) has some (or overriding) motivation to act accordingly. Only a very strong internalism (which says that everyone of necessity is completely conscientious) would make it unnecessary to ask why one should be conscientious. SP entails internalism only if we add a premise that it's logically (or causally) necessary that people always (or typically) have some (or overriding) motivation to be consistent.

[2] An intermediate view is that prescriptivity expresses, not a strict entailment, but a "presupposition" or "pragmatic implication." Along similar lines, Hoche 1990 claims that "X ought to do A" pragmatically implies "I intend that X do A."

ought to do A; but *don't* do A." This may be *inconsistent* in some nonlogical sense; we might call it *ethically inconsistent*. But why care about this? Why accept imperative P? Why be conscientious?

As we did in Section 2.6, we'll now sketch various defenses. We'll first consider two promote-desire justifications.

Let's suppose that you have idealistic desires. Accordingly, you want to be a morally good person, and hence conscientious. You want to do the right thing for its own sake. You want your ethical beliefs to penetrate your life. You value integrity. Then P expresses your desires and conscientiousness promotes your goals.

Let's now suppose that you care only about promoting your self-interest in some narrow sense. It's plausible to think that conscientiousness will do this.

I'll follow the Hobbes-Brandt account of how self-interest can justify morality.[1] Imagine a society of egoists. Unintelligent egoists would lie, steal, and kill when it was to their immediate advantage; this would make life miserable for everyone and promote no one's interest. Intelligent egoists would set up rules to make life better for themselves. There'd be rules against lying, stealing, and killing – and in favor of cooperation and concern for others. People who violated the rules would suffer both external sanctions (alienation from others, social disapproval, legal penalties) and internal sanctions (guilt, anxiety, loss of self-respect); and people following the rules would be praised and made to feel good about themselves. These would ensure that you won't be happy unless you try to do your duty; but then self-interest justifies conscientiousness. To sum up: it's in everyone's self-interest to bring about an atmosphere in which it's in no one's self-interest to violate conscientiousness – and such an atmosphere by and large exists.

This justification works fairly well. Some isolated actions that violate conscientiousness may promote self-interest. But generally a policy of conscientiousness (instead of assessing individual actions in terms of self-interest) will be in your self-interest.[2]

We'll now briefly consider the other theories. I'll omit prescriptivism, since it accepts SP.

[1] Hobbes 1651 (84–105) used the punishments of an absolute monarch as sanctions. Brandt 1972 substituted social and psychological equivalents.

[2] Another factor (perhaps related to the Hobbesian explanation) is that distressing and unpleasant "cognitive dissonance" can occur when our beliefs conflict with our actions. This gives another self-interested reason for being conscientious.

Utilitarians could claim that conscientiousness promotes the general good: it's important for the good of society that people be motivated to do their duty. Ross's theory could accept this and add that conscientiousness is inherently good.

Definist theories could defend conscientiousness as demanded by society, or by ideal observers, or by God. Conscientiousness is important for social life and survival; and ideal observers and God are seen as conscientious and as supporting conscientiousness.

Nonnaturalists could see the conscientiousness norms as self-evident, or as derived from other self-evident norms, or as coherent with our ethical intuitions, or as something that ideal moral thinking leads us to. And emotivists could say "Hurrah!" to conscientiousness; moral beliefs express feelings, and we need to keep our feelings in harmony with how we live and want others to live.

3.8 Conscientiousness Examples

This section is an exercise in distinguishing theorems from nontheorems. It has three purposes. First, it gives a convenient format for considering possible counterexamples against our system; these can lead to adjustments or clarifications. Second, it gives a way to discuss interesting formulas and distinctions. Third, it helps to sharpen our understanding of formal ethical principles; often a subtle change in wording can turn a solid principle into one that has absurd consequences.

Is each of these a theorem or a nontheorem? Answers follow.

1. If you believe that you ought to get up out of bed now, then you'll get up out of bed.

2. If you want to lose weight and you believe that eating less is necessary in order to lose weight, then you'll eat less.

3. Don't believe that you ought to vote now without acting to vote.

4. You ought to do what you think you ought.

5. Don't combine (1) believing that it's all right for everyone to steal from everyone else with (2) not consenting to the idea of everyone else stealing from you.

6. Don't combine (1) believing that one ought to remain motionless when a shark approaches with (2) not having it be the case that if a shark approached then you'd remain motionless.

7. Don't hold that people ought to be concerned only with their own self-interest (regardless of harmful effects on others) without

desiring that when others deal with you they be concerned only with their own self-interest (regardless of harmful effects on you).

8. Don't hold that it's permissible for the opponent to tackle our quarterback without permitting the opponent to do this.

9. Don't combine (1) believing that abortion is always wrong with (2) not urging and forcing others to avoid abortion.

10. If you hold that you ought to blow up city hall, then you ought to act to blow up city hall.

11. If it's wrong to kill, then don't kill.

12. If it's all right to go, then go.

13. Don't accept that your act was wrong and yet at the same time not regret that you did it.

14. Don't combine (1) wanting X to do A with (2) not thinking that it would be all right for X to do A.

15. You ought not to combine accepting "The robbery is wrong" with wanting the robbery to take place.

16. Don't have it be that yesterday you accepted "I ought to go to the movie tomorrow" while today you don't act to go to the movie.

17. Don't combine accepting "All people over sixty ought to be shot" with not desiring that when you get over sixty then you be shot.

18. Don't accept "Murderers ought in every conceivable case to be executed" without it being the case that if you were a murderer then you would want to be executed.

19. "It's causally necessary that I seek pleasure for its own sake" entails "I ought to seek pleasure for its own sake."

20. "Studying is causally necessary to become a teacher" entails "Either study or don't become a teacher."

21. "Studying is causally necessary to become a teacher" entails "You *ought* to either study or else not become a teacher."

22. You ought not to act to do something without believing that what you're doing is permissible.

23. "It's obligatory that you not do some jobs that you're doing" entails "It's causally possible that you not do some jobs that you're doing."

24. Don't accept "Racism is always wrong – and this candidate supports racism" while also supporting the candidate.

25. You ought not to combine (1) doing the right thing with (2) not being motivated to do the right thing for its own sake.

Now I'll give the answers.

1 is a nontheorem. I often know what I ought to do and yet don't do it; I'm often inconsistent. Knowledge isn't virtue. Plato might object that I don't really believe an *ought* judgment if I don't act on it; this might be a psychological truth or a semantic point about *believing* an ethical judgment. This view makes it impossible to violate conscientiousness – an implausible result.

2 is a nontheorem. It's wrong for at least three reasons: (1) you might violate it because you're weak-willed and inconsistent, (2) you might find it burdensome to eat less and so you might instead give up the goal of losing weight, and (3) eating less might be impossible or in conflict with another desire.

Some say that you don't really want the end if you don't carry out the admittedly necessary means; this might be a psychological truth or a semantic stipulation on what it is to *want* something. This view (like Plato's view mentioned above and the psychologistic view of Section 2.5 Q5) transforms our consistency norms into descriptions of how people always think and act.

This view is overstated (as is Plato's). You'd have few desires (or ethical beliefs) if their very existence depended on their being perfectly consistent with how you live. Your desire to lose weight, even when you don't act on it, may show itself in other ways. Maybe you have uneasiness or regret over how you eat. Or at cool moments (when not tempted) you may vow to eat less. Or when you overeat you may act on desires that you desire not to have; you'd modify your impulses if you knew how or if you could do this through sheer will power; so you intend that "Eat less" be an overriding action guide over your unruly nature.

3 is a theorem.

4 is ambiguous. It's a theorem if it means "You ought not to combine (1) thinking that you ought to do A with (2) not acting to do A." This forbids acting against your conscience. It's a nontheorem if it means "If you *think* you ought to do A, then you *ought* to do A." This says that your conscience can't be mistaken.

5 is a theorem. "It's all right for everyone to steal from everyone else" with P implies "Everyone else may steal from you."

6 is a nontheorem. The correct form (see Section 3.6) is about your present attitude toward a hypothetical case; you ought not to combine (1) believing that one ought to remain motionless when a shark approaches with (2) not being resolved that if a shark approached then you'd remain motionless.

7 is a theorem; this makes it difficult to hold ethical egoism consistently. But the egoist might deny that believing "X ought to do A" commits one to *wanting* X to do A (see Kalin 1970). The egoist might appeal to football and chess examples:

FB   I believe that my opponent ought to kick (or try to kick) a goal; but I don't want her to do this.

CH   I believe that my opponent ought to make this move (which would checkmate me); but I don't want her to do this.

EG   I believe that X ought to act egoistically toward me; but I don't want X to do this.

The first two seem like permissible combinations. And so EG (egoism) would also seem like a permissible combination.

However, the *ought* in FB and CH is only hypothetical. When we talk about what our opponent in a game *ought* to do, we mean what she *ought to do to achieve victory*. This is like what a robber *ought to do in order to pull off the robbery*. A hypothetical *ought* doesn't commit us to desiring the act.

We make various kinds of *ought* judgment about a game. There are strategic *ought* judgments about what one ought to do to achieve victory (as in FB and CH); these are hypothetical imperatives and don't commit us to desiring the acts. Other *ought* judgments are about good sportsmanship – like "My opponent ought not to break my leg" and "You ought not to cheat"; these are all-things-being-considered evaluations, and commit us to desiring the acts. If EG is taken as an all-things-being-considered evaluation, then it too will commit us to desiring the act.[1]

8 is ambiguous. Whether it's a theorem depends on how we take "permitting." I think that it's permissible to tackle the quarterback of an opposing team, but not to break his arm intentionally. Suppose that I'm playing football. For the sake of my team, I'll try to stop you from tackling our quarterback; and in that sense I don't consent to (permit, allow) your action. Yet if you do tackle our quarterback, I won't condemn or disapprove or object to your action (as I would if you intentionally break his arm); and in this sense I do consent to the action. My theorems use the latter sense.

---

[1] Another possible reply sees FB and CH as about all-things-being-considered evaluations, inconsistent, and permissible by way of exception (the prima facie duty to avoid inconsistency being overridden by our duty as game participants to desire only the good of our side). I'll take an "exception" approach for example 15. But this reply here would weaken the case against egoism. If FB and CH are exceptions, then EG may be too. The grounds that make FB and CH exceptions don't apply to EG; but EG may be an exception on other grounds. In any case, we needn't take the "exception" approach here.

Section 3.1 stressed that I intend "consenting" to refer to an inner attitude of a minimal sort that needn't involve favoring or advocating the action. Perhaps it's clearer to use the term "willing": I'm *willing* that the opponent try to tackle our quarter-back (although I'll try to stop him).

Gauthier 1968 used an objection like this to argue that "Act A is permissible" doesn't commit one to permitting or allowing act A. My reply is that "Act A is permissible" *does* commit one to this, at least if we take "permitting" and "allowing" correctly. Thornton 1971 replied differently, claiming that morality isn't like football and that if we claim (outside of such games) that act A is all right we must thereby permit (or allow) act A to happen.[1]

9 is a nontheorem. The person has to *will* that no one have abortions. This involves intending not to have abortions oneself and desiring that others not have them. It needn't involve blaming people who have abortions, or thinking that they're evil people. It needn't involve urging others not to have abortions or acting through legal means to stop people from having them. One might consistently think that abortion is wrong but shouldn't be against the law. What challenges this isn't formal ethics but rather our firm view that the law should protect life.

10 is a nontheorem. The correct form tells you not to combine (1) believing that you ought to blow up city hall with (2) not acting to blow up city hall. This combination is defective both because it's inconsistent and because the first element is defective.

11 is a theorem. It's equivalent to this instance of P: "If you ought not to kill, then don't kill." This doesn't need a *don't-combine* form, since axiom R isn't used in the derivation.

12 is a nontheorem. By P, we get "If it's all right to go, then you *may* go."

13 is a theorem – provided that the *wrong* judgment and the regret are qualified the same way. We often shift the standpoint with past actions. I might admit that I did wrong (based on what I

---

[1] Wilson 1988 (120) objected to my view: "It is not morally wrong for someone to put sugar in my coffee. It doesn't follow that I will consent to this – I do not like sweet coffee." This is beside the point, since I don't hold that "Act A is permissible" entails "I consent to act A." The objection would need to claim that it's consistent for me to think that it's permissible for you to put sugar in my coffee while refusing to consent to the idea of your doing this. If "permissible" is evaluative, this doesn't seem consistent. The example is odd; if I don't like sweet coffee, why should I think that it's permissible for you to put sugar in my coffee?

know now), but acted rightly relative to what I knew then – and so I don't regret the action from that standpoint. This is consistent. Relative to what I know now, the act was wrong and I regret it; but relative to what I knew then, the act was right and I approve of it.

14 is a theorem. From "Would that X do A" we can derive, using P1, "It would be all right for X to do A."

15 is a theorem. "The robbery is wrong" with P is inconsistent with "Would that the robbery take place." However, we may admit that the robbery is wrong but still want it to take place – because we set up a trap to catch the robber. What's wrong with that? This seems acceptable – but it violates our theorem.

Here other considerations override the prima-facie consistency duty. Our implicit "provided that QF" proviso recognizes such exceptions (see Section 2.3). Our consistency requirements aren't exceptionless duties.[1]

16 is a nontheorem. We shouldn't combine incompatible attitudes at the same time. But we can change our minds.

17 is a nontheorem, since there's nothing in "All people over sixty ought to be shot" to say that it covers *future* situations. The statement might be based on circumstances that will change by the time you reach sixty. The example would be a theorem if we worded it to apply to all present or future times, or to all actual or hypothetical situations.

"All A is B" can be tricky. Suppose that this statement just happens to be true at the moment:

UM Everyone in my office is a Michigan fan.

UM entails "If Clinton is in my office, then he is a Michigan fan." It doesn't entail "If Clinton *will be* in my office tomorrow, then he *will be* a Michigan fan tomorrow." For UM to entail claims about the future, we could change it to "At every time, now and in the future, everyone in my office is a Michigan fan." Similarly, UM doesn't entail "If Clinton *were* in my office, then he *would* be a Michigan fan." For UM to entail counterfactuals, we could change it to "In every actual or hypothetical situation, everyone in my office is a Michigan fan." Ethical principles work the same way.

---

[1] Here's another apparent exception (from McCann 1991). E10 tells us not to intend to do what we think is impossible. But in desperate situations this might be a sensible thing to do. Or perhaps it might only be sensible to intend to *try* to do what we think is probably impossible (the *trying* itself being possible)?

Their wording (or sometimes the context) determines whether they entail future or counterfactual claims.

18 is a nontheorem. The correct form (see Section 3.6) is about your present attitude toward a hypothetical case; you ought not to combine (1) believing that murderers ought in every conceivable case to be executed with (2) not desiring that if you were a murderer then you'd be executed.

19 is a theorem. Here's the derivation (where "S" is short for "seek pleasure for its own sake"):

> "It's all right for me not to S" entails "It's causally possible that I don't S." {From theorem **E6** (*all right* implies *can*).}
>
> ∴ "It's not causally possible that I don't S" entails "It's not all right for me not to S." {Contrapositive.}
>
> ∴ "It's causally necessary that I S" entails "I ought to S." {Substitute equivalents.}

Mill would be pleased; but I doubt that it's causally necessary that I seek pleasure for its own sake.

If we followed Frankena's suggestion that *ought*-implies-*can* expresses less than a full logical entailment (see Section 3.4 Q5), then we'd formulate this example (and some of the next few) in terms of something weaker than "entails."

20 is a theorem. The derivation is technical (here "S" is short for "study" and "B" for "become a teacher"):

> "B" entails "If your S-ing is causally necessary for your B-ing, then S." {From axiom **E**.}
>
> ∴ "Your S-ing is causally necessary for your B-ing" entails "Either S or don't B." {By $\Box(\underline{B} \supset (N \supset \underline{S}))$ ∴ $\Box(N \supset (\underline{S} \lor \sim\underline{B}))$.}

21 is a theorem. The derivation is technical:

> "It's all right that you B and not S" entails "It's causally possible that you B and not S." {From **E6** (*all right* implies *can*).}
>
> ∴ "It's not causally possible that you B and not S" entails "It's not all right that you B and not S." {Contrapositive.}
>
> ∴ "Your S-ing is causally necessary for your B-ing" entails "You *ought* to either S or else not B." {Substitute "$\Box(\sim S \supset \sim B)$" for "$\sim\diamondsuit(B \cdot \sim S)$" and "$O(\underline{S} \lor \sim\underline{B})$" for "$\sim R(\underline{B} \cdot \sim\underline{S})$."}

This example and #19 above seem to shatter Hume's Law – that we can't deduce an *ought* from an *is*. Here's another example (where Carol is my infallible older sister):

> Everything Carol says is true.
> Carol says that I ought to do A.
> ∴ It's true that I ought to do A.
> ∴ I ought to do A.

(Hare 1977 and Gensler 1990: 210–11 have other examples.) But Hume's Law may just need a better formulation. I suggest this:

> Hume's Law: If B is a consistent nonevaluative truth that doesn't quantify over truths (or anything similar) and A represents a logically and causally contingent simple action, then B doesn't entail that act A ought to be done.

This thesis is controversial – not trivially true or trivially false.

22 is a theorem, like **C6**. I mention it to bring up a possible objection. Suppose you have to act quickly, and you don't have time to gain information needed to discover a permissible alternative. Wouldn't it be consistent and all right to act while withholding judgment on whether your act is permissible?

We need to distinguish. If you have to act quickly, you might be unable to determine what is permissible *objectively* (relative to the actual facts of the situation). But you can judge at least implicitly that your action is permissible *subjectively* (relative to your limited knowledge and opportunity to reflect on this knowledge). This is what the theorem requires. In applying axiom **P**, the *ought* judgment and the imperative have to be qualified the same way. For example, both are to be taken objectively, or both are to be taken subjectively. The example shows that acting to do A is equivalent to accepting the *subjective* imperative for me to do A now.

23 is ambiguous. The antecedent is (1):

(1) O(∃x)(Dux · ~D*u*x): It's obligatory that you not do some jobs that you're doing.

The consequent could be taken as either (2) or (3):

(2) ◈(∃x)(Dux · ~Dux): It's causally possible that, for some x, you're doing job x and you aren't doing job x.

(3) (∃x)(Dux · ◈~Dux): For some x, you're doing job x and it's causally possible that you don't do job x.

(2) is self-contradictory; (1) entails (3) but not (2). However, Kant's Law **E2** at present lets us derive (2) from (1); but this is wrong. To avoid this, we hereby qualify **E** and its corollaries so that substitution instances for "E," "M," and "A" must be pure imperatives (not combinations of imperatives and indicatives, as

here). With this change, (2) is no longer derivable from (1). We can still derive (3) from (1); but the derivation is complex.

24 is a nontheorem. You could consistently claim that other factors justify supporting the candidate; perhaps the other candidates are even more racist and would cause a nuclear war.

25 is a nontheorem. Kant 1785 (393–401) thought that a virtuous person would be motivated to do the right thing for its own sake. This idea seems right to me (at least if we qualify it carefully[1]), but I haven't worked it into formal ethics; my system doesn't talk about the proper motivation for doing an act.

Kant's ideal of a virtuous person demands more than my ideal of a conscientious person. Anyone satisfying Kant's ideal would satisfy my ideal; but you might satisfy mine without satisfying Kant's – because you might be conscientious out of self-interest (see the Brandt-Hobbes approach in Section 3.7).

To be conscientious, in the sense we are dealing with here, is to live in harmony with our moral beliefs. This requires that our actions, resolutions, and desires not clash with our moral beliefs. Such conscientiousness is consistent with various sorts of motivation and justification.

---

[1] I'd allow that a virtuous person might have mixed motives. But the motivation to do the right thing for its own sake must be strong enough that it would prevail even if the other motives pulled against it. Perhaps Kant would agree.

Chapter 4

Impartiality

Consistency in a broad sense involves *impartiality* – the requirement that we make similar evaluations about similar cases, regardless of the individuals involved. Impartiality is based on universalizability.

4.1 Universalizability

Our fourth and final axiom is *universalizability*. This axiom claims that the moral category of an act depends on the *kind* of act that it is – and not on who plays what role in the situation. Here's a more precise formulation:

> U   If act A ought to be done (would be all right), then there is some conjunction F of universal properties such that (1) act A is F and (2) in any actual or hypothetical case every act that is F ought to be done (would be all right).[1]

Axiom U covers the deontic terms "ought" (required) and "all right" (permissible). It applies derivatively to "wrong" (what ought not to be done) and "neutral" (what's all right to do and all right not to do). Similar principles hold for other evaluative terms (like "good" and "bad").

U says that the moral category of an act (whether it's obligatory or wrong or neutral) depends on the act's universal properties. If an act fits in a given moral category, it's because of the *kind* of act that it is. Any act of this kind would fit in the same moral category regardless of the individuals involved.

U equivalently says that right and wrong are based on principles that apply to similar cases. A "principle" here is a universal state-

---

[1] This is short for writing U twice, with "ought" and with "all right."

ment that's expressible without proper names or pointer words and
that supports counterfactuals (and thus applies to imagined cases
as well as to actual ones). U doesn't say that right and wrong are
based on *simple* principles; it allows for principles of any degree
of complexity – including ones that specify all the universal properties of an act or that are too complicated for us to formulate.

In axiom U, a "universal property" is a nonevaluative property
expressible without proper names (like *Gensler*, *Chicago*, or *IBM*)
or pointer words (like *I*, *this*, or *now*).[1] Let's take some examples.
My neighbor Patrick just got a new computer, and I might be
tempted to steal it. The (possible) act of *my stealing Pat's computer* has several properties or characteristics; for example, it is:

- *wrong* (evaluative term),
- an act of stealing *Pat's* computer (proper name), and
- something *I* would be doing (pointer word).

These properties aren't universal since they involve evaluative
terms, proper names, or pointer words. But the act also has properties that are universal; for example, it is:

- an act of stealing a new computer from one's neighbor,
- an act whose agent has blue eyes, and
- an act that would greatly distress the owner of the computer.

U says that the morality of an act depends on its *universal* properties – like those of the second group – properties expressible without evaluative terms, proper names, or pointer words.[2]

Here's a looser but more intuitive formulation of our axiom:

> U   If act A ought to be done (would be all
>   right), then, in any actual or hypothetical
>   case, any act that is exactly or relevantly
>   similar in its universal properties also
>   ought to be done (would be all right).

This speaks of two acts being "exactly or relevantly similar in
their universal properties." What does this phrase mean?

"Exact similarity" is easy to define. Acts A and B are *exactly
similar* in their universal properties if they have the *same* universal

---

[1] Burks 1977 (554–61), in defending an inductive-logic analogue of U, gives a
fuller explanation of pointer words (which he calls "indexicals").

[2] It's sometimes said that a universal property can't mention an individual. It
would be clearer to say that it can use a definite description ("the all-time football
ground gainer") but not a proper name ("Walter Payton").

properties – so that A has every universal property that B has, and vice versa. By U, two acts that are exactly similar in their universal properties would fit in the same moral category.

It's more difficult to explain "relevantly similar." Roughly speaking, to call two acts *relevantly similar* is to say that, because of certain features that they have in common, both acts fit in the same moral category. Here's a more precise definition:

> Acts A and B are *relevantly similar* in their universal properties
> =df There's some conjunction of universal properties F such that:
> (1) acts A and B are both F, and (2) for any act that is F it is
> morally irrelevant what further universal properties it has [in the
> sense that if the act's complete description in universal terms
> would make it obligatory (wrong, neutral) then so would F].[1]

Section 8.4 will formulate this in precise logical symbolism. When we say that two acts are relevantly similar, we are making a complex moral claim.[2]

I'll often speak of two acts being "similar." When I say this, I'll mean "similar *in universal properties*" even if I don't add the italicized words. If I don't specify "exactly" or "relevantly," I'll mean "*exactly or relevantly* similar."

4.2 Is Universalizability Useful?

Universalizability, while almost universally accepted, does raise various issues. For example, many claim that the principle is true but trivial (for discussions on this see, for example, D. Locke 1968 and Hare 1978). We'll now consider some of these issues.

---

[1] Property F must include more than just the reasons for the act's moral category. Another act with these same reasons might fit in a different moral category – because of different undercutters or contrary reasons. (See Dancy 1993: 57–64, 79–90.) Property F could be very complicated and could include facts about the attitudes and beliefs of the parties involved.

[2] This paragraph defines "Acts A and B are relevantly similar" – but not "F is a morally relevant property." Here's a rough definition of the latter notion. First, a *directly relevant* property is a universal property used in formulating a basic moral principle. (On a simple utilitarianism, the property of maximizing pleasure is the only such property.) Then an *indirectly relevant* property is one that is causally, logically, or evidentially related to a directly relevant property. A non-universal property can be *indirectly* relevant – since if A hurts *me*, then A hurts *someone*; the latter might be directly relevant.

(Q1) It's true that two acts that are *exactly similar* in all
their universal properties would fit in the same moral
category. But what is the use of this? In the actual
world, no two acts are ever exactly similar.

The idea of "exact similarity" is usefully applied to hypothetical
cases. To test our impartiality, we can imagine exactly similar
actions in which the parties are in different places – in which, for
example, we are on the receiving end of the action.

Let's consider an example adapted from the good Samaritan
parable (Luke 10:30–5).[1] Suppose that, while I'm jogging, I see a
man who's been beaten, robbed, and left to die. Should I help the
man, perhaps by running back to make a phone call? I think of
excuses why I shouldn't; I'm busy, don't want to get involved, and
so on. I say to myself: "It would be *all right* for me not to help this
man." Then I consider an exactly reversed situation. I imagine
myself in the exact place of the man; I'm the one who's been
beaten, robbed, and left to die. And I imagine him in my exact
place; he's jogging and sees me in my sorry state. I ask myself,
"Would it be all right for this man *not to help me* in this situation?" Surely not! But then I'm inconsistent. By universalizability,
what's all right for me to do to another has to be all right for the
other to do to me in an imagined exactly reversed situation.[2]

In the actual world, no two acts are exactly similar. But we can
always *imagine* an exactly similar *hypothetical* act. If I'm about to
do A to X, I can imagine what it would be like for X to do A to me
in an exactly reversed situation.

What is an "exactly reversed situation"? It's a situation in which
we imagine all the universal properties switched. Suppose that we

---

[1] The heart of the parable goes like this (I take all biblical quotations from the
New American Bible 1992):

   A man fell victim to robbers as he went down from Jerusalem to Jericho. They
   stripped and beat him and went off leaving him half-dead. A priest happened to
   be going down that road, but when he saw him, he passed by on the opposite
   side.... But a Samaritan traveler who came upon him was moved with compas-
   sion at the sight. He approached the victim, poured oil and wine over his
   wounds and bandaged them. Then he lifted him up on his own animal, took him
   to an inn and cared for him.

[2] Samuel Clarke 1706 (86–7) mirrors this idea in the earliest formulation of U
that I could find: "What I judge reasonable or unreasonable, that Another should
do for Me; That by the same judgment I declare reasonable or unreasonable, that I
in the like case should do for Him."

list the universal properties of myself and of the other person (X) in the good Samaritan case:

The actual situation	
My properties	X's properties
jogging	beaten and robbed
writing an ethics book	needs a doctor
has blue eyes	has brown eyes
and so forth ...	and so forth ...

Imagine that the list contains *all* our universal properties, even complex ones. (The list would be too long to write out – perhaps infinitely long.) When I imagine an *exactly reversed situation*, I imagine one where the list of properties is reversed:

An imagined exactly reversed situation	
My properties	X's properties
beaten and robbed	jogging
needs a doctor	writing an ethics book
has brown eyes	has blue eyes
and so forth ...	and so forth ...

Here I'm beaten and robbed, and X is the jogger. We also have to reverse any relationships. So if X helped me in the past (in the actual situation), then I'd imagine my having helped X in the past (in the imagined reversed situation).

There's another way to understand exactly reversed situations. Suppose that the following conjunction of properties gives the *complete* universal description of my-not-helping-X:

My-not-helping-X is an act of a jogger who is in a hurry, has blue eyes, and so forth ... not helping someone who was beaten and robbed, needs a doctor, has brown eyes, and so forth ....

When I imagine the exactly reversed situation, I imagine X-not-helping-me having this same conjunction of properties:

X-not-helping-me is an act of a jogger who is in a hurry, has blue eyes, and so forth ... not helping someone who was beaten and robbed, needs a doctor, has brown eyes, and so forth ....

Thus I imagine a situation that is *exactly similar* to the actual one except that the place of the parties is switched; in this imagined situation, I am beaten and robbed and X is the jogger.

My good Samaritan example illustrates this theorem:

U1   If it would be all right for you to do A to X, then in an
     exactly reversed situation it would be all right for X to do A
     to you.

The two acts are stipulated to be *exactly* similar in their universal
properties; so if one act is all right, then the other must be all right
too.[1] Impartiality theorem I1 follows from U1 (using R), and tells
us not to have belief combinations violating U1:

I1   Don't combine (1) believing that it would be all right for you
     to do A to X with (2) not believing that in an exactly
     reversed situation it would be all right for X to do A to you.

This passive voice version of U1 uses "for A to be done to you"
(instead of "for X to do A to you"):[2]

U2   If it would be all right for you to do A to X, then in an
     exactly similar situation it would be all right for A to be
     done to you.

Let's take another example. Suppose that I'm driving and spot a
hitchhiker. Should I pick him up? If I don't, he may spend a long
and frustrating time waiting; I know what this is like from when
I've hitchhiked to backpacking trails. On the other hand, people
who pick up hitchhikers are sometimes robbed or hurt. Impartiality tells me that whatever judgment I make on my-picking-up-the-
hitchhiker (that it's obligatory, or wrong, or neutral), I must make
the same judgment on the imagined reversed situation act. Formal
ethics doesn't tell me what to do; and, unlike in the good Samaritan case, it doesn't push me toward an obvious answer. Rather, it
encourages me to reflect on the act from both perspectives (mine
and the hitchhiker's). And it emphasizes that, whatever I decide, I
have to apply the same standards to myself that I apply to others.

---

[1] U1 is like a principle that Carnap 1945 (78–9) proposed for inductive and
deductive logic: if evidence E about specific individuals makes hypothesis H probable (or logically entails H), then the same would hold if E and H were reformu-
lated to be about other individuals. Carnap says "All authors on probability have
assumed this principle.... Inductive logic should, like deductive logic, make no
discrimination among individuals." See also Burks 1977 (125).

[2] There's a technical problem with U1 if we substitute for "X" a phrase with
descriptive content (like "this unconscious man") – for example:

  If it would be all right for you not to help this unconscious man, then in a
  reversed situation it would be all right for this unconscious man not to help you.

This admits of a possible ambiguity. When I imagine the reversed situation, I
imagine the person (who in fact is unconscious) being a jogger and hence
conscious. I don't, of course, imagine him being both unconscious and jogging.
The passive voice formula U2 avoids the problem: I imagine myself *not being
helped* in an exactly similar situation, which doesn't mention the agent.

(Q2) When I imagine myself in X's *exact* place, do I imagine myself having X's beliefs and preferences?

Yes. You imagine a situation where you have *all* of X's current universal properties. Facts about X's beliefs and preferences can be important for how X ought to be treated. If X has certain moral beliefs about vegetarianism, for example, you may need to be sensitive to these in planning dinner arrangements.

There's no special difficulty in imagining a situation where you have beliefs which differ from your current ones. While I firmly believe that the world is round, I can still imagine a situation where I believe that the world is flat.

(Q3) When I imagine a reversed situation, do I have to imagine an *exactly* reversed situation?

No. If you prefer, you can imagine a *relevantly reversed* situation, where you switch just the properties that are *relevant* to evaluating the act. (So you normally needn't switch eye color.) We can express our theorems either way.

This approach raises the issue of which properties are relevant – an issue that may be controversial. In the good Samaritan case, is it relevant that X is well-dressed – or that X is familiar to the jogger? These factors may influence the likelihood of his being helped. But should they? I may be unsure of these things; and people of different moral perspectives may disagree about them. I can avoid this problem by imagining an *exactly* reversed situation and switching *all* the universal properties. Or I might switch every property that I (or anyone else) even suspects *may* be relevant. This gives a "safely similar" situation where the relevant similarity between the cases ceases to be controversial.

When I imagine a role reversal in real life, I generally imagine a reversed situation that is either *exactly* or *safely relevantly* similar but without carefully distinguishing between the two. Both approaches work fine.

(Q4) Do these principles, which involve putting yourself in the place of the other person, give us a precise statement of the golden rule?

Sidgwick 1901 (xvii, 209–10, 379–80, 384–5, 417) thought so. However, I distinguish more clearly between impartiality and the golden rule. Impartiality theorems prescribe that we make similar *evaluations* about similar cases; they forbid us to combine certain pairs of *beliefs*. The golden rule, on the other hand, prescribes that we not combine an *action* (toward another) with a *desire* (about how we be treated). When we get to the golden rule in the next chapter, we'll see that it flows nicely from our impartiality and conscientiousness principles.

Impartiality principle I2 is structurally similar to golden rule principle G1 in that both involve a *don't-combine* form, a similar situation qualifier, and a present attitude to a hypothetical situation. Without these features, both principles would have absurd consequences and wouldn't be provable from our axioms. Section 5.2 will investigate these features more carefully.

> (Q5) It's true that *relevantly similar* actions fit in the same moral category. But isn't this useless in comparing actual cases, since we can always appeal to trivial differences? We can say things like: "It's all right for me to kill you, but wrong for you to kill me – because I have six toes and you don't."

Let me first explain how the "relevantly similar" forms work. Here are two typical theorems:

U3   If act A is wrong and act B is relevantly similar to act A, then act B is wrong.

U4   If you ought to do A but X ought not to do A, then there's some relevant difference between the two acts.

The corresponding *impartiality* theorems would tell us not to have belief combinations that violate these.

The Bible mentions a technique that mirrors U3 (see 2 Samuel 12:1–13; 14:1–13; 1 Kings 20:38–42). The Israelite kings sometimes did evil things. For example, King David once brought about the death of Bathsheba's husband, so he could marry this beautiful woman. The prophets had to make the king realize his errors; but it was dangerous to criticize the king directly. So they sometimes did the following. After the king did wrong by doing A-B-C, the prophet would describe a case where someone else did A-B-C. The king would respond "That man did wrong!"; and the prophet would shout "You condemned yourself!" Then the king (who saw that the acts were *relevantly similar*) would realize his error.

What happens if the king appeals to trivial differences between the cases? Suppose that the king is the only person with six toes.[1] Then he could say: "It's all right for me to kill you, but wrong for you to kill me – because I have six toes and you don't." But we can easily defeat such claims by using hypothetical cases. Does the king honestly believe that *if* the other person had six toes (instead of him), *then* it would be all right for the other person to kill him? No one would believe this.

Also, the king can only appeal to differences that he's aware of. He only knows a few things about the two cases. In particular, he only knows that the second act has factors A-B-C (and others inferable from them); he has to propose a relevant difference from these. And in proposing a difference, he must be factually accurate (that the factor applies in one case but not the other) and logically consistent (giving the factor equal weight regardless of which side is imagined to have it). The king would have difficulty doing these things. It isn't so easy to satisfy the requirement to make similar evaluations about relevantly similar actions.

> (Q6) Your examples use universalizability to counter self-interest and help us to recognize responsibilities toward others. Can U also help us to recognize responsibilities toward ourselves?

Yes. Let me give an example from the movie *Babe* (which also illustrates theorem U4). The great athlete Babe Didrikson Zaharias (1914–56) got cancer and would die if she didn't have a colostomy operation. Mainly out of fear, she decided that she shouldn't have the operation. Her husband thought she should have it. To encourage her to change her mind, he had her talk with another woman in similar circumstances, who also had to choose between dying and having the operation. Babe instinctively told the other woman, "You ought to take courage and have the operation – for life is the greatest gift there is." But then Babe realized she had to apply the same principles to herself that she applied to others. She decided that she too ought to have the operation.

---

[1] We each have universal properties that distinguish us from everyone else. For example, I'm the third person to hike the length of the 1000-mile trail over ice-age glacial hills (the Wisconsin Ice Age Trail). Try to think of some universal property that only you have. If you lead an undistinguished life, you might use the conjunctive property of having n_1 hairs on your head on day 1 of your life, n_2 hairs on day 2, ..., and n_{1000} hairs on day 1000. Ask your parents for the specific numbers.

Let's consider the case more carefully. Babe combined these three judgments:

(a)   I ought not to have the operation.

(b)   You ought to have the operation.

(c)   Our cases are relevantly similar.

She held (a) because she feared the consequences of the operation, she held (b) because of the value of life ("the greatest gift there is"), and she held (c) because she thought that any reasons that would justify one operation would justify the other. She saw that her beliefs were incoherent and that she had to change something; she could reject (a), (b), or (c). She in fact rejected (a), saying that she too ought to have the operation, just as the other woman in her similar situation should have it. She could have rejected (b), saying that neither should have the operation; she didn't take this option because she so strongly believed that the other woman ought to have it. Or she could have rejected (c), saying that the operation was right in one case but not the other, because of such and such differences; she didn't take this option, because she couldn't think of any reason that would justify one operation but not the other. So consistency considerations, although not telling her what to believe, helped her to form her beliefs.

Formal ethics forbids us to accept inconsistent combinations but doesn't tell us which consistent combinations to accept or what to think about ethical issues. Rather, it gives us guides for working out our own answers in a consistent way.

> (Q7) Could we apply an "actual situation" analysis to the good Samaritan case?

Yes. Suppose that I believe that it was all right (permissible) for me to refuse to help a man X who was beaten, robbed, and left to die even though I could easily have helped. This belief might conflict with my beliefs about how I ought to have been treated in the past (or ought be treated in the future) in my actual situation – so long as I admit a relevant similarity between the cases. Let me sketch three scenarios to illustrate this.

- I was recently a victim of a similar crime, and a stranger refused to help me. I believe that I was treated wrongly. Yet this action is so similar to my refusal to help X that it's obvious to me that both fit in the same moral category. Here I'm clearly inconsistent.

Such parallel cases have an immediacy and vividness that is difficult to match with merely hypothetical cases. But such neat parallels are rare.

- I've never been beaten up, but I can recall having been refused help in a situation that is somewhat analogous. I believe that I was treated wrongly. So I'm inconsistent if I believe that these cases are relevantly similar to my refusal to help X.

Here the analogy is less close and the relevant similarity more tenuous. If I don't see that these cases are relevantly similar to my refusal to help X, then I am not inconsistent in making different evaluations about them.

- I might in the future be robbed and left to die in a similar way. I believe that it would then be wrong for people to refuse to help me. So I'm inconsistent if I believe that these cases are relevantly similar to my refusal to help X.

I might escape this inconsistency if I know that I'll never be robbed in this way or if I regard X's situation as relevantly different from mine because he has a different skin color.

This "actual situation" analysis is sometimes useful. When it runs into problems, we can return to the "hypothetical situation" approach where we *imagine* ourselves in place of the other (either the *exact* place or a *safely relevantly similar* place).

(Q8) I see how universalizability is useful in testing our consistency. Does it have other uses in moral thinking?

Yes. For example, it encourages us to ask "Why?" about our inherited ethical beliefs (see Brandt 1959: 19–26). U says that if act A ought to be done, then there's a reason – a principle – behind this. Searching for the principles behind our beliefs can be a powerful force in criticizing these beliefs.[1]

Recall Ima Racist from Section 2.2. Imagine that society taught him that we ought to treat white people well but black people poorly. When Ima starts asking "Why?" he's made a big step forward. His society may tell him, "Because blacks are inferior"; but we saw (in Section 2.2) how to demolish this argument.

---

[1] Strictly speaking, you're committed to there being a principle that backs up your judgment (that is, to the act having some universal property F such that any act with that property would be obligatory) – but you don't have to produce the principle. It's often difficult to formulate clear principles; but if you have no idea (not even a rough one) what the principle is, then you haven't thought about the matter very deeply. And how can you know that there is such a principle if you have no idea what it is?

(Q9) Universalizability lets any universal properties be morally relevant. It permits claims like "All who have black skin ought to be treated poorly." Doesn't this make it trivial and useless?

No. U doesn't restrict which universal properties can be morally relevant. Ima Racist could take advantage of this, and claim:

BW All blacks ought to be treated poorly – just because they have black skin. And all whites ought to be treated well – just because they have white skin.

BW is consistent with U, since the properties are universal. Some think this is a major weakness of U. But perhaps not. Perhaps U lets BW stand up tall for a moment – to better enable us to knock it out decisively.

How do we respond to BW? Should we give an ethical argument against it? Then Ima won't accept our premises. Should we demand that Ima prove BW? Then we won't accept *his* premises. Should we just ridicule BW as unintuitive? Then Ima will ridicule *our* principles. These strategies will likely end in a stalemate where each party just rejects the views of the other.

Instead, we should appeal to consistency. Does Ima consistently hold BW? Does he consistently discriminate by skin color? Let's ask him these questions:

- Ima, you know that many blacks (especially albinos) have fairly light skin – lighter than that of many white people. Do you believe that these people ought to be treated well?

- Ima, suppose that a cosmetic called *Skin So Pale* turns black skin permanently white. Should (former) black people who use this gain instant equality? Should we only discriminate against blacks who don't use this cosmetic?

- Ima, you know that many whites (especially sun worshippers) have dark skin – darker than many black people. Do you believe that these people ought to be treated poorly? Do you despise white people on the beach who have deep, dark tans? Do you think they should live in ghettos and have poor jobs?

- Ima, imagine that a color-changing germ infects everyone in the world. It turns originally white skin permanently black, and originally black skin permanently white. In this case, should the newly white people be treated well, and the newly black people be treated poorly? This involves your friends being put into the ghetto, while your enemies gain the upper hand. (This delightful example is from Hare 1963: 218.)

- Ima, tell me where to draw the line between white and black skin. My neighborhood has people from every racial group and mixture. Skin shades vary over a wide spectrum. And we have beautiful beaches where many tan their skin during the summer. Ima, what skin colors correspond to what sort of treatment?

After a few such questions, Ima will realize that BW is a crazy principle. Again, the appeal here is only to consistency; but this can be very powerful.

We might also quote to Ima some words from Abraham Lincoln (1854: 105) – words that also appeal to consistency:

- You say A is white, and B is black. Is it *color*, then; the lighter, having the right to enslave the darker? Take care. By this rule, you are to be slave to the first man you meet, with a fairer skin than your own.

- You mean the whites are *intellectually* the superiors of the blacks, and, therefore, have the right to enslave them? Take care again. By this rule, you are to be slave to the first man you meet, with an intellect superior to your own.

- But, say you, it is a question of *interest*; and, if you can make it your *interest*, you have the right to enslave another. Very well. And if he can make it his interest, he has the right to enslave you.

Lincoln wrote these words before his presidency – at a time when most Americans accepted the rightness of slavery.

Ima may see that his racist orientation is foolish. Or he may regroup, and respond this way:

I see that skin color isn't the issue. I'm confused on the issue but I'm not ready to give up my judgments about how we ought to treat black people. I don't know the *principles* behind these judgments; but I'll keep working on it.

To pursue the argument further, we need ammunition that we'll develop in the next few chapters. We'll return to the issue of racism in Section 7.3.

(Q10) Some of your theorems involve a role reversal in which you imagine yourself in the place of X. Do these presume that X is a human being – or perhaps a member of your tribe or social group? Can we apply these theorems to our treatment of animals or things?

The theorems hold regardless of what X is, but are vacuous if X is a nonsentient being. Consider this instance of theorem U2:

ST   If it's all right for me to step on X, then if I were in X's
     exact place then it would be all right for me to be stepped on.

X here might be a rock, a dog, a stranger, or a friend. The proof
goes the same way for all four cases:

It's all right for me to step on X. {Hypothesis.}
∴ It's all right for X to be stepped on.
∴ Any act exactly similar in its universal properties to X-being-
   stepped-on would be all right. {By U.}
   If I were in X's exact place, then my-being-stepped-on would
   be exactly similar in its universal properties to X-being-
   stepped-on. {This is true by the definition of "exact place."}
∴ If I were in X's exact place, then it would be all right for me to
   be stepped on. {From the last two steps.}

These steps don't presuppose that X is any particular kind of
being. So ST holds even if X isn't a human being.

However, theorem ST is vacuous if X is a nonsentient being.
Consider the consequent of ST for the case where X is a rock:

RK   If I were in this rock's exact place, it would be all right for
     me to be stepped on.

I take RK's first part to be logically impossible.[1] My essential
nature as a person is to be a center of (actual or potential) experiences. I'm totally baffled by the idea of my having all and only the
properties of this nonsentient rock – being identical with *this rock*
instead of *that rock*. Putting myself in X's place involves imagining myself having X's experiences. So I can't consistently put
myself in the exact place of a totally nonsentient rock. Even if I
could do it, I don't care if I'm stepped on in the place of the rock;
rocks feel no pain. These problems don't arise for the other cases;
theorem ST can be significantly applied to the dog, stranger, and
friend. So I step on rocks, but not on dogs, strangers, or friends.[2]

> (Q11) Universalizability says that whether an act *ought*
> to be done depends on its *universal properties*, where
> these are *nonevaluative* properties expressible without
> proper names or pointer terms. Why can't a universal
> property be *evaluative*?

---

[1] This would make RK vacuously true – just as "~◇A" would make
"□(A ⊃ B)" vacuously true regardless of what B is.

[2] See also Mulholland 1988 and Sher 1977. We'll discuss these matters further
when we talk about the scope of the golden rule. For now, the important point is
that the derivation of theorem U2 doesn't presuppose that X is a human being.

I'm concerned that universalizability not be trivialized. Suppose that nonnaturalism is true and that there is a nonempirical but objective property of obligatoriness. Then whether an act ought to be done would depend on whether it has the property of obligatoriness. Without our "nonevaluative" stipulation, that would be enough to satisfy U; whether an act ought to be done needn't depend on what it is like in some more ordinary sense. This would trivialize U and go against the understanding of most nonnaturalists. The "nonevaluative" stipulation avoids trivialization by specifying that what ought to be done must depend on properties other than evaluative ones like obligatoriness.

But there's still a problem. Suppose that naturalism is true. Then the line between evaluative and nonevaluative properties would be blurred and our stipulation that universal properties can't be *evaluative* would be unclear. So then we might drop the *nonevaluative* stipulation and instead require that universal properties be *empirical*. This wouldn't matter much in how we apply U.

Suppose that noncognitivism is true and there are no evaluative truths or properties. Then our stipulation that universal properties can't be *evaluative* is unnecessary – since there are no evaluative properties. So how we understand "universal property" (and hence universalizability) depends on our approach to metaethics.

> (Q12) Is impartiality always good? Don't we need at times to be partial to our friends and loved ones? Wouldn't complete impartiality destroy friendships and other close relationships?

You're objecting to a kind of impartiality different from the one that I'm defending. My impartiality only requires that we make similar evaluations about similar cases, regardless of the individuals involved. I'm not advocating either of these:

(1) Give equal weight to everyone's interests, regardless of how the person relates to you.

(2) Have no particular desires – but always desire the same sort of thing for the same sort of case, regardless of the individuals involved.

You might violate (1) by giving greater weight to your children's interests. This needn't involve conflicting *evaluations* about similar cases; you could consistently hold that it's all right for *anyone* in similar cases to give greater weight to their children's interests.

You might violate (2) by desiring that you win the lottery but not desiring that others in similar situations win it. Again, this needn't involve making conflicting *evaluations* about similar cases.

So I'm defending only a very weak sort of impartiality – that we make similar evaluations about similar cases, regardless of the individuals involved. This is compatible with having a special consideration or "partiality" toward friends and loved ones.

4.3 Why Be Impartial?

The *ought* part of our *universalizability* axiom goes this way:[1]

U   If act A ought to be done, then there is some conjunction F
       of universal properties such that (1) act A is F and (2) in any
       actual or hypothetical case every act that is F ought to be
       done.

U generates *impartiality* duties: that we ought to make similar evaluations about similar cases, regardless of the individuals involved. How can we justify axiom U? Why be impartial?

Our answer depends on whether we think axiom U is logically necessary. Let's call U *weak universalizability*, to distinguish it from *strong universalizability* SU:

SU   "Act A ought to be done" logically entails "There is some
       conjunction F of universal properties such that (1) act A is F
       and (2) in any actual or hypothetical case every act that is F
       ought to be done."

While U is a plain if–then, SU asserts an entailment. We might base U on SU. Or we might reject SU and defend U differently.[2]

Let's suppose that SU is true. Then this statement is logically inconsistent: "Act A *ought* to be done – and act B is exactly similar to act A in its universal properties; but act B *ought not* to be done." SU would solve the problem of justifying U and impartiality. For then U would be derivable from the true logical-entailment principle SU. And violations of impartiality would be violations of logical consistency (which we've already defended).

SU holds on many definist views. Suppose that we define "Act A *ought* to be done" to mean "Act A has F" (where F is some universal property). If act A *ought* to be done, it then logically

[1] What I say here about the *ought* part applies analogously to the *all right* part.

[2] We can't combine SP and SU – we can't have both prescriptivity and universalizability express logical entailments. I'll explain why in Section 6.5.

follows that act A has universal property F and that in any actual or hypothetical case every act that's F ought to be done. So SU is true on any view that defines *ought* in universal terms. This justification works with the ideal observer theory but not with cultural relativism (since "is demanded by *my* society's *current* norms" has indexical references). It works with supernaturalism if "God" is a nonevaluative description (like "The supremely powerful, knowing, and loving creator") instead of a proper name (like "Yahweh") or an evaluative notion (like "The all-good creator").

SU is plausible on other views as well. Nonnaturalists could accept SU as a self-evident truth. Emotivists could take *ought* to express impartial feelings that apply to similar cases (like "Hurrah for anything like that!"). Ayer suggests this view when he says:

> The common objects of moral approval or disapproval are not particular actions so much as classes of actions; ... if an action is labeled right or wrong, or good or bad, ... it is because it is thought to be an action of a certain type.[1]

(Ayer 1946: 21)

Hare accepts SU, since he takes *oughts* to be universalizable prescriptions (like "Let every act like A be done"); he's done much to show the usefulness of universalizability.

Philosophers who reject SU may still defend U and impartiality on another basis. Let's now suppose that SU is false. In this case, axiom U and impartiality have no special logical credentials. There's then no logical inconsistency in saying this: "Act A *ought* to be done – and act B is exactly similar to act A in its universal properties; but act B *ought not* to be done." This may be *inconsistent* in some nonlogical sense; we might call it *ethically inconsistent*. But why care about this? Why accept U? Why be impartial?

One consideration is that universalizability and impartiality have a crucial social function (see Levin 1979). They make possible important kinds of moral reasoning, and they promote a neutral (intersubjective) standpoint for settling disputes and reaching a moral consensus, thus making life better for everyone. These ideas can be important for various views.

We'll now sketch various defenses of impartiality. Those who hold SU could appeal to these, not to show the truth of U, but to show why we'd want to use a moral language with U built into it. We'll first consider two promote-desire justifications.

---

[1] See also D. Hume 1751 (IX, i). Sartre 1957 (17–19) also endorses U.

Let's suppose that you have idealistic desires. Accordingly, you want to be fair and impartial – both for its own sake and for its social benefits. So you want to make similar evaluations about similar acts, regardless of the individuals involved. Then impartiality promotes your goals.

Let's now suppose that you care only about promoting your self-interest in some narrow sense. It's plausible to think that impartiality will do this. In the Hobbes-Brandt account, enlightened egoists set up moral rules to protect their interests. These rules, to be viable, have to be expressible in universal terms and thus satisfy U (since other people won't accept a rule like "Everyone is to serve *me*"). In addition, U and impartiality give a neutral standpoint for settling disputes;[1] this is important for avoiding social chaos and protecting our interests. So egoists would agree to enforce impartiality with external and internal sanctions, which give self-interested reasons for following U and impartiality.[2]

We'll now briefly consider the other theories. I'll omit Hare's prescriptivism, since it accepts SU.

Utilitarians could claim that impartiality helps people settle disputes by reasoning together from a neutral standpoint – and thus it promotes the general good.[3] Ross's theory could accept this and add that impartiality is inherently good and a prima facie duty.

Definist theories could defend impartiality as demanded by society, or by ideal observers, or by God. Impartiality is important

[1] P. Singer 1988 says that if we limit the concern of moral reasoning to our own group (family, social class, nation, or whatever), then we can't object to others who do the same thing against us. So in seeking to defend our concerns, we need to appeal to a non-arbitrary perspective independent of our personal concerns – a perspective expressed in unrestricted universalizability.

[2] Another factor (perhaps related to the Hobbesian explanation) is that a painful and distressing "cognitive dissonance" can occur when our beliefs violate universalizability. This provides another self-interested reason for being impartial.

Cognitive dissonance can occur when we combine beliefs that don't "fit together" in a broad sense, even if they are logically consistent (see Aronson 1969 and Festinger 1957). For example, suppose that I learn that my highly intelligent PhD cousin married a simple-minded high-school dropout; this improbable (but logically consistent) combination will distress me cognitively until I find further information to make it more understandable.

[3] In addition, U is deducible from many forms of utilitarianism. Let F be the universal property of maximizing pleasure. Suppose that, in every actual or hypothetical case, all and only acts that are F are obligatory. Then U follows: if act A ought to be done, then there's some universal property F such that act A is F and in any actual or hypothetical case every act that is F ought to be done.

for social life and survival; and ideal observers and God are seen as impartial and as supporting impartiality.[1]

Nonnaturalists could see U or the impartiality duty as self-evident; Moore 1912 (71) and Ross 1930 (109, 123) accepted U on this basis. Or they could accept it as derived from other self-evident norms, as coherent with ethical intuitions, or as something that ideal moral thinking leads us to. Ideal nonnaturalists have a further commitment to impartiality, as a necessary ingredient in reasonable ethical beliefs.

Emotivists could say "Hurrah!" to impartiality in light of its benefits to ourselves and to others. Ideal emotivists have a further commitment to impartiality, as a necessary ingredient in reasonable ethical beliefs. The emotivist C.L. Stevenson, in the last course he gave at Michigan (where I was a doctoral student), saw the neglect of U as a defect in his earlier work. He claimed that it's normally self-defeating to violate U. Our attitudes, unless we support them with universal reasons, will receive ridicule and abuse. This goes against our purpose in making ethical judgments: to express our attitudes and influence the attitudes of others.

Also, many thinkers include U and impartiality as part of the moral point of view (or as needed to make a *moral judgment*[2] or as presumed by rational ethical discourse – see Habermas 1990). So if following the moral point of view can be justified (perhaps as promoting our desires or as reasonable by certain standards), then this too would provide a justification for U and impartiality.

Maybe U holds because right and wrong are based on universal natural laws – or Platonic forms – or rules that we'd choose behind a veil of ignorance. Or maybe U follows from the fact that all

[1] A computer search found over 20 verses in the Bible supporting impartiality. Here are some examples: "You shall not distort justice; you must be impartial. You shall not take a bribe; for a bribe blinds the eyes even of the wise." (Deuteronomy 16:19) "To show partiality in judgment is not good." (Proverbs 24:23) "God shows no partiality." (Acts 10:34) "By the standard by which you judge another you condemn yourself, since you, the judge, do the very same things." (Romans 2:1) "Why do you notice the splinter in your brother's eye, but do not perceive the wooden beam in your own eye?" (Matthew 7:3)

[2] The term "moral judgment" is very fluid in ordinary speech. Suppose that a primitive tribe follows norms that violate U; are their norms thereby not "moral judgments" but instead perhaps "quasi-moral judgments"? Other than clarifying terms, what does it matter what we say? The important issue is whether there are solid reasons for U. Linking "moral" semantically with U doesn't by itself provide such reasons; it only implies that if there are no solid reasons for U then there are no solid reasons for making "moral judgments" either (in this sense of "moral").

basic *a priori* concepts (duty, goodness, causality, probability, entailment, and so forth) depend on principles. Or maybe U is so clearly true that it needs no justification; perhaps every argument for U appeals to premises less secure than U. Or maybe we're unsure which justification to accept; but with so many plausible justifications, we can be sure that at least one of them works.

4.4 Impartiality Examples

Universalizability frequently gets mangled. People are often very loose on what the principle says and what follows from it. These examples may help to firm up our understanding of U. Is each of them a theorem or a nontheorem? Answers follow.

1. If X does A to me, then it would be all right for me to do A to X in relevantly similar circumstances.

2. If it's all right for you to do A, then it's all right for me to do A.

3. If others ought to listen to me when I talk, then in similar circumstances I ought to listen to others when they talk.

4. If it's wrong for Japan to invest heavily in the United States and yet it's all right for the United States to invest heavily in the Dominican Republic, then there are relevant differences between the two cases.

5. If I do something, then in relevantly similar circumstances it would be all right for you to do what I'm doing.

6. If it's all right for X to do A, then it would be all right that everyone in similar circumstances do A.

7. If you ought to refuse to pay taxes and your situation is relevantly similar to that of everyone else, then everyone ought to refuse to pay taxes.

8. If it was all right for Sis to take out the car and stay out all night when she was my age, then it's all right for me to do this too.

9. If Sandy ought to teach class when she's a little sick, then in similar circumstances I ought to do this also.

10. If the president lies, then it's all right for me to lie.

11. Don't combine believing that you ought to be allowed to spank your child with believing that teachers ought not to be allowed to spank your child.

12. If you ought to study harder and my case is just like yours in the relevant respects, then I ought to study harder too.

13. Don't combine (1) believing that this concrete action ought to be done with (2) believing that there's no reason why this concrete action ought to be done (no principle under which it falls).

14. Don't combine (1) believing that you ought to let people take advantage of you with (2) believing that in similar circumstances others ought not to let people take advantage of them.

15. If it's wrong for others to hurt me and my case isn't different in relevant respects from theirs, then it's wrong for me to hurt others.

16. If in one situation you do A and then in a relevantly similar situation you don't do A, then one time or the other you acted wrongly.

17. Under relevantly similar circumstances one ought always to act in the same way.

18. Don't combine (1) believing that you ought to spank little Jimmy with (2) not having it be the case that if you were in his exact place then you'd believe that you ought to be spanked.

19. If it's all right for me to do A, then in relevantly similar conditions it would be wrong for another not to do A.

20. If you hold that you ought to do A, then you're committed to blaming others for not doing A in the same sort of situation.

21. If it's all right for Jones to take the test late and my situation is relevantly similar, then it's all right for me to take the test late.

22. If you believe that act A is wrong and you believe that act B is relevantly similar to act A, then you'll believe that act B is wrong.

23. If Dr Jones ought to remove my appendix, then I ought to remove Jones's appendix.

24. If you believe that Dr Jones ought to remove your appendix and you believe that the two cases are relevantly similar, then you ought to remove Jones's appendix.

25. Don't combine (1) believing that others ought to give up smoking, (2) believing that your case is relevantly similar to theirs, and (3) not believing that you ought to give up smoking yourself.

Now I'll give the answers.

1 is a nontheorem (since the first part lacks "all right") and a form of the *lex talionis* (law of retaliation).[1] It entails: "If X pokes out your eye, then it's all right for you to poke out X's eye." People who harm you thus *forfeit their right* not to be harmed by you.[2]

---

[1] The Old Testament endorsed the *lex talionis* (Exodus 21:23–5 and Leviticus 24:17–20). The law was intended to discourage wrongdoing and to keep you from inflicting *greater* harm on others than you received yourself. Jesus rejected the law and instead endorsed GR and the law of love (Matthew 6:37–9, 43–5, and 7:12).

[2] The *lex talionis* when combined with U has a surprising result: if X does A to you, then it's *all right* for X to do A to you! The proof is complicated:

X does A to you. {Hypothesis.}

∴ In relevantly similar circumstances it would be all right for you to do A

2 is a nontheorem since it doesn't say that the cases are *relevantly or exactly similar*. Maybe it's all right for you to operate but not all right for me, because you're a doctor but I'm not.

3 is a theorem. When I say "similar" by itself, I mean "exactly or relevantly similar."

4 is a theorem. Are there relevant differences? In proposing a factor to be a relevant difference, we need to be factually accurate (that the factor applies in one case but not the other) and logically consistent (giving the factor equal weight regardless of which side is imagined to have it).

5 is a nontheorem, since I could be doing wrong. To make it a theorem, change the if-part to "If what I'm doing is *all right*."

6 is a nontheorem. It follows that it's all right for *anyone* (not "*everyone*") in similar circumstances to do A. If it's all right that *any* available woman marry Al, it doesn't follow that it's all right that *every* available woman marry Al (massive polygamy).[1]

7 is a theorem. This leads to a form of the "What if everyone did that?" argument. Let's suppose that you admit that not everyone ought to do A (since this has very bad results). Then you're inconsistent if you go on to hold that you ought to do A and that your case is relevantly similar to that of everyone else.

8 is a nontheorem. There may be relevant differences between the two cases; maybe Sis was more responsible at this age than you are – or maybe you can't drive. Children appreciate U; they often ask why it's all right for X to do A but not all right for Y.

9 is a theorem. I take "in similar circumstances" broadly, to include all the features of the situation. The example would be a nontheorem if we took this phrase more narrowly, to include just the "external circumstances" and to exclude, for example, ways in which Sandy's health and my health may differ.

to X. {By the *lex talionis*.}
∴ It's not the case that in relevantly similar circumstances it would not be all right for you to do A to X. {From the previous step.}
∴ If it's not all right for X to do A to you, then in relevantly similar circumstances it would not be all right for you to do A to X. {From U.}
∴ It's all right for X to do A to you. {From the two previous steps.}
So if X lies or steals from you, then it's *all right* for X to do so to you. If you accept the *lex talionis*, then you can't consistently criticize as *wrong* how others treat you. In this sense, you forfeit your right to be protected by morality.

[1] "It's all right for *anyone* to do A" ("(x)RA$\underline{x}$") doesn't entail "It's all right that *everyone* do A" ("R(x)A$\underline{x}$"). This is like "It's possible for *anyone* to win" ("(x)◇Wx") not entailing "It's possible that *everyone* win" ("◇(x)Wx").

10 is a nontheorem. To apply U, we'd need "all right" in the first part and a *similar situation* qualifier.

11 is a nontheorem. There may be relevant differences. Maybe parents and teachers have different relationships to the child that would justify different judgments.

12 is a theorem. Giving advice to others can commit us to giving similar advice to ourselves.

13 is a theorem.

14 is a theorem. A person with a low self-image could violate this theorem.

15 is a theorem.

16 is a nontheorem. You might have a Coke, and then later in a similar situation have a Pepsi. You needn't have acted wrongly in either case; both acts may be morally neutral.

17 is a nontheorem. It doesn't violate formal ethics to eat carrots one day and celery the next – even if circumstances haven't changed. Again, the act may be neutral. It would be boring to always do the same thing in the same circumstances. Unspontaneous people who do this are sometimes called *consistent*. Such people might *consistently* contradict themselves – that is, always contradict themselves in the same sort of situation. This is a different sense of *consistency*.

18 is a nontheorem. The correct form (see Section 3.6) involves your present attitude toward a hypothetical case; you ought not to combine (1) believing that you ought to spank little Jimmy with (2) not believing that if you were in his exact place then you ought to be spanked.

19 is a nontheorem. It follows that in relevantly similar conditions it would be *all right* for another to do A. This doesn't entail that it would be *wrong* for the person *not* to do A.

20 is a nontheorem. You're committed to holding that others in the same situation *ought* to do A – but not necessarily to *blaming* them if they don't. A well-known philosopher once attributed this view to Hare, whose views often get mangled – perhaps because of their subtlety. Hare should do an article listing ingenious theses (like this one) that are wrongly attributed to him; the list would be long but interesting.

21 is a theorem. This is typical student reasoning, and perfectly correct. In giving an exception for one student, we should consider that others may ask for the same exception.

22 is a nontheorem. People are sometimes inconsistent.

23 is a nontheorem. To get a theorem, we could add a *relevantly similar* qualifier: "If Dr Jones ought to remove my appendix and our two cases are relevantly similar, then I ought to remove Jones's appendix." Here the same reasons would have to apply in both cases (which is unlikely). Or we could use an imagined *reversed situation*: "If Dr Jones ought to remove my appendix, then if the situation were exactly reversed I ought to remove Jones's appendix."

24 is a nontheorem, since it doesn't have the *don't-combine* form. Your beliefs might be wrong.

25 is a theorem. It's another form of "Practice what you preach" (see C4 of Section 3.5).

Many of my nontheorems stem from misinterpretations of universalizability by students and philosophers. Often when people hear some principle of formal ethics, they say "*Yes* – that sounds reasonable." But they misformulate the principle when you ask them to repeat it. Few people are good at expressing principles of formal ethics carefully and correctly.

Chapter 5

The Golden Rule

The golden rule requires that we treat others as we want to be treated. GR is the most important principle of formal ethics – and perhaps the most important rule of life. We'll discuss GR in this chapter and the next.[1]

5.1 A GR Theorem

This golden rule theorem (expressed in precise and intuitive ways) is derivable from our axioms:

> **G1** Don't combine (1) acting to do A to X with (2) not consenting to the idea of A being done to you in an exactly similar situation.
>
> = Treat others only in ways that you're willing to be treated in the same situation.

To apply **G1**, you'd imagine yourself in the exact place of the other person on the receiving end of the action. If you act in a given way toward another, and yet are unwilling to be treated that way in the same circumstances, then you violate the rule.

Let's take an example. President Kennedy (1963) appealed to the golden rule in an anti-segregation speech at the time of the first black enrollment at the University of Alabama. He asked whites to consider what it would be like to be treated as second class citizens because of skin color. Whites were to imagine themselves being black – and being told that they thus couldn't vote, or go to

---

[1] Hare 1963 and Wattles 1996 have important extended treatments of GR; I've learned a lot from both. Shorter discussions of GR include Blackstone 1965, Broad 1950, Cadoux 1912, Gewirth 1978a, Goodman 1688, Lewis 1957 and 1969, Mackie 1977 (83–102), Ricoeur 1990 and 1992, Weiss 1941, and Whately 1857. Further footnotes mention other discussions. My GR theorem has an original wording and derivation.

the best public schools, or eat at most public restaurants, or sit in the front of the bus. Would whites be content to be treated that way? He was sure that they wouldn't – and yet this is how they treated others. He said the "heart of the question is ... whether we are going to treat our fellow Americans as we want to be treated."

To apply the golden rule adequately, we need knowledge and imagination. We need to *know* what effect our actions have on the lives of others. And we need to be able to *imagine* ourselves, vividly and accurately, in the other person's place on the receiving end of the action. When combined with knowledge and imagination, GR is a powerful tool of moral thinking. We'll discuss these and other elements in Chapter 7.

The golden rule, construed as G1, is a consistency principle. It doesn't replace regular moral norms. It isn't an infallible guide on which actions are right or wrong; it doesn't give all the answers. It only prescribes consistency – that we not have our actions (toward another) be out of harmony with our desires (toward a reversed situation). It tests our moral coherence. If we violate the golden rule, then we're violating the spirit of fairness and concern that lie at the heart of morality.

We begin our proof of G1 by giving this derivation:[1]

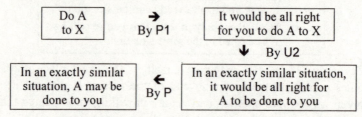

Then by R you ought not to accept the first box without also accepting the last. These involve acting (to do A to X) and consenting (to A being done to you in an exactly similar situation). So you ought not to act to do A to X without also consenting to the idea of A being done to you in an exactly similar situation. Moving from "ought not" to "don't" (using axiom P) gives us G1 – our GR theorem.

Violating G1 involves violating either *conscientiousness* or *impartiality*. Equivalently, if you're conscientious and impartial then you'll follow G1. To see this, assume that you're conscien-

---

[1] Our proof appeals to previous axioms and theorems: R (Section 3.2), P and P1 (Section 3.5), and U2 (Section 4.2).

tious (keep your actions, intentions, and desires in harmony with your ethical beliefs) and impartial (make the same ethical judgments about actions that have the same universal properties). Then you won't act to do A to X unless you also consent to the idea of A being done to you in an exactly similar situation:

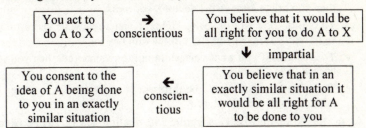

This argument doesn't depend on our axioms or on our analysis of *willing* as accepting an imperative. The argument leads to this hypothetical-imperative form of **G1**:

> If you want to be conscientious and impartial, then you ought not to combine (1) acting to do A to X with (2) not consenting to the idea of A being done to you in an exactly similar situation.

If we assume that you *ought* to be conscientious and impartial, it follows that you *ought* to follow GR theorem **G1**.

5.2 GR Misformulations

G1 is more complex than the literal golden rule **G1a** ("Treat others as you want to be treated"):

G1 (correct)	G1a (incorrect)
Don't combine acting to do A to X with not consenting to the idea of A being done to you in an exactly similar situation.	If you want X to do A to you, then do A to X.

G1 has three refinements that we needed before:

- a *don't-combine* form (Sections 2.1 and 2.2),
- a *similar situation* qualifier (Sections 4.1 and 4.2), and
- a *present attitude* to a hypothetical situation (Section 3.6).

Without these three refinements, GR has absurd consequences and can't be proven from our axioms.

The literal golden rule **G1a** is often plausible. If you want Sara to be kind to you (or respect you, or keep promises made to you), then you are to do these things to her. And if you want Tom not to hurt you (or rob you, or be selfish to you), then you are not to do these things to him.

But **G1a** can have absurd implications. For example:

- To a patient: If you want the doctor to remove your appendix, then you are to remove the doctor's appendix.
- To a little boy who loves to fight: If you want your sister to fight with you, then you are to fight with her.
- To a parent: If you want your child not to punish you, then you are not to punish him.
- To a person who wants to be tortured: If you want X to torture you, then you are to torture X.

Also, our Alice-and-Betty argument in Section 1.2 (Q10) showed that **G1a** can have self-contradictory consequences. Could we avoid the absurdities by applying GR only to "general" actions (like treating someone with kindness) – and not "specific" ones (like removing someone's appendix)? This wouldn't work, since we can reword our torturing example to be about hating, which is surely a general action.

A better way to deal with the specificity problem is to imagine yourself in the exact place of the other person. My father is hard of hearing. Since I want him not to speak more loudly to me, **G1a** tells me not to speak more loudly to him. But this is silly and ignores differences in circumstances. I'd do better to ask how I'd want to be treated if I were in my father's exact place (and thus also hard of hearing). This suggests:

G1b If you'd want A done to you if you were in X's exact place, then do A to X.

This would lead me to talk more loudly to my father.

Consider the patient who needs her appendix removed. Using **G1b**, the patient would imagine herself in the exact place of her doctor (who has a healthy appendix). Since in this situation she'd want *not* to have her appendix removed by a sick patient ignorant of medicine, she is *not* to do this to her doctor. This is an improvement over **G1a**.

Consider also the little boy who loves to fight. The boy would imagine himself in the exact place of his little sister (who hates fighting). Since he'd want *not* to be fought with in this situation, he is *not* to fight with her. Again, this is better.

The case of a parent punishing a child is tricky and brings out an ambiguity. Suppose that you, the parent, imagine yourself as a child who wants not to be punished. If you were in this position, then you'd want *not* to be punished. So **G1b**, oddly, seems to tell you *not* to punish your child. This takes **G1b** to be about how you'd react under different conditions – as in this formulation:

> **G1c** Given that if you were in X's exact place then you'd desire that A be done to you, then do A to X.

You might apply **G1b** another way. You see that the punishment is justified and in the child's best interest. So you say, "I now (as an adult) desire that if I were in my child's exact place then I be punished." Given this, **G1b** seems to imply that you are to punish your child. This takes **G1b** to be about your present attitude to a hypothetical case – as in this formulation:

> **G1d** If you desire that if you were in X's exact place then A be done to you, then do A to X.

Consider the question: "Would you want to be punished if you were in your child's exact place?" This could be taken in two ways (reflecting **G1c** and **G1d**):

(c) Incorrect form: how you'd react under different conditions	(d) Correct form: your present attitude to a hypothetical case
If you were in your child's exact place, would you then (as a child) desire to be punished? – No!	Do you now (as an adult) desire that if you were in your child's exact place then you be punished? – Yes!

The difference is subtle but important.[1]

If the child desires not to be punished, the answer to (c) is *no*. If you were in your child's *exact* place, you'd then (as a child) have *all* his characteristics, including his desire *not* to be punished. So **G1c** implies, implausibly, that you are *not* to punish the child. By like reasoning, **G1c** implies that you are always to follow the other person's desires. This would lead to spoiled children – and

---

[1] The distinction parallels one that we made in Section 3.6 about pacifism:

(c)   If I were in a panic situation, then I'd desire not to kill.

(d)   I now desire that if I were in a panic situation then I not kill.

Hare 1963 (108) was perhaps the first to apply this distinction to GR. He (1972c: 44) noted that this common mistranslation obscures the issue: "Do unto others as you *would have* them do unto you." See also Hare 1981 (95–6) and Hoche 1982 (76–9).

incompatible judgments when different people desire conflicting things.[1]

G1d and (d) give better results. Since the punishment is just and in the child's interest, you'd now desire that you'd be punished if you were in your child's place. You might add, "I'm glad that my parents punished me in such circumstances." So G1d implies that you are to punish the child. G1d is an improvement over G1c.

Let me give another example. Suppose that you're thinking about robbing a person who is asleep. Consider the question: "Would you want to be robbed if you were in this sleeping person's exact place?" The question is ambiguous:

(c) Incorrect form: how you'd react under different conditions	(d) Correct form: your present attitude to a hypothetical case
If you were in this sleeping person's exact place, would you then (while asleep) desire to be robbed? – Huh?	Do you now (while awake) desire that if you were in this sleeping person's exact place then you be robbed? – No!

Most of us would be perplexed by (c) but would answer no to (d). The distinction is crucial when we deal with someone who isn't very rational – such as one who is confused, senile, or in a coma. Then we shouldn't ask *what we'd desire if we were* confused, senile, or in a coma. Rather, we should ask *what we now desire* be done in a hypothetical or future case where we picture ourselves as confused, senile, or in a coma.[2]

---

[1] This is how G1c implies that we are always to follow X's desires:

> If X desires that A be done to him, then if you were in X's exact place then you'd desire that A be done to you. (True by the meaning of "exact place.")
> Given that if you were in X's exact place then you'd desire that A be done to you, then do A to X. (G1c)
> ∴ If X desires that A be done to him, then do A to X.

People sometimes criticize GR as being "too soft" – as telling us to do whatever people want. This criticism holds against G1c, which forbids us to punish the child against his will. G1 isn't "too soft"; it lets us punish the child.

[2] Hale 1805 (406) suggested something like this (see also Section 4.2 Q2):

> Given that if you were in X's exact place except for keeping your ordinary discretion then you'd desire that A be done to you, then do A to X.

But I may need to deal with X in special ways because X lacks ordinary discretion. X may be in a coma. If I imagine myself being in X's exact place except for keeping my ordinary discretion, then I imagine myself *not* being in a coma. So I have to ignore this fact about X; I am to treat X as if X was normal. This won't work.

Let's compare *don't-combine* theorem G1 to *if–then* nontheorem G1d (which, while an improvement, still isn't right):

G1 (correct)	G1d (incorrect)
Don't combine acting to do A to X with not consenting to the idea of A being done to you in an exactly similar situation.	If you desire that if you were in X's exact place then A be done to you, then do A to X.

I violate G1 if I *combine* an action (toward another) with a certain desire (about the reversed situation). To avoid the inconsistency, I'd have to change either my action or my desire; either of the two may be defective. G1 doesn't assume that my desires about how I be treated are fine and provide a correct guide on how to treat others. The *if–then* G1d does assume this – and this is its downfall. I'll give two objections to G1d.[1]

First, G1d can imply absurdities – for example, that a masochist is to torture others. Suppose that Ima Masochist wants to be tortured and desires that if she were in X's exact place then she be tortured. It follows that she is to torture X. So G1d can prescribe that an agent with perverted desires do evil things.

G1 is better. It tells Ima not to combine (1) acting to torture X with (2) not consenting to the idea of herself being tortured in an exactly similar situation. The combination is defective both *logically* (because it's inconsistent) and *ethically* (because the first element is defective). G1 doesn't tell Ima to do anything evil. In this respect, G1 is better than G1d.

But suppose that Ima tortures X and consents to the idea of herself being tortured in similar circumstances. Then she satisfies G1. Our G1 is a consistency principle; it forbids combinations that violate GR consistency. But Ima doesn't violate GR consistency. She treats others as she wants to be treated – by torturing them. Despite this, however, she acts wrongly.

Both forms show a weakness. G1d prescribes evil actions; G1 doesn't do this, but it doesn't convict Ima of inconsistency either.

---

[1] There are two other differences. First, G1 uses "acting (in order) to" and deals with *intentional* actions. There's no inconsistency if you *accidentally* spill soup on another but don't consent to this being done to you in a similar situation. Second, G1 uses "consent" (which is weaker than "desire"). Acting commits you to thinking that the act is *permissible* – and thus to thinking that the reversed-situation act is *permissible* – and thus to *consenting* to this reversed-situation act.

G1 seems weak here. We'd like GR to lead Ima to do the right thing; but G1 taken by itself doesn't do this.

The problem lies in taking G1 *by itself*. GR works best as part of a team; it may carry the ball, but it needs other team members to block. GR appeals to factors like understanding, imagination, and desires; any of these may be flawed and thus criticized further. Ima's desires, in particular, need rational criticism. Ima has enormous self-hatred; she hates herself so much that she desires that she be tortured even if she were in the place of a nonmasochist.[1] Maybe we can get Ima to understand herself better and thus appreciate her self-worth. Or maybe we can get her to understand what caused her self-hatred and to experience positive ways of living. If Ima developed a love for herself, then GR could extend this love-of-self to love-of-others. So G1 may not suffice *by itself* to show Ima her error; but it would likely suffice when combined with other factors. We'll discuss these other factors in Chapter 7.

My second objection is that G1d can imply contradictions. Imagine this three-party case. You're a robber, and your fellow robber X asks you to help him to rob Y.[2] What should you do? You get conflicting results depending on whether you imagine yourself in the place of X (fellow robber) or of Y (victim). You desire that if you were in the place of X (fellow robber), then you be helped to rob Y. So you *are* to help X to rob Y. But you also desire that if you were in the place of Y (victim), then X not be helped to rob you. So you *are not* to help X to rob Y. So facts plus G1d can entail contradictions.[3]

G1 tells you to be consistent in your treatment of another person – whether this person be X or Y. You have to satisfy the golden rule toward both parties. To do this, you must come to consent to a certain kind of action regardless of where you imag-

[1] Typical masochists desire physical or emotional abuse because this brings physical or emotional satisfactions (perhaps of a sexual, athletic, or religious sort). Let's suppose that X wouldn't get these satisfactions. Then, to satisfy G1, Ima would have to desire that she be abused even if she were in X's place and thus didn't get these satisfactions from being abused. This requires great self-hatred.

[2] This is like Sidgwick's 1901 (380) objection to GR, that "One might wish for another's cooperation in sin and be willing to reciprocate it." My objection is stronger, since it shows that G1d can prescribe, not only a wrong action, but also a pair of self-contradictory actions. The *don't-combine* G1 avoids these problems.

[3] The *if–then* forms of GR and of the hypothetical imperative (see Section 3.3) fall to similar objections. Both forms can, for a person with certain desires, prescribe absurd or self-contradictory actions.

ine yourself in the situation – in the place of X or of Y. Otherwise, you'll violate **G1** whatever way you act. This suggests a three-party version of **G1**:

> Don't act in a given way toward X and Y without consenting to the idea of this act being done when you imagine yourself in the place of X and also consenting to the idea of this act being done when you imagine yourself in the place of Y.

We'll develop this and other formulations in the next section.

5.3 GR Variations

So far we've taken **G1** to be our formulation of the golden rule:

> **G1** Don't combine acting to do A to X with not consenting to the idea of A being done to you in an exactly similar situation.

But it's inaccurate to speak of "the" golden rule – as if there were only *one* such formula. There are *thousands* of golden rules – *thousands* of GR theorems. For given purposes, one theorem may be better than another.

G1 uses an imperative format; but we also could express the golden rule using four other formats (for the blank put "combine acting to do A to X with not consenting to the idea of A being done to you in an exactly similar situation"):

> **Go1** Ought: You ought not to ….
>
> **Gv1** Virtue: Consistency is a virtue – and involves being disposed not to ….
>
> **Gd1** Description: It isn't consistent for you to ….
>
> **Gi1** Imperative (same as **G1**): Don't ….
>
> **Gh1** Hypothetical imperative: If you want to be consistent, then you ought not to ….

(These take *consistency* in a wide sense, to include logical consistency in believing and willing, ends–means consistency, conscientiousness, and impartiality.) I prefer the imperative for its brevity; but I see it as based on the *ought* form.

G1 uses an imagined *exactly similar* situation in which we are on the receiving end of the action. But we could instead refer to an imagined *relevantly similar* situation:[1]

---

[1] In giving variations, I'll use the simpler "Don't … without …" wording instead of the equivalent and more explicit "Don't combine …" As before, two acts are *relevantly similar* if, because of certain features that they have in

G2 Don't act to do A to X without consenting to the idea of A
being done to you in an imagined *relevantly similar* situation.

To avoid controversies about which properties are relevant, we
might switch all those that we even suspect *may* be relevant; this
gives us a "safely relevantly similar" situation. The "relevantly
similar" situations of G2 are more realistic than the "exactly similar" situations of G1, since they are closer to the situations that we
occupy in real life; this may be an advantage.

Or we might refer to relevantly similar *actual* situations:

G3 Don't act to do A to X without consenting to the idea of A
being done to you in any relevantly similar *actual* situation.

Recall the example where I refuse to help the stranger who was
beaten, robbed, and left to die (see Section 4.2 Q7). I might violate
G3 if I have a conflicting desire about how I be treated in an
actual situation so long as I admit a relevant similarity between
the cases. When we can't find sufficiently clear parallel cases in
our own lives, we can always go back to G1 or G2 and *construct* a
clearly parallel hypothetical case in our imagination.

We can use the active "X doing A to you" instead of the passive
"A being done to you":

G4 Don't act to do A to X without consenting to the idea of *X
doing A to you* in an exactly reversed situation.

Or we can imagine some other person Y (such as the town bully)
doing A to you:

G5 Don't act to do A to X without consenting to the idea of *Y*
doing A to you in an exactly similar situation.

Or we can imagine some other person Z (such as your daughter)
on the receiving end of the action:

G6 Don't act to do A to X without consenting to the idea of A
being done to Z in an exactly similar situation.

These variations may sometimes be more intuitive.[1]

---

common, both actions fit in the same moral category; see Sections 4.1 and 4.2.

[1] The novelist Jack London (1903: 212–13) used something like G6 to protest
about the poverty of the East End of London (see also Dickens 1854: 43):

> Here, in the East End, the obscenities and brute vulgarities of life are ram-
> pant.... The application of the Golden Rule determines that East London is an
> unfit place in which to live. Where you would not have your own babe live and
> develop ... is not a fit place for the babes of other men to live and develop.... It
> is a simple thing, this Golden Rule, and all that is required. Political economy
> and the survival of the fittest can go hang if they say otherwise.

Section 5.2 mentioned a three-party form of the rule:

G7 Don't act in a given way toward X and Y without consenting to the idea of this act being done when you imagine yourself in the place of X and also consenting to the idea of this act being done when you imagine yourself in the place of Y.

Here's an n-party formulation:

G8 Don't act in a given way toward X_1, ..., X_n without consenting to the idea of this act being done when you imagine yourself in the place of X_1, ..., and consenting to the idea of this act being done when you imagine yourself in the place of X_n.

= Don't act in a given way without consenting to the idea of this act being done in this kind of situation regardless of where you're placed in the situation.

The formula of universal law, which we take in the next chapter, expresses this idea more elegantly.

G1 prescribes a consistency between our actions (toward another) and our desires (about a reversed situation). But **G9** prescribes a consistency between our actions (toward another) and our *evaluation* (about a reversed situation):

G9 Don't act to do A to X without *believing that it would be all right* for A to be done to you in an exactly similar situation.

G10 prescribes a consistency between our *desires* (about how another be treated) and our desires (about a similar action):

G10 Don't *desire that A be done* to X without consenting to the idea of A being done to you in an exactly similar situation.

G11 and **G12** prescribe a consistency between our *evaluation* (of our act) and our desires (about a reversed situation):

G11 Don't *accept that it would be all right* for you to do A to X without consenting to the idea of A being done to you in an exactly similar situation.

G12 Don't *accept that you ought* to do A to X without desiring that if you were in an exactly similar situation then A be done to you.

These give consistency conditions for holding ethical beliefs.

G1 prescribes that we not combine doing one thing *with not* doing another. But **G13** prescribes that we not combine doing one thing *with* doing another:

G13 Don't combine *acting* to do A to X with *demanding* that A not be done to you in an exactly similar situation.

Here the second part ("demanding ...") is equivalent to "accepting that A *may not* be done to you." **G14** gives yet another variation:

> **G14** Don't combine *demanding* that if you were in X's exact place then A be done to you with *not acting* to do A to X.

This is like "Treat others as you *demand* to be treated."

We can combine these options in various ways. We can make our GR formulation like:

> **Go1, Gv1, Gd1, Gh1,** or **Gi1** (5 options); **G1, G2,** or **G3** (3 options); **G1, G4,** or **G5** (3 options); **G1** or **G6** (2 options); **G1, G7,** or **G8** (3 options); **G1** or **G9** (2 options); **G1, G10, G11,** or **G12** (4 options); and **G1, G13,** or **G14** (3 options).

Multiplying the options together, we get 6,480 combinations. All of these are theorems.[1]

The variations that aren't theorems typically lack one of three key features:

- a *don't-combine* form,
- a *similar situation* qualifier, or
- a *present attitude* to a hypothetical situation.

Given three defects (A, B, and C), there are 7 possible combinations of one or more of these (A, B, C, AB, AC, BC, and ABC). This gives 7 bad forms for each of the 6,480 good forms – or 45,360 bad forms in all.

So GR has many forms, including at least 45,360 bad forms. People who criticize "the" golden rule as having absurd implications are usually criticizing a bad form. But at least 6,480 forms would be perfectly correct; these are provable from our axioms and don't entail absurdities or self-contradictions.

5.4 GR Questions

(Q1) Is the golden rule a widely held principle?

Yes. The golden rule has been prominent among the different cultures and religions of the world for the last 2500 years. GR is the wisdom of the ages – not the fad of the moment.

---

[1] There are some further GR theorems that don't fit neatly into my schema, such as "Treat X only as it would be permissible for you to be treated if you were in X's exact situation" and "Treat X in whatever ways you ought to be treated if you were in X's exact situation."

Zoroaster, Buddha, and Confucius had the earliest recorded instances of the rule:[1]

- Zoroaster (630–550 BC): "That nature alone is good which refrains from doing unto another whatsoever is not good for itself."
- Buddha (563–483 BC): "Hurt not others in ways that you yourself would find hurtful."
- Confucius (551–479 BC): "Is there one maxim which ought to be acted upon throughout one's whole life? Surely it is the maxim of loving-kindness: Do not unto others what you would not have them do unto you."

The Rabbi Hillel and Jesus Christ used GR to summarize the ethical teachings of the Jewish scriptures:

- Hillel (70 BC–10 AD): "Do not to others that which you would not have others do to you. That is the whole Bible. The rest is commentary. Now go and learn it." (Talmud, *Shabbat* 31a)
- Jesus (6 BC–29 AD): "Do to others whatever you would have them do to you. This is the law and the prophets." (Matthew 7:12)

In addition, the golden rule occurs in:

- All the other major world religions (and many minor ones), including Baha'i, Hinduism, Islam, Jainism, Mormonism, Sikhism, Taoism, and Urantianism.
- Other traditional Christian sources, including Luke 6:31, the western text of Acts 15:21 and 29, the *Didache*, and many patristic writers and later theologians.
- Other traditional Jewish sources, including Tobit 4:15, Philo of Alexandria, and Moses Maimonides.
- King Alfred, Aristotle, Augustine, Joseph Butler, Samuel Clarke, Charles Darwin, Epictetus, Thomas Hobbes, Isocrates, John Locke, John Stuart Mill, Thomas Paine, Thomas Reid, Seneca, Emperor Severus, Baruch Spinoza, Thales (allegedly), and many others.

Many of these give GR a central status in moral thinking – as being somehow the summary of all morality. It is sometimes said that all peoples of all cultures agree on the golden rule; this is an exaggeration, but not far from the truth.[2]

[1] The first three quotes are from Browne 1946 (xv); the Hillel quote is from Heifetz 1991 (50). Dates and authorships are subject to the usual controversies.

[2] I combined notable members of GR lists from Browne 1946 (xv), Brussel 1970 (235), Hertzler 1934, R. Hume 1959 (121, 276–9), Laertius 1925 (39, 463, 465), McArthur 1967, F. Mead 1965 (191–4), and Runes 1959 (vii). See also Butler 1726 (198–9), Clarke 1706 (86–91), Darwin 1871 (317), J. Locke 1706

A defender of GR needn't fear what Habermas 1990 (197) calls the *ethnocentric fallacy* – that our central norm is "just a reflection of the prejudices of adult, white, well-educated, Western males of today." Confucius was neither white nor Western nor modern. The female Calypso in Homer's *Odyssey* (9th century BC) had perhaps the earliest recorded example of GR thinking (see Wattles 1993: 71). GR is close to being a global principle – a norm common to all peoples of all times.

The golden rule, with roots in a wide range of world cultures, is well suited to be a standard that different cultures could appeal to in resolving conflicts. As the world becomes more and more a single interacting global community, the need for such a common standard is becoming more urgent.

(Q2) Is the golden rule the summary of all morality?

This depends on how we take the question. Are we looking for a complete moral theory in a single principle that, when combined with factual premises, tells us whether each act is right or wrong? GR doesn't do this. Forms that directly guide action, like G1a and G1d, lead to absurdities or contradictions when an individual has evil, deranged, or inconsistent desires.

The golden rule, properly interpreted, doesn't prescribe or forbid individual actions. Rather, it prescribes consistency – that we not have our actions (toward another) be out of harmony with our desires (about a reversed situation). Thus GR doesn't compete with principles like "It's wrong to steal" or "One ought to do whatever maximizes enjoyment." GR operates at a different level.

The golden rule captures the *spirit* behind morality. It helps us to see the point behind specific moral rules. It engages our reasoning, instead of imposing an answer. It motivates us and counteracts our limited sympathies. It concretely applies ideals like fairness, concern, and impartiality. And it doesn't assume any specific theoretical approach to ethics. If you had to give one sentence to express what morality is about, you couldn't do better than GR. In this sense, the golden rule *is* the summary of all morality.

(1:27–8), the Mormon 3rd Nephi 14:12, Rost 1986 (for Baha'i), and the Urantia Foundation 1955 (1650–1). The moral relativist Westermarck (1912: 105), who delights in showing how cultures differ on moral issues, attests to the near universality of the golden rule.

(Q3) Does the golden rule give a necessary condition for right (permissible) actions?

No. Such a view would say something like this:

> It's *permissible* for you to do A to X, *only if* you consent to the idea of A being done to you in an exactly similar situation.

This is equivalent to the following:

> If you don't consent to the idea of A being done to you in an exactly similar situation, then it isn't permissible for you to do A to X.

Substituting "ought not" for "not permissible," we get:

> If you don't consent to the idea of A being done to you in an exactly similar situation, then you ought not to do A to X.

This is much like **G1d** (see Section 5.2) and leads to the same absurdities and contradictions.

The golden rule doesn't give necessary or sufficient conditions for individual right actions. Rather, it forbids certain inconsistent combinations. And satisfying GR is a necessary condition for being conscientious and impartial (see Section 5.1).

(Q4) Suppose that we violate GR, and thus our action (toward another) is out of harmony with our desires (about how we be treated). How do we know which to change – the action or the desires?

When we violate GR, usually our desires are fine but our actions are defective. So a rough rule is that, unless we have a special reason to doubt the rationality of our desires, we should change how we act toward the other person.

Various things could lead us to question our desires. For example, maybe other people criticize our desires. Or maybe our desires are mostly based on ignorance and early upbringing. Chapter 7 talks about how to make our desires more rational.

(Q5) Can one satisfy GR and yet act wrongly?

Yes. Suppose that you act to do A to X, this act is wrong, and you consent to the idea of A being done to you in similar circumstances. Then you satisfy GR and yet act wrongly. Section 5.2 had a more dramatic example. Here Ima Masochist tortures others and desires that she be tortured in similar circumstances. Ima satisfies GR and yet acts wrongly.

In general, it doesn't discredit a principle if you can satisfy it and still act wrongly. Consider "One ought not to lie." You can satisfy this and still do wrong – since you might torture or kill, instead of lying. However, it *does* discredit a principle if we can derive absurd implications from it.

GR is a consistency principle, not a direct guide to action. It doesn't tell us which individual acts are right or wrong; it just tells us to be consistent. We might be consistent and still act wrongly.

On the other hand, the golden rule is an unusually powerful consistency principle. *If* the other elements that GR depends on (such as understanding, imagination, and desires – see Chapter 7) are in proper working order, then we'll generally *tend* to act rightly toward others if we follow GR.

(Q6) Does the golden rule hold without exception?

No. Qualification **QF** (see Section 2.3) is implicitly tacked on to **G1** and to other principles derived using axiom **R**. GR is overridden or doesn't apply if, for example:

- Dr Evil will destroy the world unless you violate GR,
- you're a small child who can't grasp the idea of being on the receiving end of the action, or
- you're psychologically unable to follow GR.

In practice, these qualifications aren't very important.

(Q7) What's the difference between the positive and negative forms of the golden rule?

We can formulate the positive (**p**) and negative (**n**) forms of the literal golden rule in this way:

G1p If you want X to do A to you, then do A to X.

G1n If you want X not to do A to you, then don't do A to X.

Some hold that the two have different implications – the positive implying "Do good to others" (beneficence) and the negative implying "Don't harm others" (nonmaleficence). Then perhaps the positive form is more elevated and idealistic, while the negative form imposes the stronger and more essential duty. One form may be preferred – or the two may be viewed as complementary.[1]

---

[1] Atkinson 1982, Hale 1805, *Interpreter's Bible* 1951 (7:329–30), Sedgwick 1993, Tasker 1906, and Votaw 1904 prefer the positive GR. Abrahams 1967 (18–29), Allinson 1992, Eisler 1947, *Jewish Encyclopedia* 1962 (6:21–2), Kaufman 1963 (224–5), and Rieser 1958 prefer the negative GR. Chan 1955, Henry

The Christian gospels have a positive form, while the classic Jewish GR is negative. While some Christian writers claim that the positive form is superior and uniquely Christian, some Jewish writers say that the negative form is more important. But both traditions have both forms. Christianity has the negative form in the western text of Acts 15:21 and 29, the *Didache*, and many later writers; the Jewish thinker Moses Maimonides used both forms. Islam and Sikhism use the positive form, while Taoism has both forms. So the positive form isn't uniquely Christian.

The forms are logically equivalent if taken to cover all actions.[1] To derive G1n from G1p (or G1p from G1n), first substitute "omit doing" for "do"; then rephrase to simplify the wording. We could avoid the equivalence by taking G1p and G1n to cover only positive actions (not negative ones like "to omit doing A"). But this distinction between *positive* and *negative* actions is unclear. Is the act of going away (not staying), in itself and apart from how we talk about it, positive or negative? What would this mean?

The distinction between doing good and not harming is important and fairly clear. But it doesn't correspond well to the distinction between positive and negative actions. Matthew 5:42 says "Give to the one who asks of you, and do not turn your back on one who wants to borrow." This is about doing good, whether we use the positive "Give" or the negative "Do not turn your back."

The various religious traditions tend to mix beneficence and nonmaleficence duties in a balanced way, regardless of their positive or negative GR preference. Jesus formulates GR positively in the Sermon on the Mount, but he gives both kinds of duties. In the five places in the sermon where he explicitly disagrees with then-current standards (Matthew 5:21–48), he gives two beneficence duties and three nonmaleficence duties – so we have a 2:3 ratio of beneficence to nonmaleficence duties. This is the same as the 2:3

1827 (4:63–4), King 1928, McKenzie 1968, Rowley 1940, Sharp 1928 (140–1, 334–43), and M. Singer 1963 held both to be equivalent. Kohlberg *et al.* 1990 (158) and Von Wright 1963 (155–216) also discuss the two forms.

[1] This logical equivalence is compatible with a psychological difference. Empirically, we may find that many people apply the two forms differently.

Confucius took GR to cover all actions (both positive and negative). While he formulated GR negatively, he gave many positive GR implications: we are to serve our fathers as we would expect our sons to serve us; we are to serve our rulers as we would expect our ministers to serve us; we are to serve our older brother as we would expect our younger brother to serve us; and we are to serve our friends as we would expect them to serve us. (See Chan 1955 and 1963: 101.)

ratio of positive to negative precepts in the Jewish Law, which had 248 positive and 365 negative precepts (see Abrahams 1967: 23).

> (Q8) St Augustine (400: 161–2) and others have suggested forms like "Do unto others whatever *good* things you want done to yourself" or "Do unto others as you *ought* to want them to do unto you." Can your system generate anything like these?

Yes – we can prove these two theorems:

(1) If you *ought not* to consent to the idea of A being done to you in an exactly similar situation, then *don't act* to do A to X.[1]

(2) If you *ought* to demand that if you were in X's exact place then A be done to you, then *act* to do A to X.

You can add these to the 6,480 GR theorems sketched earlier.

The Augustinian forms provide another way to avoid masochist objections (see Section 5.2).[2] However, I prefer our *don't-combine* form because it's simpler to apply and doesn't require a previous moral appraisal of our desires.

Yet another way to avoid masochist objections is to appeal to *rational desires*. Here are two possible formulations:

(3) If it would be rational for you to demand that if you were in X's exact place then A be done to you, then act to do A to X.

(4) If it would be rational for you to demand that if you were in X's exact place then A be done to you, then it would be rational for you to act to do A to X.

Here (3) can tell you to do the wrong thing in cases where your desires are rational but mistaken; (4) avoids this problem and seems correct for some suitable interpretation of "rational." But (4) would be hard to use: to show that you violate it, we'd need to show that it would be *rational* for you to demand that if you were in X's exact place then A be done to you – not an easy task. Also,

---

[1] The derivation of (1) goes as follows (where D = act to do A to X, and C = consent to the idea of A being done to you in an exactly similar situation):

You ought not to combine D-ing with not C-ing. {The *ought* form of G1.}

∴ If you ought not to C, then you ought not to D. {By O~($\underline{D} \cdot$ ~$\underline{C}$) ∴ (O~$\underline{C}$ ⊃ O~$\underline{D}$).}

∴ If you ought not to C, then don't D. {By P.}

We can similarly derive (2) from the *ought* form of G14.

[2] As far as I can tell, St Augustine (400: 161) was the first author to point out that the literal GR has absurd implications. He imagined someone who wants to be challenged to get drunk – and who thus ought to challenge others to get drunk.

(4) would make it circular to use GR-consistency as part of the criterion of "rational desire" (as I want to do in Section 7.1).

Instead, I suggest that we formulate GR without using the notion of moral rationality – as G1. Then we can add further rationality requirements to supplement it. GR requires these additional elements, not in its formulation, but to lead us most effectively into knowing the right or reasonable thing to do. To arrive at this knowledge, we need GR plus factual information, imagination, and so forth. GR is itself one element of moral rationality; but we need various elements working together.

> (Q9) Section 5.1 used the example of Kennedy asking white Americans to put themselves in the place of black people. How would it be possible for me to be in another person's place? If I'm white, wouldn't it be impossible for me to be black?

Kennedy's use of GR requires that I be able to *imagine* myself in the place of a black person. This is surely possible. After seeing Michael Jordan lead the Chicago Bulls to a third straight National Basketball championship, I might imagine what it would be like to be in his place. Imagining ourselves in different situations is a common experience. We do it when we watch movies or read novels, or even when we make moral judgments. A slave owner might imagine himself in the place of his black slaves, in order to understand better how to manipulate them. There's no logical impossibility in these cases.

It would be logically impossible for me to be both white (as I am) and also black, but the hypothetical situation doesn't require this. And it might be factually impossible (without color-altering drugs) for me to become black. But I can imagine something factually impossible as long as it isn't logically impossible. If I can imagine myself leaping to the top of tall buildings (like Superman), I can surely imagine myself with a different skin color.

A "white essentialist" might disagree with this and claim: "I logically couldn't have been black – 'I'm black' is self-contradictory with the 'I' referring to me – I have the essential property of being nonblack." He might argue in this way:[1]

---

[1] The argument goes the same way if we used this second premise instead: "If I'm white, then necessarily a nonwhite wouldn't be me."

I'm white.

If I'm white, it would be impossible for me to be black.

∴ It would be impossible for me to be black.

But this is an example of a classic modal fallacy.

The second premise here is ambiguous. It could mean this:

"If I'm white then I'm not black" $\Box(W \supset \sim B)$
     is logically necessary.

On this interpretation, what's necessary is the *relationship* between the parts. Being white necessarily excludes being black. What's necessary is that if-I'm-white-then-I'm-not-black. This doesn't talk about the necessity of being white or being black by itself. On this interpretation, the second premise is true but the argument has an invalid form ("W, $\Box(W \supset \sim B)$ ∴ $\Box \sim B$").

Or the second premise could mean this:

If I'm white, then $(W \supset \Box \sim B)$
"I'm not black" is logically necessary.

On this interpretation, if I happen to be white then my-not-being-black is itself logically necessary. If I'm white in the actual situation, then in all imaginable situations I'm nonblack. On this interpretation, the second premise is false. The argument is plausible only because of the ambiguity of the premise.

If we ignore the ambiguity, we can similarly "prove" that any true proposition A is logically necessary:

A is true.

If A is true, then it would be impossible for A to be false.

∴ It would be impossible for A to be false.

∴ A is logically necessary.

This commits the same fallacy as before.[1]

> (Q10) To imagine myself in X's exact place, I have to imagine myself having all of X's characteristics. But isn't this impossible – since I don't know all of X's characteristics?

You don't have to know *all* of X's characteristics. When you reflect on your own situation, you bring to mind those features of your situation that you're aware of. Since you can never know *all*

---

[1] Hare 1978 and Wiseman 1978 further defend the possibility of imagining ourselves in another person's shoes. MacKay 1986 (305) calls this the *mental shoehorn maneuver* but admits its importance. Hare (in Seanor and Fotion 1988: 286) says that we can view "imagining being in the same qualitative conditions as another person" as the same as "imagining being that person."

the details, you fill them in as best you can. The same holds if you reflect on the situation of another – or if you reflect on what it would be like to be in another's situation. In all these cases, you fill in the details as best you can.

We can put this point more formally. "You accept the idea that, if act B were exactly similar to what act A is like now, then..." is analyzed as (1) not as (2):

(1)   You accept that [for some F, F is the complete description in universal terms of act A, and, if act B were F, then...].

(2)   For some F, F is the complete description in universal terms of act A and you accept that [F is the complete description in universal terms of act A, and, if act B were F, then...].

Here (2) requires that you be aware of every detail of the case, but (1) doesn't require this.

> (Q11) Returning to the Kennedy example, couldn't the racist easily, if he knew that he wasn't black, desire that he'd be treated poorly if he were black?

No. Try to desire this, and see how difficult it is. Say to yourself slowly the words, "I really desire that if I were black then I'd be treated poorly" – and see if you can mean it.

To desire this is to accept a counterfactual: "If I were black, then would that I be treated poorly." The falsity of the antecedent doesn't make the counterfactual vacuous. Causal counterfactuals are similar in this respect. "If I had dropped this glass, it wouldn't have broken" doesn't become trivially true or acceptable just because the antecedent is false.

Material implications work differently. "(A ⊃ B)" is true if "A" is false. Similarly, material implications with an indicative antecedent and an imperative consequent (like "(A ⊃ B̲)" – "if A is true then do B") can be vacuously assented to if the antecedent is false. Suppose that a government passes a law that all blacks are to be enslaved. The law entails this imperative (where the if–then expresses a material conditional):

> If I'm black, then I'm to be enslaved.

The racist could easily assent to this, since he knows that he isn't black and isn't likely to become black. Since this if–then is a material conditional (not a counterfactual), the falsity of the antecedent makes it easy to assent to the conditional.

Counterfactuals are different. Section 3.6 talked about my pacifist friend Jim. His pacifism committed him to the counterfactual, "If a madman *were* about to kill my family and the only way to prevent this was by killing him, then *would that* I not kill him." Jim had to desire that if this situation were to occur then he wouldn't kill. Since this is a counterfactual, the falsity of the antecedent didn't make it vacuously easy to give assent. It was very difficult for Jim to assent to the conditional – even though the antecedent was false.

GR uses counterfactuals, not material conditionals. The counterfactuals come from universalizability (see Section 4.1).[1]

> (Q12) Isn't it difficult to imagine in a realistic way what it's like to be in another person's position – especially when it differs from what you've experienced yourself?

Yes, it can be difficult. We're never perfectly informed on the situations of others. And we're never perfectly able to imagine their situations and inner lives in a vivid and accurate way. But we can get better at these important capacities if we try.

Section 5.3 mentioned that some GR forms are less taxing on our imagination. If we imagine a *relevantly* similar situation (G2) instead of an *exactly* similar one, we imagine ourselves in a situation closer to our actual one. And it may be more intuitive to imagine some other person Z (such as our daughter) on the receiving end of the action (G6) – or to imagine some other person Y (such as the town bully) doing A to us (G5). Or we might reflect on how we want to be treated in our actual situation (G3).

> (Q13) In applying the golden rule, what weight should we give to the desires of the other person?

GR doesn't force us to give *overriding* weight to the desires of another; we needn't always treat others as they desire to be treated. We often go against desires that are confused, unreasonable, or impossible to satisfy. GR lets us do this, if we are willing that people go against our desires in similar circumstances.[2]

As we apply GR, we'll normally give *some* weight to the desires of others. Suppose that you know that Ima wants a bicycle. You'll normally have some desire that if you were in Ima's exact place

---

[1] See also Hare 1978 and my response to #17 in Section 3.8.

[2] See Section 5.2 – especially G1c and the punishment example.

(and thus wanting a bicycle) then you'd get one. So this "conditional reflection" principle seems correct:

CR If you're aware that X has desire D, then you'll normally have some desire that if you were in X's exact situation (and hence had desire D) then your desire D be satisfied.

CR has qualifications: "normally" and "some desire." You may give little or no weight to desire D if it's confused, unreasonable, immoral, or in conflict with similar desires of other people. But normally you'll give it more weight than this.[1]

By GR, roughly, I am to give to the desires of others whatever weight I want given to *my* desires. I find that the weight I want given to my desires depends on how rational these desires are. I now want you to give little weight to my clearly confused desires[2] – for example, when I order my tenth drink or I tell you (by mistake) to turn right (over the cliff); when I become more rational, I'll thank you for acting against these desires. On the other hand, I now want you to give much weight to my desires that are firm and well thought out (even if you disagree with them), because in this way you respect me as a person.

So my rough suggestion is that in applying GR we give weight to the desires of others to the extent that these desires are rational.

(Q14) Is the golden rule the principle of reciprocity?

A "reciprocity principle" is one that connects our actions toward others with their actions toward us. While GR is a reciprocity principle, there are many others. This principle, for example, tells us to reciprocate the treatment that we receive:

RP1 Treat others as they treat you.

A group of reciprocators will often treat each other well – in the hope that they'll be treated well in turn. But reciprocating also can lead to revenge; RP1 entails "If X hurts you, then hurt X" – the law of retaliation (see #1 of Section 6.4). Kohlberg notes that children at lower stages of moral thinking often confuse GR with the law of retaliation:

[1] Hare 1981 (94–6) defends a version of CR and uses it to defend utilitarianism. There's much dispute over how to formulate CR and whether specific formulations are correct and support utilitarianism. See Hare 1984, Rønnow-Rasmussen 1993 (177–221), Schueler 1984, and Seanor and Fotion 1988.

[2] If frustrating my irrational desire would cause me distress, then you need to take account of this distress. But you needn't give my irrational desire any weight in itself.

My young son thought if Eskimos killed and ate seals, it was right to kill and eat Eskimos.... My son interpreted reciprocity not as reversibility (doing as you would wish to be done by) but as exchange (doing back what is done to you).... We have systematically asked children who "know" or can repeat the Golden Rule the question, "If someone comes up on the street and hits you, what would the Golden Rule say to do?" Children at the first and second moral stages say "Hit him back. Do unto others as they do unto you."

(Kohlberg 1979: 265–6)

According to Piaget 1948 (322–3), children get the idea that it's fair to treat others as they treat you, not from adult teaching, but from the natural evolution of their thinking processes and socialization. Eventually they see that this approach leads to endless revenge – and so they switch to the golden rule.[1]

Here are some further reciprocity principles:

RP2   Treat others as people in general have treated you.

RP3   Treat others as they wish to be treated.

RP4   Treat others as they wish to treat you.

RP5   Treat others as they'd treat you if the situation were reversed.

RP6   Treat others as they in turn treat others.

RP7   You will in fact be treated as you treat others.

RP8   Return good for good; resist evil; don't do evil in return; make reparation for the harm you do.

The last of these (from Becker 1986) preserves much of what is good in RP1, but moderates it in a way that GR can support.[2]

---

[1] Kohlberg (1979), Kohlberg *et al.* (1983, 1990), Piaget (1948), and Erikson (1964) all take higher forms of GR to reflect psychologically advanced forms of moral thinking. Kohlberg's (1973: 632) stage 6 of moral reasoning resembles my formal consistency principles (my equivalents are in square brackets):

Stage 6: *The universal-ethical-principle orientation.* Right is defined by the decision of conscience in accord with self-chosen *ethical principles* appealing to logical comprehensiveness, universality, and consistency. These principles are abstract [formal] and ethical (the Golden Rule, the categorical imperative [formula of universal law]); they are not concrete [material] moral rules like the Ten Commandments. At heart, these are universal principles of *justice*, of the *reciprocity* and *equality* of human *rights*, and of respect for the dignity of human beings as *individual persons*.

Kohlberg claims that everyone would reach this stage if developmental conditions were optimal. Bachmeyer 1973, Urantia Foundation 1955, and Wattles 1987 suggest other ways to relate GR to stages of moral thinking. All of these theories about moral stages are controversial.

[2] Little and Twiss 1978 (179–206) discuss various reciprocity principles in Matthew's gospel. They define a "reciprocity principle" as a principle that says

(Q15) What is the scope of the golden rule? Does it apply just to human beings – or perhaps just to members of your tribe or social group? Does it apply to animals or things?

G1 says that you [agent] are to treat another [recipient] only in ways that you're willing to be treated in the same situation. So there are two questions. First, what *agents* does "you" apply to? Second, what *recipients* does "another" apply to?

G1 applies to *rational agents* – in the sense of agents who are capable both of acting intentionally (to do A to X) and of consenting to being treated in a given way in a hypothetical situation. **G1** forbids an inconsistent combination of activities. Those who are incapable of such activities couldn't violate the principle; in this sense, the principle wouldn't apply to them (as agents). We put a similar restriction into qualification **QF** (see Section 2.3), which is tacked on to axiom **R**, from which theorem **G1** is derived.

G1 applies to *sentient recipients* (beings capable of having experiences). While formula **G1** literally holds even for nonsentient recipients, such instances are vacuous.

Section 5.1 used this derivation in the proof of **G1**:[1]

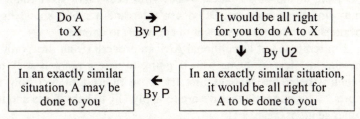

These steps don't presuppose that X is any particular kind of being. The derivation works even if X is nonsentient. It would be very difficult to limit any of the steps to cases where X is of the same tribe or social group as yourself; the steps clearly have a greater scope than that.

The crucial step here is the one involving **U2**. Section 4.2 Q10 noted that instances of **U2** that involve nonsentient beings are true

that there ought to be an equivalence of some sort between how others treat you and how you treat others (190).

[1] We went on to use **R** to conclude that you [agent] ought not to accept the first box without also accepting the last. This brings in the limitation to agents who are rational in the sense indicated a few paragraphs ago – but has nothing to do with what recipients the X can refer to.

but vacuous. We considered this instance of U2 (where X might be a rock, a dog, a stranger, or a friend):

ST   If it's all right for me to step on X, then if I were in X's
      exact place then it would be all right for me to be stepped on.

I claimed that theorem ST is vacuous if X is a rock (or any other nonsentient being), since then:

(1)   It's logically impossible for me to be in the exact place of
      the (totally nonsentient) rock. So I can't consistently imagine
      myself in its exact place.

(2)   Even if I could consistently imagine this, I don't care about
      whether I be stepped on in the place of the rock; rocks feel
      no pain.

I argued that these problems don't arise if X is a sentient being; in these cases, U2 applies nonvacuously. Since G1 is based on U2, analogous comments apply to G1.

Consider this instance of G1 which uses a dog recipient:

DG   Don't act to torture your dog without consenting to the idea
      of your being tortured in an exactly similar situation.

This works like GR applied to humans. Of course, it's more difficult to understand what it's like to be a dog and to imagine yourself in the dog's place. Those who deal more with canines may find this easier; but DG doesn't demand a subtle knowledge of dogs. So I see no reason not to apply GR to animals.[1]

I'm reminded of a traditional African proverb (from the Yoruba people in Nigeria): "One who is going to take a pointed stick to pinch a baby bird should first try it on himself to feel how it hurts." This suggests that we are to apply GR to baby birds and to other sentient creatures.

(Q16) Bernard Shaw 1903 (217) wrote: "Do not do unto
others as you would that they should do unto you. Their
tastes may not be the same." What do you say about
this?

[1] Hare 1963 (222–4) defends the application of GR to animals. He claims (in Seanor and Fotion 1988: 283) that we *can* put ourselves in the place of nonsentient beings like stoves, but that we don't care about how we be treated in such a case. This has the same practical implications as my view. Hare 1993 (219–35) argues that applying GR to animals needn't lead to complete vegetarianism.

From a more practical standpoint, Eckhoff 1994 advocates applying the golden rule to our pets. She claims that as we work and care for animals they also work and care for us. She gives examples relating to a cure for loneliness, a rescue from physical attack, and comfort after a death in the family.

This is a clever objection to the literal golden rule. Suppose that I find spinach nauseating. I'm a waiter and my customer who likes spinach orders it. Should I bring the person spinach? In applying GR, I could ask myself either of these questions:

(1) Do I want to be served spinach myself? – No.

(2) Do I consent to the idea of myself being served spinach in a hypothetical case in which I am in the exact place of the other person who likes spinach? – Yes.

The literal golden rule **G1a** asks question (1) and would tell me not to serve the person spinach – an absurd result. Our improved formulation **G1** asks question (2) and allows for differences in taste. **G1** would let me serve spinach to someone who likes it, even though I don't like it myself. Thus **G1** (unlike **G1a**) doesn't force us to impose our tastes on others.

(Q17) Suppose that you live in a dog-eat-dog society. Wouldn't people take advantage of you if you followed the golden rule?[1]

Not necessarily. GR permits self-defense. You can defend yourself against the attacks of evil people in ways that you consent to others defending themselves against you in a similar case. To further the analogy, you can eat the other dog (who tries to eat you) if you consent to your being eaten in a similar case (where you try to eat another). Even in a dog-eat-dog world, however, GR would limit how harshly we could treat others. And it may lead us to work toward a better society in which everyone follows GR.

(Q18) Can we express GR as a rights-claim?

Yes. We can rephrase the *ought* form of **G1** this way: "You have the *right* to be treated by others only in ways that they themselves are willing to be treated in similar circumstances."

Here are two related formulas: "Rights are best guarded when each person and group guards for all others those rights they wish for themselves" (Flynn 1990) and "A just society is one in which everyone follows the golden rule" (Wulff 1994).

---

[1] This may be the idea behind some GR corruptions – like "Step on others before they step on you" or "Those who have the gold make the rules."

(Q19) Is it difficult to satisfy the golden rule?

Yes. All our consistency principles are difficult to satisfy. Since we have limited intellectual clarity, we find it difficult to be logically consistent in our beliefs. Since we have limited self-control, we find ends–means consistency difficult. Since we have a tendency toward selfishness, we find GR difficult.

A saint might complain that our GR isn't demanding enough. G1 is phrased in terms of how we *consent* to being treated, or how we are (minimally) *willing* to be treated ourselves. This doesn't call us to heroic generosity so much as to minimally acceptable standards. If you're a saint, you might want to go further – to treat others with the generosity with which you'd *prefer* to be treated. This GR goes beyond the demands of my system of formal ethics.

(Q20) How does the golden rule relate to religion?

The great world religions have also been the great teachers of the golden rule (see Q1). All of them endorse GR, and most of them put GR near the center of how we are to live.

A religious world-view is particularly congenial to GR. For example, Christianity sees the world as created by a loving God. Because God has first loved us, as a father loves his children, we are motivated to share his love with other members of his family. Wattles 1996 puts it this way: "Treat other people as brothers and sisters, as sons and daughters of God, as you want others to treat you.... The golden rule becomes the principle of the practice of the family of God."[1] Christianity sees the origin and destiny of the world as deeply in harmony with the golden rule – not as indifferent to it, as on the atheistic view. So Christianity sees an atheistic GR ethics as incomplete and as existing in an alien environment.[2]

---

[1] Wattles 1996 has a fine discussion of how the golden rule relates to religion. See also Wattles 1987 and Ricoeur 1990.

[2] Some atheists emphasize the chasm between ethics and nature, while others try to tone it down. Romig 1984 is more aggressive; he contends that reasonable religion involves giving up religious beliefs (including the belief in God) as unreasonable, foolish, and harmful – and instead following the ethical insight common to all religions that is expressed in the golden rule.

Chapter 6

Universal Law

The formula of universal law requires that we act only as we're willing for anyone to act in similar circumstances – regardless of imagined variations of time or person. UL is a generalization of the golden rule. So this chapter continues our study of the golden rule, but from a broader perspective.

6.1 Concern for Self and Future

The formula of universal law includes two consistency constraints in addition to those implied in the golden rule. These have to do with concern for oneself and concern for the future.

We violate consistency if we treat *others* as *we* aren't willing to be treated. But we also violate consistency if we treat *ourselves* as we aren't willing to have *others* treat *themselves*. Maybe you have so much concern for your children that you never think of your own needs; but you aren't willing that your children live in a similar way when they grow up. Or you go through college without putting much effort into it; but you don't consent to the idea of a daughter of yours doing this in the same situation. Or, because you lack courage and a sense of self-worth, you refuse to seek treatment for a drug habit that's ruining your life; but you aren't willing that your younger brother do this in a similar case. All these violate theorem O1:

> O1   Don't act to do A without consenting to the idea of X doing A in a similar case.

I call this the *self-regard* principle. To use it effectively, you must put someone you care about in place of X.[1]

---

[1] "O" is for Omni-perspective (willing the act from all perspectives); "U" and "L" (for "universal law") were already taken. I use the "Don't … without …" wording in this chapter, since the equivalent "Don't combine …" gets awkward.

We tend to think of people as too selfish and too little concerned for others. But people often don't have much concern for themselves either. Various factors (laziness, fear, habit, lack of self-appreciation, lack of discipline, and so forth) can drive us into ways of living that are useful neither for ourselves nor for others. Formal ethics recognizes the importance of both concern for others and concern for ourselves.[1]

The golden rule and self-regard principles imaginatively shift the *persons* in the situation. But we also can shift the *time* – and imagine that we *now* experience the future consequences of our actions. We violate consistency if we treat ourselves (in the future) as we aren't willing to have been treated by ourselves (in the past). Maybe you cause yourself a future hangover by your drinking; but, when you imagine yourself experiencing the hangover *now*, you don't consent to the idea of your having treated yourself this way. Or you cause yourself a future jail sentence by your stealing; but when you picture yourself suffering these consequences *now* because of your past actions, you don't consent to these actions. These violate theorem O2:

O2   Don't act to do A to yourself later without consenting to the idea of your having done A to yourself now in a similar case.

I call this the *future-regard* principle. More crudely: "Don't do what you'll later regret."[2]

The following theorem shifts both time and person:

O3   Don't act to do A to X *later* without consenting to the idea of A having been done to you *now* in a similar case.

So you are not to act to destroy the environment for future generations without consenting to the (imagined) idea of past generations having destroyed the environment for you *now* in a similar case.

Practical reason has a more unified structure than many philosophers realize. Mackie 1977 (228–9) contrasts three seemingly unrelated kinds of practical rationality: ends–means rationality, concern for yourself (especially your future), and concern for

[1] Gilligan 1982 claims that women go through three stages of moral development: (1) selfishness, (2) concern for all but themselves, and (3) universal concern. While I'm not competent to evaluate her theories, some women (and men) seem to have concern for all but themselves (stage 2); they need O1 and O2.

[2] By now we know that the *if–then* form leads to absurdities and contradictions. Suppose that (1) if you do A then you'll regret doing A next year, and (2) if you omit A then you'll regret omitting A two years hence. Then the *if–then* form tells us "Don't do A" (from (1)) and "Do A" (from (2)).

others; he complains that there is little unity among the three. Formal ethics finds a great unity. Ends–means rationality rests on E1, concern for yourself (especially your future) rests on O1 and O2, and concern for others rests on G1. All are *don't-combine* consistency principles and are provable from our formal axioms in much the same way. So formal ethics gives a unified approach to important elements of practical reason.

6.2 UL Theorems

This universal law theorem (expressed in precise and intuitive ways) is derivable from our axioms (but the parts in parenthesis aren't strictly part of the theorem):

O4   Don't act to do A without also consenting to the idea that any exactly similar act may be done (regardless of the place of the various individuals or the time of the action).

=   Act only as you're willing for anyone to act in exactly similar circumstances regardless of imagined variations of time or person. (These variations include cases where you're on the receiving end of the action, where someone you care about is in your place, and where you're at some future time experiencing the consequences.)

This formula, which applies to exactly similar hypothetical cases, is a generalization of the golden rule. It also includes the insights of the self-regard and future-regard theorems.

Like the golden rule, the formula of universal law is a consistency principle. It forbids an inconsistent combination but doesn't tell us concretely what to do. Applying UL adequately requires other factors such as knowledge and imagination.

We begin our proof of O4 by giving this derivation:

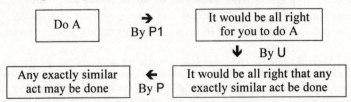

Then by R you ought not to accept the first box without also accepting the last. These involve acting (to do A) and consenting (to the idea that any exactly similar act may be done). So you

ought not to act to do A without also consenting to the idea that
any exactly similar act may be done. Moving from "ought not" to
"don't" (using axiom P) gives us theorem O4.

A conscientious and impartial being would follow O4. To show
this, let's assume that you're conscientious (keep your actions,
intentions, and desires in harmony with your ethical beliefs) and
impartial (make the same ethical judgments about actions that
have the same universal properties). Then you won't act to do
something unless you also consent to the idea that any exactly
similar act may be done:

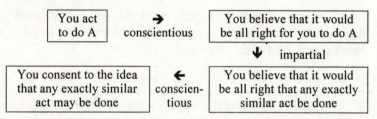

In a Kantian spirit, we might call UL the principle of autonomy.
This means, not that you are to do as you feel like, but that you are
to regulate your life by principles that you accept as holding for
everyone equally and that you will to be followed regardless of
where you imagine yourself in the situation. A conscientious and
impartial being would be "autonomous" in this sense.

Theorem O4 differs from these two misformulations:

O4a It's all right for you to do A, only if you desire that everyone
do A.

O4b It's all right for you to do A, only if you consent to the idea
that any exactly similar act may be done.

Both formulas entail absurdities and contradictions.[1]

Many variations on O4 are theorems (see Section 5.3). We
could use *ought, virtue, descriptive, imperative,* and *hypothetical
imperative* formats. We could speak of *relevant similarity.* We
could prescribe a consistency between our action and our *evalua-*

---

[1] Assuming O4a, suppose that Ima Law-Student (1) doesn't desire that everyone become a lawyer and (2) doesn't desire that everyone refrain from becoming a
lawyer. From (1), it follows that it's not all right for her to become a lawyer, and
so she *ought not* to become a lawyer. But this is absurd. From (2), it follows that
it's not all right for her to refrain from becoming a lawyer, and so she *ought* to
become a lawyer. This contradicts the previous conclusion.

O4b is a generalized version of G1d; it implies absurdities and contradictions
using our Ima Masochist and Ima Robber examples (see Section 5.2).

tion of similar actions. Or we could prescribe a consistency between our *ought* or *all right* judgment and our desires toward similar actions. Many variations aren't theorems – especially ones that lack a *don't-combine* form or a *similar situation* qualifier.

My "formula of universal law" is so called because it resembles Kant's famous formula (1785: 402):

> Act only on that maxim through which you can at the same time will that it should become a universal law.

Consider this wording of O4:

> Don't accept "Do A" without also accepting "Any act exactly similar to act A may be done."

Let's call a present-tense imperative addressed to yourself a "maxim"; and let's take "willing the maxim to do A as a universal permission" to mean "accepting 'Any act exactly similar to act A may be done.'" Then we can express O4 in a quasi-Kantian way:

> Don't act on the maxim to do A without willing the maxim to do A as a universal permission.

I'm not claiming that Kant intended his formula this way.[1]

6.3 GR and UL Analogues

GR and UL give ideals of how we are to treat others. Now we'll look into some related ideals.

Christianity has various love norms, including:

LN   Love your neighbor.

LA   Love your neighbor as yourself.

LG   Love God above all things.

LE   Love your enemies.

LC   Love others as Christ has loved you.[2]

I'll focus on how GR relates to the first two (which I see as significantly different from each other).

"Love your neighbor" (LN) tells us to have concern (considera-tion, regard, respect, kindness) for others – to care about them. I take LN to mean: "Seek to do good and not harm to others, and do

---

[1] See Kant 1785 (402–3, 421–4, 436–7), 1788 (30, 72), 1797 (24–5), and 1924 (42–4). People interpret Kant's formula in many different ways.

[2] Discussions on the first two include Crombie 1966, Frankena 1970 and 1973 (56–9), Gerhardsson 1987, Little and Twiss 1978 (179–206), and Outka 1972. Ricoeur 1990 says that LE+LC and GR supplement each other: LE+LC make greater demands than GR, but we can't build a practical ethics on them alone.

this for their sake." This is about what we seek to do, but may or
may not achieve in practice. LN differs from "Do good and not
harm to others" (beneficence-nonmaleficence) in that it specifies a
motivation. You might do good and not harm to others out of habit
or fear of punishment. But if you *love* others, then you're
concerned for them at least in part for their sake; your love can be
more or less pure depending on the purity of your motivation.

LN expresses an important orientation to life; but it's not
precise enough to be a complete ethical theory. If we wrongly take
it as such a theory, we'll be disappointed because it leaves so
many questions unanswered – for example:

- What is it to do good and not harm to others? Is this the same as
  promoting their pleasure and minimizing their pain? Or are
  there other things of value – perhaps knowledge and virtue?
  Does breaking a promise to X in itself harm X?

- Do we have an equal duty to promote everyone's good? Or do
  we have a stronger duty toward people closely related to us?

- How can we balance goods and harms? Do we total them up
  and maximize the total? Or is the duty not to harm stronger
  than the duty to do good? Are there some harms that we should
  never bring about, even when these bring about great good?

LN isn't an alternative to ethical theories (such as utilitarianism or
Ross's view) that try to answer such questions.

This chart compares LN and GR:

Love your neighbor	*The golden rule*
Do good to others.	Do what-you-want-done-to-yourself to others.
Don't do harm to others.	Don't do what-you-don't-want-done-to-yourself to others.
Do this for their sake.	————

The two are more complementary than equivalent. Love provides
the highest motive for following GR (which we also might follow
for lower motives like self-interest), while GR gives a workable
way to operationalize the vague idea of "loving your neighbor."

GR has a phrase ("what you want done to yourself") where LN
has a single word ("good"). GR provides a *method* to discover
what this "good" is that you are to do to another. The phrasing in
my chart is from the literal GR and is too crude; we can't identify
what is good (for the other) with what you want done to yourself –

since (1) your desires for yourself might be misinformed or evil, and (2) what is good for you (like an appendix operation) might not be good for the other. We refined the phrasing of GR to avoid such objections, and we recognized the need to supplement GR with rationality conditions (see Chapter 7) about knowledge, imagination, and desires. Thus refined and supplemented, GR gives a concrete and useful method for applying LN.[1]

GR normally leads to beneficence-nonmaleficence, which is an important part of LN. If you have normal desires, you'll want to have good and not harm done to you; so GR will lead you to do good and not harm to others. But we can conceive of people who follow GR while violating beneficence or nonmaleficence:

- Ima Hater treats others as he wants to be treated – by harming them. He wants others to harm him, and he harms them.

- Ima Individualist treats others as she wants to be treated – by doing them neither good nor harm.[2]

Both desires are unusual and can be rationally criticized; again, we need to supplement GR with rationality conditions. Properly functioning individuals (in terms of practical rationality or psychological health) presumably want good and not harm done to them.[3]

Now let's consider "Love your neighbor *as yourself*" (LA), which adds two crucial words to "Love your neighbor." LA is close to GR conceptually, since both model our treatment of others after our concern for ourselves. They're also close in the Bible, since Matthew's gospel (7:12 and 22:37–40) claims that each of the two norms sums up "the law and the prophets."

LA tells us, roughly, to treat others as we treat ourselves (or perhaps with the same concern as we have for ourselves). If you have normal desires, you'll do good and not evil to yourself. So LA will lead you to do good and not harm to others. But, as with GR, this implication fails if you don't love yourself:

---

[1] Ricoeur 1992 similarly claims that GR is a transitional principle (a bridge) between our basic concern for others and concrete moral principles. And Kohlberg *et al.* 1990 (164) says that GR operationalizes our intention to respect persons.

[2] To refrain from doing good to those who are weak and greatly need help, Ima has to be willing that others refrain from doing good to her in similar imagined or future situations where she's weak and greatly needs help. Few could do this.

[3] Carl Rogers's 1959 notion of a psychologically mature person includes elements like self-regard; it's difficult to imagine a view that would see Ima Hater and Ima Individualist as psychologically mature. However, the logical status of these claims about "maturity" is somewhat perplexing. So my more basic appeal would be to the rationality conditions of Chapter 7.

- Ima Hater treats others as he treats himself: he hates and harms everyone (himself included).
- Ima Individualist treats others as she treats herself: she does neither good nor harm to anyone (herself included).

So both LA and GR lead to beneficence-nonmaleficence only if we presume certain desires that are normal and rational to have.

I've been interpreting LA as "Treat others as you treat yourself." We can't take this literally, just as we can't take the usual GR phrasing literally. But the idea behind GR can be expressed in a clear, literal way – as **G1**. I don't know how to do this for LA. Am I literally to treat others as I treat myself? Do I have to brush your teeth too? And is it possible or desirable to have the same concern for a stranger that I have for myself? I suggest that we look to **G1** if we want a clear, literal, plausible way to model our treatment of others after our concern for ourselves; to love others as yourself, then, is to treat them only in ways that you're willing to be treated in the same situation.

Here are some further principles that resemble GR:

- Treat everyone as a brother or sister.
- Be humane toward others; treat others as human beings.
- Put yourself in the other person's place.
- Take into consideration the feelings, interests, and perspectives of each individual as if they were your own.
- Act as if you were at once yourself and your neighbor, with the experiences of both included in one life (Royce 1886: 148–9).
- Treat people as ends and not just as means (Kant 1785: 429).

These maxims, while emotionally powerful, are difficult to take literally. If we want to express the insight behind them in a clear, literal way, we'd do well to appeal to GR.

Consider "Treat everyone as a brother or sister." If you send your brother a birthday card, are you to do this to everyone else? If you hate your brother, are you to hate everyone else? The maxim is better seen as a colorful way to express GR. The maxim's aptness comes from the fact that many tend to follow GR better toward their brothers and sisters than toward strangers.

Consider the in-place-of-another principle. Should doctors consider vividly the situation of their patients (including their suffering and anxieties) before performing operations? Maybe not – maybe doing so would impair their ability to operate. And manipulative people might put themselves in the place of their victims in order to manipulate them better. The idea behind the in-place-of-another maxim is better captured by GR.[1]

Kant's ends formula sets people apart from things. It's permissible to treat things as mere means to our ends; but it's wrong to treat people that way – as mere objects to satisfy our desires. We ought to treat people as ends in themselves, as worthy of respect and consideration in their own right. Treating people as ends can be seen as treating them only in ways that we consent to being treated ourselves in like circumstances.

While GR focuses primarily on our treatment of another individual, UL has in mind cases where our actions influence various people. UL gives a perspective that encourages people to act in a harmonious, cooperative manner instead of at cross purposes. Here are some principles that resemble UL:

- Act according to norms that could ideally meet with the consent of all the affected parties (Habermas 1990: 197).
- Act as if you were to live out in sequence your life and the lives of those affected by your actions (Lewis 1946: 547).
- Act toward others as if the effects of your actions were to be realized with the poignancy of the immediate – hence, in your own person (Lewis 1955: 91).
- See all beings in your own self and your own self in all beings (Upanishads, quoted in Erikson 1964: 221).
- Act as if everyone else were going to pattern their lives after how you live (Sartre 1957: 20).[2]
- Act as if there were a natural law under which your mode of action would inevitably be turned on you (Nelson 1956: 115).

These are roughly like UL in that they require that we have an *impartial will* in making ethical judgments.

It's only in a limited sense that formal ethics requires an *impartial will*. We aren't forbidden to have particular desires; if I desire to marry Ima, I needn't desire to marry everyone else with similar qualities. Nor need I keep my desires impartial; I'm not forbidden to desire the victory of one side in a football game. But I must

---

[1] GR doesn't demand that you always go through the process of imagining yourself in the other person's place. You can satisfy GR dispositionally – where this roughly means that if you did go through the process then you'd consciously consent to being treated likewise. Many key terms in our consistency principles (like "believe," "intend," and "consent") are dispositional.

[2] Sartre, an unlikely supporter of formal ethics, states (47): "Though the content of ethics is variable, a certain form of it is universal." He stresses (and I agree) that this form doesn't eliminate the need for personal decision.

keep my actions and desires within the bounds of what I judge to
be permissible. And what I judge permissible in one case I must so
judge (and consent to) in all similar cases.

Phrased to parallel UL, Rawls's 1971 "veil of ignorance" says:

VI   Act only in ways that you'd consent to if you didn't know
      your place in the situation.[1]

UL and VI achieve fairness differently. UL requires that you *now
consent* to the action when you imagine yourself in the place of
any of the parties; VI requires that you *would consent* to the action
if you were robbed of the potentially biasing information of where
you fit in the situation. In our segregation example (Section 5.1),
GR would ask, "Do you now consent to the idea of your being
treated as a second class citizen if you were black?" VI would ask,
"If you didn't know what skin color you had, would you then
consent to the idea of blacks being treated as second class citizens
because of skin color?" The result is similar.

Rawls uses the veil of ignorance as part of his specification of
the "original position" – a hypothetical choice situation used to
generate the principles of justice. Very roughly:

OP   The principles of justice that ought to regulate a given
      society are the principles that its members would agree to if
      they didn't know their place in society but were otherwise
      informed, free, clearheaded, and self-interested.

OP can generate substantive ethical principles. Given information
about what the parties would agree to, OP entails conclusions
about how we ought to live. On the other hand, UL is just a consistency condition to counter biases. You can't derive substantive
ethical principles from UL; formulations that try to do this (like
O4a and O4b) lead to absurdities and contradictions – and can't
be derived from our axioms.

We can formulate OP in different ways to generate different
ethical principles. The parties will choose utilitarianism if we
specify that they want to maximize their expected utility and know
they're equally likely to play any role in society. They will pick
nonutilitarian norms if we specify that they care more to avoid
disaster than to maximize their utility. We can tailor OP to fit our

---

[1] To mirror future-regard theorem O2, we could add "or which moment of time
is the present one." Suppose that you could have ten enjoyable drinks *now* which
would bring a painful hangover *tomorrow*. Imagine yourself not knowing what
moment is the present one. Do you consent to the act being done – not knowing if
this will bring you the enjoyment of the drinks or the pain of the hangover?

moral intuitions. But there's a natural way to specify UL. Correct forms follow from clear and widely accepted formal axioms; incorrect ones (like **O4a** and **O4b**) lead to absurdities and contradictions. UL is cleaner and simpler – but less ambitious.[1]

To sum up, there are many formulas that express roughly the same core insight about morality. We can appeal to GR – or loving your neighbor as yourself – or treating others as brothers and sisters – or choosing behind a veil of ignorance – or other formulas. Which is better in a given context depends on our audience and purposes. Our main theorems (GR and UL) are technical and depend on subtle distinctions. But they have two big advantages: they can be formulated in clear, literal, plausible ways – and they can be justified on the basis of formal axioms of reason.

6.4 Why Follow GR and UL?

This section focuses on GR, but also applies to UL. It may seem redundant, since we've already defended axioms **U**, **P**, and **R** – and GR follows from these. However, we may be able to give *additional* support for GR beyond that provided by the axioms.[2] Many theories support GR more clearly than they support the axioms. And GR is so important that it's useful to sketch how it fits into various approaches to ethics.

One initial consideration is that GR, especially when combined with knowledge and imagination, can help to resolve conflicts in a way that people find acceptable. Thus GR can make life better for everyone, which can be important for various approaches.

We'll begin with two promote-desire justifications. Let's suppose first that you have idealistic desires. Accordingly, you care about others and respect their dignity; you desire to treat them with the same concern with which you want to be treated. And you see that GR would make the world a better place. GR then promotes your altruistic and idealistic goals.

---

[1] Barry 1973 (12–13); Brook 1987; Hare 1973; Kohlberg 1979, 1986; Kohlberg *et al.* 1983, 1990; and Mackie 1977 (97) also compare these principles. Kohlberg 1979 (262) supports UL and calls it *reversibility*, *ideal role-taking*, and *moral musical chairs*.

[2] An axiomatic system can be a convenient way to organize and defend a body of claims; but it needn't assume that the theorems (like "2+2=4" or GR) are less solidly based than the axioms.

Most people have at least some altruistic desires. There are various overlapping explanations for this. Behaviorists appeal to classic conditioning. Pavlov's dogs associated a bell with food, and later salivated when the bell rang without food. So too we associate pain behavior (such as crying) with our inner distress, and later experience the same distress from observing another's pain behavior; so we develop empathetic motivation to prevent in another what would cause pain if done to us. Other approaches talk about evolutionary selection for altruism (sociobiology), the advantages of altruistic norms for social survival (anthropology), how adults teach altruism by example and other methods (social learning theory), and how reason moves us to construct rules for mutual benefit (developmentalism). And various religions believe that we are made in the image and likeness of a loving God, and thus have an inner orientation toward concern for others.[1]

Let's now suppose that you care only about promoting your self-interest in some narrow sense. The Hobbes-Brandt account sees us as enlightened egoists who agree to social rules to protect our interests. So we agree to respect the property of others because we want them to respect our property. The GR-like pattern goes: "We want others to treat us in such and such a way, and so we agree to treat them likewise." So GR is a social convention that we accept out of self-interest (see Hobbes 1651: 84–105). We also agree to enforce GR with external sanctions (disapproval, aliena-tion, legal penalties) and internal sanctions (guilt, anxiety, loss of self-respect); and those who follow GR will be praised and made to feel their self-worth. But then to be happy we must follow GR. To sum up: it's in everyone's self-interest to bring about an atmos-phere in which it's in no one's self-interest to violate the golden rule – and such an atmosphere by and large exists.[2]

This justification works for the most part. Some isolated actions that violate the golden rule may promote self-interest. But a dispo-

[1] See Brandt 1976; Erikson 1964; Hoffman 1981; Kohlberg 1979; Kohlberg *et al.* 1983, 1990; Krebs 1982; Piaget 1948; Rushton and Sorrentino 1981; Rushton 1982; Schulman and Mekler 1994; and Trivers 1971. Anyone skeptical of genuine altruism should read Monroe *et al.* 1990; this is a psychological study of thirteen people who risked their lives to help Jews escape from the Nazis.

[2] Another factor (perhaps related to Hobbes) is that a painful and distressing "cognitive dissonance" can occur when our beliefs violate GR consistency; this provides a further self-interested reason for following GR. A nice research area for some psychologist would be "GR inconsistency and cognitive dissonance."

sition to have altruistic desires and follow GR (instead of assessing individual actions in terms of self-interest) is likely to promote your happiness.[1] There's a lot of truth in the old idea that to be happy in life you have to reach out and show concern for others. So self-interest can justify GR fairly well.[2]

Certain common beliefs would facilitate a self-interest justification. Many believe that God, through rewards and punishments, will give us the kind of treatment later that we give to others now. And many believe that a karma-force will result in our receiving the treatment that we give to others; a hiker once told me that, since I helped her, I will at some later time receive similar help from someone else. On either of these beliefs, GR would clearly promote our self-interest.

Self-interest can lead us toward a purer altruism. Suppose that I desire to do only what promotes my self-interest. Since I see that people are happier if they desire to do good to others for their own sake, I try to develop this desire myself. If I succeed, then I'll no longer desire to do only what promotes my self-interest. Instead, I'll desire to do good to others for their own sake.

The promote-desire justification of GR doesn't presume that you make ethical judgments. Section 5.3 had *nonethical* formats of GR – as descriptions, imperatives, and hypothetical imperatives. You could accept and follow these while rejecting ethical judgments. You might even revise formal ethics to remove ethical terms. To do this, drop axioms U, P, and the ethical formats of

[1] Intelligent crooks seemingly might promote their interest by *not* following GR. To avoid guilt and other internal sanctions, they could become callous inside. To avoid external sanctions, they could fool others into thinking that they're honest. But this involves heavy costs – a life lived in the fear of being caught and likely a shallow and unsatisfying existence. This strategy is rarely successful in the end. So enlightened self-interest would seldom (if ever) support such a life.

[2] Rimland 1982 claims that a simple classroom experiment gives empirical support for GR. Ask your students to list up to 10 names of people that they know well. Have them put H/N (happy/not happy) after the names – and then S/U (selfish/unselfish). Tell them to cross out names where they couldn't assign H/N or S/U with confidence. Then count and add up the combinations. Strikingly, almost no happy people are selfish; statistically, your odds of being happy are seven times better if you're unselfish. So self-interest is claimed to support GR.

Kantians and Aristotelians would have mixed reactions. Kantians would be pleased that altruistic people, who *deserve* happiness, tend to attain it; but altruism is good whether or not it promotes self-interest – and appealing to self-interest cheapens our moral motivation. Aristotelians would be pleased to see their view confirmed that virtuous living brings contentment; but a life isn't virtuous *because* it brings contentment – rather, it brings contentment *because* it's virtuous.

axiom R (Ro and Rv); for axioms, use E and nonethical formats of axiom R and O4. This "formal (non)ethics" drops impartiality and conscientiousness while keeping nonethical formats of the logicality, ends–means, GR, and UL theorems.

We'll now briefly consider the other theories. I'll omit prescriptivism, since we'll consider it in the next section.

Utilitarians could see GR as a useful principle for promoting the good of society; groups that follow GR prosper better than those who don't. So Mill 1861 (22) praised GR as expressing "the complete spirit of the ethics of utility" and "the ideal perfection of utilitarian morality." Ross's theory could see GR as a useful way to apply the beneficence and nonmaleficence norms – and as forbidding inconsistent and inherently bad combinations.

Definist theories could defend the golden rule as demanded by society, or by ideal observers, or by God. We already sketched how GR is important for social life and survival, how impartiality and conscientiousness require following GR, and how GR is important in Christianity and all the other major world religions.

Nonnaturalists could see GR as self-evident, or as derived from other self-evident norms, or as coherent with our ethical intuitions, or as something that ideal moral thinking leads us to. Emotivists could have feelings in favor of GR, and thus say "Hurrah!" to it. And ideal nonnaturalists and emotivists could see GR as a partial test of the reasonableness of our ethical beliefs – since to violate GR is to violate conscientiousness or impartiality.

I've been sketching *further* reasons for following GR beyond those provided by our axioms. For each of the theories, we could add "and GR follows from axioms U, P, and R – which we showed how to defend on this theory."

Or maybe we're unsure of which justification to accept; but with so many plausible justifications, we might think that at least one of them works. Or maybe the golden rule is so obvious that it needs no further justification; perhaps any justification would appeal to premises less plausible than the rule itself.

6.5 Universal Prescriptivism

I'll now sketch how R.M. Hare bases the golden rule on his universal prescriptivism. While I'm critical of Hare's approach, I find it ingenious and stimulating. My own work in formal ethics and the golden rule owes a great debt to Hare.[1]

Hare 1963 claims that a form of GR reasoning depends on the meaning of "ought" and "all right." We use these words to issue universal prescriptions (imperatives) and permissions. We can explain the main sense of these words using these definitions (which Hare doesn't give but are implicit in his work):

df-O Act A ought to be done = Let every act like A be done = For some conjunction F of universal properties, act A is F and in any actual or hypothetical case let every F act be done.

df-R Act A is all right = Every act like A may be done = For some conjunction F of universal properties, act A is F and in any actual or hypothetical case any F act may be done.[2]

Ethical judgments are like imperatives in that they aren't factually true-or-false but instead express our will – our commitment to act or our desire that others act in certain ways. They differ from ordinary imperatives in being universalizable – in expressing a will that applies to all similar situations.

Definitions df-O and df-R make universalizability and prescriptivity true by definition. So this view accepts SU (strong universalizability) and SP (strong prescriptivity). It also accepts these two GR logical entailment principles:

gr-O "I *ought* to do A to X" entails "If the situation were reversed, let X do A to me."

gr-R "It is *all right* for me to do A to X" entails "If the situation were reversed, X may do A to me."[3]

I'm inconsistent if I think I *ought* to torture X but don't prescribe that if the situation were reversed then I be tortured. Likewise, I'm inconsistent if I think it's *all right* for me to torture X but don't

[1] My philosophical interest in the golden rule dates back to a talk that Hare gave in Detroit in 1968. I found his approach to GR so intriguing that I read his book *Freedom and Reason* twice the next week. GR still intrigues me.

[2] Hare 1972c (125–6, 134) speaks of moral judgments as "universal or universalizable prescriptions, permissions or prohibitions"; see also 1972b (101). He often speaks of the universalizability and prescriptivity principles as being true by virtue of the *meaning* of the moral terms. These claims presume that "ought" and "all right" can be defined in some manner like df-O and df-R. Hare 1952 (191) guardedly equates "all As ought to be B" with the imperative "all As being B, please." Moral judgments may fail to be prescriptive in cases of moral weakness; but in serious moral argument we must presuppose that the moral terms are used prescriptively (1963: 20, 52–3, 62–8, 77–9, 90).

[3] Hare 1963 (86–111) uses gr-O extensively. He uses gr-R in 1963 (102, 196, 221–3), 1964 (411), and 1972a (78, 82).

consent to the idea of my being tortured in the reversed situation. Definition df-O entails gr-O, and df-R entails gr-R.

Hare's view here is semantic. It doesn't tell us what we *ought* to do; rather, it tells us what "ought" and "all right" mean, and what we logically commit ourselves to if we use these words. We could refuse to use them, and hence avoid the game of morality. But if we use "ought" and "all right" consistently, then we have to satisfy the GR consistency conditions built into their meaning.

Compare these three versions of the golden rule:

- Classic GR: Treat others as you want to be treated.
- Our G1: Don't combine acting to do A to X with not consent- ing to the idea of A being done to you in an exactly similar situation.
- Hare's GR: You're logically inconsistent if you believe that you ought to do A to X but don't prescribe that if you were in an exactly similar situation then A be done to you.

G1 is midway between the classic GR and Hare's GR. Like the classic GR, G1 can be expressed either as an imperative without evaluative terms, or as an *ought* judgment. Like Hare's GR, G1 deals with an inconsistent combination and includes an *exactly similar situation* qualifier. Hare's GR is a consistency condition on our use of ethical judgments. We have theorems like this too (see G11 and G12 of Section 5.3); but we left it open whether this inconsistency is *logical* inconsistency.

I have two main objections to Hare's approach, one strategic and one logical. My strategic objection is that Hare's GR reason- ing is so important and useful that it needs to be shared. Natural- ists, emotivists, and nonnaturalists need the golden rule too. So I've tried to express Hare's GR in a generic way that doesn't rest on Hare's analysis of moral judgments and that can be defended from practically any approach to ethics.

My logical objection is that his theory is self-contradictory. Definitions df-O and df-R together let us prove *both* the truth *and* the falsity of GR principles gr-O and gr-R. The argument for this is very technical.

Let's suppose that definition df-R is true. Then accepting that an act *ought* to be done is logically equivalent to *not* universally permitting the *omission* of the act. We can show the equivalence as follows (where "=" stands for logical equivalence):

I ought to do A to X	=	It is not all right for me to omit doing A to X	= by df-R	Not every act like my omitting to do A to X may be done

The first "=" is based on a common deontic equivalence.[1] The second "=" is based on df-R; to see this, omit each "not." But then *ought* judgments are too weak to sustain GR arguments:

Box 3 doesn't logically entail "If the situation were reversed, let X do A to me." {Important premise.}

∴ Box 1 doesn't logically entail "If the situation were reversed, let X do A to me." {Substituting equivalents.}

The "important premise" (which has no ethical terms) is clearly true. It holds on Hare's view because ordinary imperatives and permissives aren't universalizable[2] and don't entail reversed-situation prescriptions. The conclusion *denies* gr-O.

So from df-R we can show the *falsity* of gr-O. But from df-R we also can show the *truth* of gr-R. But then:

H1 If df-R is true, then gr-R is true and gr-O is false.

So df-R makes one GR principle true and the other false.

Now suppose that df-O is true. Then accepting that an act is *all right* is logically equivalent to *not* universally prescribing the *omission* of the act. We can show the equivalence as follows:

It is all right for me to do A to X	=	It is not the case that I ought to omit doing A to X	= by df-O	Let not every act like my omitting to do A to X be done

Again, the first "=" is based on a deontic equivalence. The second "=" is based on df-O; to see this, omit each "not." But then *all right* judgments are too weak to sustain GR arguments:

Box 3 doesn't logically entail "If the situation were reversed, X may do A to me." {Important premise.}

∴ Box 1 doesn't logically entail "If the situation were reversed, X may do A to me." {Substituting equivalents.}

The conclusion *denies* gr-R. So from df-O we can show the *falsity* of gr-R. But from df-O we can show the *truth* of gr-O. So then:

H2 If df-O is true, then gr-O is true and gr-R is false.

[1] This deontic equivalence ("O$\underline{A}$ = ~R~$\underline{A}$") is common and Hare (1952: 182, 1972d: 36) is committed to it. The argument can be rephrased to require only the one-way entailment from "~R~$\underline{A}$" to "O$\underline{A}$." As far as I know, this entailment is universally accepted among deontic logicians – although some qualify it by adding the proviso that act A is contingent (which we could add to our argument).

[2] See Hare 1963 (36), 1972b (106), and 1972d (36).

So df-O also makes one GR principle true and the other false.

Given H1 and H2, it's inconsistent to accept both definitions (df-O and df-R) at once. For then we could deduce that gr-O and gr-R are each both true and false. So we must give up at least one definition. There are three possible approaches:

#1   Keep df-R and reject df-O.
#2   Keep df-O and reject df-R.
#3   Reject both df-O and df-R.

We'll consider these three approaches in turn.

Approach #1 keeps df-R but rejects df-O. Then by H1, gr-R is true but gr-O false. There are two problems with this. First, both GR principles seem equally good. So gr-O and gr-R are both true or both false. But this approach says that the first is false and the second true. This seems implausible and arbitrary.

Second, approach #1 impoverishes moral reasoning through the loss of gr-O. By H1, if df-R is true then gr-O is false:

gr-O   "I *ought* to do A to X" entails "If the situation were reversed, let X do A to me."

But then this is consistent:

"I *ought* to torture X; but if the situation were reversed, let X *not* torture me."

Then it's consistent to believe that I *ought* to torture X while prescribing that in the reversed situation X *not* torture me. A torturer who wants to be consistent can shift from "It's *all right* for me to torture X" (which gr-R can attack) to "I *ought* to torture X." He can then avoid Hare's arguments. But it's incredible that *all right* has to conform to GR while *ought* doesn't.[1] So keeping df-R while rejecting df-O isn't an acceptable option.

Approach #2 keeps df-O but rejects df-R. Then by H2, gr-O is true but gr-R false. Hare takes this approach (1981: 182–7, 1989b). He gives this analysis of indifference:

> To say that an act would be morally indifferent, therefore, is to refrain explicitly from expressing any desire that acts of just this sort should be done in *all* circumstances of just this sort, or any desire that they should not.
>
> (Hare 1981: 185)

---

[1] Aaron Bunch suggested to me that approach #1 could still use GR arguments against *ought* judgments, since "ought" entails "all right" and approach #1 accepts gr-R. But the problem here is that df-R (which is part of approach #1) also invalidates the principle that "ought" entails "all right." (See also Gensler 1976.)

Now "Act A is morally indifferent" means "It's all right to do A and it's also all right not to do A." So Hare's analysis of indifference leads to this analysis of "all right":

> To say that it is all right to do A is to refrain explicitly from expressing any desire that acts of the same sort as A not be done in *all* circumstances of just this sort.

Putting this in terms of prescriptions instead of desires (and simplifying the wording) gives this definition:

> Act A is all right = Let not every act like omitting A be done.

So accepting that an act is *all right* is equivalent to *not* universally prescribing the *omission* of the action. This is as it should be if we base our definition of "all right" on the definition of "ought" (df-O) plus the familiar deontic equivalence ("all right to do" = "not obligatory to omit" – "R$\underline{A}$ = ~O~$\underline{A}$"). Hare is thus rejecting his earlier view that *all right* judgments are universalizable permissions. So he no longer holds definition df-R:

> df-R Act A is all right = Every act like A may be done.

Given the new understanding of "all right," golden rule arguments using "all right" no longer work. This follows our earlier result:

> H2   If df-O is true, then gr-O is true and gr-R is false.

Hare seems to accept this. He no longer uses golden rule arguments with "all right." While he hasn't said explicitly that he now rejects gr-R, his new approach commits him to this.

There are two problems with approach #2. First, both GR principles seem equally good. Then gr-O and gr-R are both true or both false. But this approach says that the first is true and the second false. This seems implausible and arbitrary.[1]

Second, approach #2 impoverishes moral reasoning through the loss of gr-R. By H2, if df-O is true then gr-R is false:

> gr-R "It is all right for me to do A to X" entails "If the situation were reversed, X may do A to me."

But then this is consistent:

---

[1] This view involves rejecting half of strong prescriptivity SP: while an *ought* judgment still entails an imperative, an *all right* judgment no longer entails a permissive. This could be made plausible if some independent reason were given for modifying SP – some good objection to the "all right" part that didn't hold for the "ought" part. Example #7 of Section 3.8 has the most plausible objection to the "all right" part that I can think of; but #8 gives a similar objection to the "ought" part. Both fail once we make needed distinctions (see my responses to #7 and #8). For more about the permissive form "You may do A," see Sections 3.1 and 8.1.

> "It is all right for me to torture X; but if the situation were reversed, X may *not* torture me."

Then it's consistent to believe that it's *all right* for me to torture X while demanding that in the reversed situation X *not* torture me. A torturer who wants to be consistent can shift from "I *ought* to torture X" (which gr-O can attack) to "It's *all right* for me to torture X." He then can avoid Hare's arguments. But it's incredible that *ought* has to conform to GR while *all right* doesn't. And gr-R is more useful than gr-O, since moral respectability demands that our action be permissible, not that it be required. So it would be more useful to attack "It is *all right* for me to torture X." Thus, keeping df-O while rejecting df-R isn't an acceptable option.

In view of the loss of gr-R, Hare tries to conduct his moral discussions using what he calls the "ought"/"ought not" dichotomy. He avoids claims about what is *all right* (permissible). Sometimes, as Brandt 1989 points out, this is awkward. In discussing abortion, for example, we want to know whether abortion is generally *all right*. But Hare's theory, while it can still argue about *ought* judgments, can't argue very well about *all right* judgments.[1]

Hare tries to assimilate judgments of indifference to amoralism (which refrains from moral judgments). He asks on what basis one is sometimes to use judgments of indifference and sometimes to admit the "ought"/"ought not" dichotomy. But this has an easy Hare-like answer:

> I try to approximate to ideal moral thinking – full information, imagination, consistency, and so forth. Then, if I universally prescribe acts like A, I say "Act A ought to be done." If I universally prohibit acts like A, I say "Act A is wrong." If I universally permit acts like A, I say "Act A is all right." If I both universally permit acts like A and also universally permit omitting acts like A, I say "Act A is indifferent." Probably most actions are indifferent.

This makes the same sense for "all right" and "indifferent" as it does for "ought" and "wrong."

Approach #2 makes Hare's theory arbitrary (in accepting gr-O but rejecting gr-R) and weak (in rejecting GR arguments using "all right"). I think that Hare made a mistake in adopting approach #2; he'd do better to adopt a version of my third approach.

Approach #3 rejects both definitions. There's a strong argument for this rejection. Since both GR principles are equally good, both

---

[1] Hare, by picking approach #1, could have had it the other way. Then he could argue about *all right* judgments but not about *ought* judgments.

are true or both are false. By H1, if df-R is true then one of the GR principles is true but not the other; so df-R isn't true. Similarly, by H2, df-O isn't true. So neither definition is true.

This doesn't necessarily leave universal prescriptivism in shambles. We can, by rearranging the "universal" element, provide for golden rule arguments using both "ought" and "all right." This is approach #3+.[1] It defines "all right" as a simple permissive:

df-r   Act A is all right = Act A may be done.

Then, given the deontic equivalence "$O\underline{A} = {\sim}R{\sim}\underline{A}$," this definition of "ought" follows:

df-o   Act A ought to be done = Act A may not be omitted.

Here "Act A may not be omitted" entails (but isn't entailed by) the simple imperative "Do A" (see Section 8.1).

We seem to have lost universalizability. But we can bring it back by a further thesis about "ought" and "all right":

EV   "Ought" and "all right" are typically used in evaluative judgments; it's misleading to use them otherwise. By definition, to make an *evaluative judgment* you must prescribe the same thing about similar cases and thus satisfy universalizability.

Universalizability comes in, not by the definition of "ought" and "all right," but by the definition of "evaluative judgment."[2] Universalizability isn't analytic (so SU is rejected); but it's analytic that if you make an evaluative judgment then you satisfy universalizability. Suppose you say, "Act A is all right and act B is wrong – but the two have the same universal properties." While your claim is logically consistent, you aren't making an *evaluative* judgment – and your use of "all right" and "wrong" is misleading.

This view accepts these golden rule entailment principles:

gr-o   "I *ought* to do A to X" with U entails "If the situation were reversed, let X do A to me."

gr-r   "It is *all right* for me to do A to X" with U entails "If the situation were reversed, X may do A to me."

Then I'm inconsistent *or not making an evaluative judgment* if I believe that I *ought* to torture X but don't prescribe that if the

---

[1] I'm *not* endorsing approach #3+. Rather I'm presenting it as part of my strategy of showing how to defend formal ethics from various perspectives.

[2] It doesn't matter if EV captures the ordinary sense of "evaluative judgment." We might, to avoid begging questions, speak of "impartial evaluative judgment" or "U-type prescription." The term doesn't matter. What matters is that there are good reasons (as we sketched in Section 4.3) for wanting to make such judgments.

situation were reversed then I be tortured. Likewise, I'm inconsistent *or not making an evaluative judgment* if I believe that it is *all right* for me to torture X but don't consent to the idea of my being tortured in the reversed situation.

Does it weaken U to have it built into "evaluative" instead of "ought"?[1] I can't see how it does. Either point by itself is merely verbal; we could avoid these words (or use them differently) if we wanted to avoid U (see Hare 1963: 165). We might reject or modify the notions that we've inherited to guide our lives. So the verbal points aren't decisive. The real issue is whether, after reflection, we really do want to guide our lives by universalizable prescriptions and permissions. I think that Hare can handle this problem; but I don't see how having U built into "evaluative" instead of "ought" makes the problem any easier or any harder.

In practice, then, this new view would work much like the original. In theory, however, there's a big gain. This new view is logically consistent (as Hare 1963 wasn't) and accepts both kinds of golden rule arguments (as Hare 1981 didn't).

Before ending this section, I'd like to prove a related result – that universalizability and prescriptivity can't both be necessary truths (and thus express logical entailments). In other words, SU (strong universalizability) and SP (strong prescriptivity) can't both be true. My proof goes as follows:

> "Do A" with U and P entails "Any exactly similar act may be done." {See the proof for O4 in Section 5.2.}
> ∴ If U and P are both necessary truths, then "Do A" by itself entails "Any act exactly similar to act A may be done."
> "Do A" doesn't by itself entail "Any act exactly similar to act A may be done." {Important premise.}
> ∴ U and P aren't both necessary truths.

The "important premise" is clearly true; it holds on Hare's view because ordinary imperatives and permissives aren't universalizable – and hence don't logically entail prescriptions about exactly similar cases.[2] So SU and SP can't both be true. This result has

---

[1] Hare 1955 tied U to "moral" instead of to "ought" (see also 1972b: 17–21, which is from a 1954 article). Hare 1963 (37) shifted on this: "The word 'moral' plays here a far smaller role than I was at one time tempted to assign to it. It is the logic of the word 'ought' in its typical uses that requires universalizability, not that of the word 'moral.'" But now further shifts are needed to make the view more coherent and powerful.

[2] If the "important premise" were false, then "Do A to X" would by itself entail "In an exactly similar situation, A may be done to you" – thus making it *logically*

application to other theories besides universal prescriptivism. Nonnaturalists and emotivists might be tempted to accept both SU and SP. But this won't work. At least one of the pair {U, P} doesn't express a logical entailment.

6.6 GR and UL Examples

Philosophers sometimes point out that the golden rule has absurd implications. It indeed does have absurd implications if we don't formulate it with great care. GR is more subtle than it looks. People who hear my G1 remark that it makes sense; but they usually phrase it wrongly when they try to repeat it. The following exercise is designed to help us understand how to formulate GR.

Is each of the following a theorem or a nontheorem? Keep in mind that GR theorems generally involve:

- a *don't-combine* form,
- a *similar situation* qualifier, and
- a *present attitude* to a hypothetical situation.

Answers will follow.

1. You ought to treat others as they treat you.
2. People will treat you as you treat them.
3. If you don't want others to keep you awake after midnight by loud radio playing, then you ought not to do this to others.
4. Don't act to go through college doing the least work possible without consenting to the thought of a daughter of yours doing this same thing in similar circumstances.
5. Don't combine (1) accepting that it's all right for the United States to do nothing to help starving people in other countries with (2) not consenting to the idea of the United States doing nothing to help you if you were a person starving in such circumstances.
6. Given that if you were in this criminal's place then you wouldn't want to be jailed, it follows that you ought not to jail this criminal.
7. If you believe that you ought to rob another but don't desire that you be robbed in the reversed situation, then your belief is false.
8. If in the reversed situation you'd want to rob Jones, then you ought to let Jones rob you.
9. Don't act to drive drunk and hence threaten the lives of others without consenting to the idea of others doing this in parallel circumstances and thus threatening the lives of your loved ones.

inconsistent for you to act to do A to X without consenting to the idea of A being done to you in an exactly similar situation. This seems implausible.

10. Don't combine (1) believing that it would be all right for you to take hostages to further your political goals with (2) not consenting to the idea of others taking your loved ones hostages to further their political goals in relevantly similar circumstances.

11. If you demand that in similar circumstances your wife not lie to you about your terminal illness, then don't act to lie to your wife about her terminal illness.

12. Don't combine (1) believing that it's all right for you to leave your dirty dishes around with (2) demanding that in admittedly similar circumstances others not leave their dirty dishes around.

13. If you want others not to enslave you, then you ought not to enslave them.

14. Don't act to pay your employees in a given way without consenting to the idea of yourself (or one dear to you) being paid that way in such circumstances.

15. If your slave consents to the idea of your beating him, then it's all right for you to beat him.

16. Don't accept "If the situation were reversed then she ought to help me" without acting to help her.

17. If it's wrong for Aunt Alice to tell me nasty things about you and if your situation is relevantly similar to hers, then don't you tell me nasty things about Aunt Alice.

18. Don't act to refuse forgiveness to others without consenting to the idea of your being refused forgiveness in similar circumstances.

19. Don't accept that it's all right for you to bump into others in the pool without consenting to the idea of others doing this to you in similar circumstances.

20. Don't accept "It would be all right not to cancel rental car reservations I'm not going to use even though there are others who might be thereby deprived" without consenting to someone doing this in a similar situation where you might be thereby deprived.

21. Don't accept "It's all right for me to take drugs even though this may mean that my child won't be born normal" while also demanding that in the hypothetical situation where you're the child about to be born this risk not be taken with you.

22. Don't act to have an abortion without consenting to the idea of your mother having had an abortion while pregnant with you in imagined similar circumstances.

23. Don't combine (1) desiring that not everyone litter, (2) believing that there's no relevant difference between your case and that of other people, and (3) believing that you ought to litter.

24. To the president deliberating on whether to veto a bill: Don't act to veto (or not veto) the bill without consenting to this act being done regardless of where you imagine yourself in the situation.

25. To a wilderness backpacker: Don't act to shampoo your hair in this spring which is the sole drinking water for future campers without consenting to the idea of someone in a similar case shampooing their hair in a spring which is your sole drinking water.

Now I'll give the answers.

1 is a nontheorem. It has instances like "You ought to knock out X's eye if X knocks out your eye" – so leads to the law of retaliation (see Section 4.4 #1 and Section 5.4 Q14). It's sometimes confused with the golden rule (even by theologians – see Robinson 1966 and Ricoeur 1990). But GR says you ought to treat others as you *want* to be treated – not as you actually *are* treated.

2 is a nontheorem. This "tin rule" describes behavior; it isn't an imperative or an *ought*. It's sometimes confused with GR, perhaps because a hypothetical imperative GR follows from it. Suppose that Sue is kind to you only if you are first kind to her. Then this hypothetical imperative GR follows: "If you want Sue to be kind to you (the end), then you ought to be kind to her (the means)."

Often others are kind (or unkind) to us depending on how we treat them. In these cases, it pays to follow GR to get people to treat us as we want to be treated. But often others are kind (or unkind) to us no matter what we do. Then only the categorical GR applies – that we ought to treat others as we want to be treated *regardless* of whether others reciprocate. The categorical GR is the more usual understanding of the golden rule.

This hypothetical imperative GR might remind you of our self-interest GR justification (Section 6.4). But there we appealed to the external and internal sanctions behind GR, including social disapproval and our sense of self-worth. We didn't assume that individuals will return the treatment that we give them.[1]

3 is a nontheorem. This example isn't absurd, but other examples with this form are. One correct form would tell you not to act to play your radio loudly after midnight (thus keeping others awake) without consenting to the idea of others doing this same thing to you in similar circumstances.

---

[1] In the Bible, the immediate context of the golden rule has traces of both the tin rule and the self-interest justification of GR (see Matthew 7:1–2 and Luke 6:35–8). These may seem unworthy of the exalted tone of the Sermon on the Mount. But a religion that appeals to both saints and sinners has to be understandable to people at different levels of moral maturity – from those who follow GR out of self-interest (including divine rewards and punishments) to those who follow it out of genuine love for others as God's children.

4 is a theorem.

5 is a theorem. There used to be a "Golden Rule Sunday" (see Vickrey 1928) after Thanksgiving that applied GR to world hunger. People ate substandard meals to help them appreciate the situation of hungry people and the urgency of the problem. Now many do this before Thanksgiving, but without the GR reference.

6 is a nontheorem, since it lacks the *don't-combine* form and isn't about your *present attitude* to a hypothetical situation. One correct form would tell you not to act to jail this criminal without consenting to the idea of your being jailed in similar circumstances. If the sentence is just, judges should be willing that they (or their loved ones) be jailed for similar crimes in similar circumstances. (See also Hoche 1982: 77–8.)

Kant (1785: 430) in a footnote[1] used this (misformulated) example to object to GR. He had three other objections to GR:

(1)   GR is a deduction from UL instead of a basic principle.

But UL isn't basic either (since it's provable from axioms U, P, and R); and a theorem needn't be of less value than an axiom.

(2)   GR doesn't cover duties to oneself, while UL does.

I admit this; see Sections 6.1 and 6.2.[2]

(3)   GR doesn't contain the principle of duties of benevolence to others, since you could gladly consent that others not benefit you if you be excused from showing benevolence to them.

UL has the same limitation, but both lead to benevolence if we assume certain desires which, I argue, it would be rational to have. (Kant himself sometimes appeals to rational desires.) Recall that, to avoid benevolence toward those who are weak and greatly in need of help, you must consent to the idea that others not do good to you in similar imagined or future situations where you are weak and greatly in need of help. See Section 6.3.

---

[1] Wattles 1987 notes that Kant's GR footnote "almost completely silenced a previously energetic European tradition of reflection on the golden rule for 150 years." He later (1996) speculates that Kant's formulation of the categorical imperative may have been prompted in part by the need to reform the golden rule. Hoche 1982 has a good discussion of Kant's footnote.

[2] Hoche's 1982 (83) version of GR (which I'd classify as a relative of GR, like my O-formulas) covers some duties to oneself. If I worded his formula to be a theorem of my system, it would say: "For every X and Y (whether yourself or another), don't act to do A to X without consenting to the idea of A being done to Y in an exactly similar situation." You violate this if you do something that hurts yourself but don't consent to the idea of your being hurt in this way.

7 is a nontheorem. You're inconsistent, but your belief needn't be false.

8 is a nontheorem.

9 is a theorem.

10 is a theorem.

11 is a nontheorem, since it lacks the *don't-combine* form.

12 is a theorem.

13 is a nontheorem. A better form would tell you not to act to enslave others without consenting to the idea of your being enslaved in the same situation. Those condemning slavery on the basis of GR include the Stoic Epictetus (90: 33), the Quakers in 1688 (see Phipps 1982: 195), *Uncle Tom's Cabin* (Stowe 1852: 126), and Abraham Lincoln (see Phipps 1982: 195).

14 is a theorem. Supporters of GR in business include Handlin 1992, Holoviak 1993, Management 1985, Nash 1923, Sheridan 1991, and Training 1992. These claim that using GR to run a company leads to employees who are more productive and customers who are more loyal – and thus it brings greater profits.

15 is a nontheorem.

16 is a theorem.

17 is a theorem. This doesn't need a *don't-combine* form, since we can derive it without axiom R. Suppose that it's wrong for Aunt Alice to tell me nasty things about you – and your situation is relevantly similar to hers. By U, it's wrong for you to tell me nasty things about Aunt Alice. By P, don't do it.

18 is a theorem. The Our Father prayer (Matthew 6:9–13) asks God to forgive us as we have forgiven others. We can't sincerely pray this unless we've forgiven others as we want to be forgiven.

19 is a theorem. The pool where I learned to swim had a big sign with the golden rule – which is the YMCA motto.

20 is a theorem. I almost violated this out of laziness, at the very time that I was writing my dissertation on the golden rule.

21 is a theorem.

22 is a theorem. I doubt that most people having abortions satisfy it. The theorem sidesteps the ambiguous question of whether the fetus is a "person"; neither the theorem nor the axioms it depends on (U, P, and R) use the notion of "person" in the relevant places. Applying GR to abortion is tricky (see Gensler 1986a).

23 is a theorem. This is a version of the "What if everyone did that?" argument. Section 4.4 (#7) had another version.

24 is a theorem. If you were the president, you could test whether you satisfy this by imagining yourself in the place of the various kinds of people affected by the action and seeing whether you then consent to the action.

25 is a theorem. This example is relevant to the Appalachian Trail (A.T.) which I hiked from Georgia to Maine in 1977 – and on which I did a 450-mile hike after I sent this book off to Routledge. The handbook for long distance A.T. hikers says this about wilderness ethics and the golden rule:

> Rules on the A.T. are relatively few and far between, and the ones that do exist are not meant to limit your freedom but have been designed to allow as much freedom to as many people as possible.... The Golden Rule, "Do unto others as you would have them do unto you," is a good standard to live by on the A.T. (as it is in the rest of life), and the relatively few problems that develop among hikers could be eliminated if this simple rule were observed by everyone. It requires that you value and respect your fellow hikers in the same way you expect them to value and respect you. It also requires you to consider the effect your actions will have on those around you and, equally important, on those behind you.
>
> (Bruce 1995: 6)

Chapter 7

Moral Rationality

M oral rationality pertains to how we ought to make moral judgments. Equivalently, it's about practical reason – or wisdom – or the qualities of an ideal moral judge.[1] Moral rationality has formal aspects, like logical consistency and impartiality. It also has semiformal aspects, like factual data and imagination; these can't usefully be systematized using variables and constants. The various factors supplement each other and yield a strong account of moral rationality.

7.1 Rationality Conditions

Our ethical beliefs are more or less reasonable to the extent that we satisfy various rationality conditions. I'll divide the conditions into four groups: (1) consistency, (2) factual data, (3) imagination, and (4) personal qualities.

(1) *Consistency.* We need to be *consistent* in a broad sense that includes consistency in beliefs, ends–means consistency, conscientiousness, impartiality, the golden rule, and the formula of universal law. We've already talked about these.

(2) *Factual data.* We need to know the nonmoral facts: circumstances, alternatives, consequences, pros and cons. We learn these mainly from personal experience and expert opinion. To the extent that we're misinformed or ignorant, our thinking is flawed.[2]

We also need to know about ourselves – especially about how we developed our feelings and moral judgments. Some people are hostile toward a group because they were taught this when they

---

[1] Readers for whom the word "rational" has a cold and alien feel might try rephrasing what I say using words like "wise," "authentic," or "sensible."

[2] An exception to this is that it may be desirable to eliminate information that may bias or cause cognitive overload.

were young. They might change their attitudes if they understood the source of their hostility; if so, their attitudes are defective – since they exist because of a lack of self-knowledge.

We also need to know the possible moral views on the case, including their implications and arguments for or against them. It's important to consider both sides of a complex issue.

I'm describing an ideal of full rationality – of what Hare 1981 (44–64) calls the *critical level* of moral thinking. In practice, we can't know all the facts. Nor can we always try to be as informed as possible, since then we'd have to research every trivial decision. We can only try to be as informed as reasonably practical, in view of our limited time and the relative importance of the issue. We have to make most of our moral judgments quickly, on the basis of our moral habits, although we strive for greater rationality when we make important choices or criticize our moral habits. Perfect rationality is beyond our reach; but the ideal is important, because it suggests concrete ways to improve our ethical thinking.

(3) *Imagination*. We need a vivid and accurate awareness of the situation of another (or of our own situation at another point of time) and what it would be like to be in that situation. This differs from just knowing facts.[1] We need, for example, not only to know facts about poor people, but also to appreciate what these facts mean to their lives. Movies, literature, and personal experience can help us to imagine the place of another.[2]

We also need to appreciate future consequences. Knowing that drugs will have harmful effects differs from being able to imagine these effects in a vivid and accurate way. An essay about drug addiction might give us the facts, while a story or play about drug addicts might bring these facts to life for us.

---

[1] Imagination involves non-propositional knowledge (knowing what it's like to experience such and such) plus a vivid appreciation of this and of facts that we grasp propositionally. Many philosophers include knowledge and imagination together, saying that we need a vivid awareness of the facts and of what these facts mean to the parties involved. This is the same view, but organized differently.

[2] George Mead 1934 pointed out how common it is to imagine oneself in the place of another. A child pretends to be a mother or a soldier. A chess player asks, "If I were in my opponent's place, how would I respond to this move?" A writer dialogues with an imagined reader who misunderstands and raises objections. A teacher imagines being in the place of a student and asks, "How would I respond to this assignment?" Mead thinks that the idea of the self can only arise when we learn to take the perspective of another and see ourselves from that perspective; whether or not this is true, the operation is important in human life.

The term "imagination" is misleading, since it suggests fantasy and unreality. Better words perhaps are "sensitivity," "appreciation," or "understanding." We need a vivid and accurate awareness of a real situation, and what it would be like to be in that situation. Imagining the place of another is often called "empathy"; Carl Rogers 1959 (210) defined this as perceiving "the internal frame of reference of another with accuracy, and with the emotional components and meanings which pertain thereto, as if one were the other person, but without ever losing the 'as if' condition." Empathy is important for moral thinking.[1]

(4) *Personal qualities.* This covers a mixed assortment.[2] My first subgroup applies to any activity that involves thinking:

- Be intelligent, creative, clear, careful, attentive, thorough.
- Don't let anger, drunkenness, or psychological defects determine your views.
- Feel free to develop your own ideas; don't think that you have to conform to what others say.
- Recognize that many of your intuitive beliefs may come from social conditioning and might not withstand rational criticism; be open to the possible revision of your views.
- Avoid beliefs, desires, and attitudes that you only have because you (or those influencing you) violated rationality in the past.

My next subgroup is more specifically about ethical thinking:

- Seek to find out how you ought to live.
- Look for moral principles that explain your moral convictions and that survive your best attempt to find objections.
- Have a broad experience of life; come into personal contact with different sorts of people and their circumstances.
- Have feelings of concern for yourself and for others.

My last subgroup is about limitations in our moral rationality:

- Don't be dogmatic on areas where rational people differ.
- In areas where you don't have the time or ability to be very rational, give weight to the views of those who are more rational – especially if there's a consensus.

[1] Katz 1963 has a good discussion of empathy, mostly from the perspective of psychology and counseling. See also Hoffman 1981 and Stotland 1969.

[2] Many philosophers give fewer rationality conditions. Hare 1979b, for example, includes analogues of my first three groups but not of my group (4). We needn't be disagreeing; Hare may accept my group (4) as implicit in (or derivable from) his conditions. I don't claim that my conditions are all basic; some may be redundant or derivable from others. Section 7.2 suggests how we might take some rationality conditions as basic and then derive further conditions from these.

- Dialogue with others in your society and in other societies.[1] In practice, we can't arrive at rational moral beliefs by ourselves. We need others to point out our inconsistencies and to make us aware of factors to which we'd otherwise be blind.

- Be aware that these rationality conditions are idealized and that no one can satisfy them completely.[2]

I'm sure that my list needs further additions and refinements.[3]

Our four groups link up in various ways. Impartiality in a formal sense requires that we make similar evaluations about similar cases; in a wide sense, it also includes seeking the facts on both sides of an issue and imagining these vividly. Conscientiousness in a formal sense requires that we live in harmony with our ethical beliefs; in a wide sense, it also includes trying to find out how we ought to live. Concern for others relates to the golden rule; but it also involves finding out how our actions affect others, imagining ourselves in their place, and having feelings of concern for them.

Ends–means rationality also covers various elements. Recall Ima Lazy (from Section 3.3), who wants to be a doctor:

- Ima needs to be *consistent*. She doesn't take the means she sees as necessary to fulfill her goal. She has goals that are incompatible (to become a doctor and to party all the time), given her beliefs about ends and means. And her goal of becoming a doctor conflicts with her belief that she's incapable of doing so.

- Ima needs *factual data*. What means will promote her goals? How did her goals originate – because of parental pressure? Is she capable of becoming a doctor? What alternative occupa-

---

[1] Dialogue can be required, not only by rationality, but also by autonomy and respect for persons. Someone named "Joan" who was interviewed by Kohlberg *et al.* 1990 (170) put it this way: "No person has the right to make a decision that affects the dignity and integrity of another person without there being cooperative discussion among the people involved."

[2] Friedman 1989 emphasizes how difficult it is to satisfy demands of impartiality, information, and imagination. We humans are a mixture of consistency and inconsistency, impartiality and bias, knowledge and ignorance, sensitivity and insensitivity. We have ideals for moral wisdom that far exceed our capacities. We can only do as well as we can, knowing that we'll fall short of the ideal. Only God could satisfy the rationality ideals completely.

[3] One might be tempted to add a *content* requirement, like Gert 1990. But it's hard to avoid controversial content (see Postow 1991), and the notion of "moral rationality" that I'm trying to capture is about *method* rather than *content*. "Rational" can mean different things in different contexts (see Sapontzis 1979, Foley 1993, and Plantinga 1993a: 132–46). A content definition like Gert's is about which actions are "rational" in the sense of "sane"; my "moral rationality" relates instead to how we ought ideally to form our moral beliefs.

tions are open to her? What are the probable consequences of pursuing various occupations?

- Ima needs to be able to *imagine* vividly and accurately the different ends and means. When she visualizes the hard work required by medical school and the practice of medicine, she may find that she doesn't want to be a doctor after all.

- Ima needs certain *personal qualities*. She needs to be motivated to find out what she ought to do. She needs creativity in exploring different means. And she needs to be open to the advice of others, especially those who are wiser than she is.

Ends–means rationality involves various factors working together.

I propose these two definitions of "rational desire":[1]

DS   Your *desire* that A happens is *rational* (in *how* you desire it) =df In desiring that A happens, you satisfy to a high degree the conditions needed for practical rationality.

DO   Your *desire* that A happens in situation S is *rational* (the content of the desire, abstracting from how you hold it) =df If you satisfied the conditions needed for practical rationality as far as possible, you'd desire that A happens in situation S.

DS is the *subjective* sense; it has to do with flaws (like inconsistency and ignorance) in *how* you hold your desire. DO is the *objective* sense; it's about the *content* of the desire – whether you'd desire the content if you were as rational as possible. Your desire not to smoke might be rational in its *content* (sense DO – since you'd have this desire if you were ideally rational) yet irrational in *how* you hold it (sense DS – because you don't follow it consistently). I'll generally use the subjective sense.[2]

[1] I've borrowed many ideas on rational desires from Brandt 1970 and 1983. His "cognitive psychotherapy" is a good model for what I'm trying to do in this book in that it gives clear and useful rationality constraints that can be incorporated into different approaches to ethics. DO is somewhat like his definition of an *irrational desire* as one that wouldn't survive in the presence of a vivid awareness of knowable facts. He gives this as a rough definition; he also recognizes the importance of logical criticism and other factors.

I've also borrowed ideas from Carson 1984. He calls a desire *irrational* if, for example, we only have it because we (or those influencing us) were once ignorant or misinformed. Such a desire might satisfy Brandt's conditions if it's so deeply entrenched that further information can't dislodge it; this addition improves on Brandt's method. The later point on emotional displacement is also from Carson.

[2] The phrase "in situation S" in DO is an important addition to Brandt's definition. Without this, *desiring to be more rational* would be irrational – since if you were as rational as possible, then you wouldn't have this desire. But you'd then desire that *in the present situation* (where you're only partly rational) you'd be more rational. DO (like G1) uses a counterfactual desire – desiring that something happen in a hypothetical situation.

We can be irrational about desires by being inconsistent about them. Ima's desire to be a doctor can be inconsistent with an action, another desire, an ethical belief, or a belief about what's causally possible – either alone or combined with a belief about ends and means. We also can use factual data, imagination, or personal qualities to criticize a desire. Your desire might be:

- to do what in fact is impossible. You desire to do A, but you're incapable of doing A.
- based on *current* false beliefs. You desire A because you believe that it leads to B; but this belief is false.
- due to *previous* false beliefs. You avoid yogurt only because you once believed that it was poisonous. You gave up this false belief; but your desire to avoid yogurt remains.
- due to a misgeneralization. You avoid a certain group because of personal experiences. But your experiences weren't typical, and if you expanded them then your desire would change.
- due to social conditioning. You avoid a certain group because you were so taught. But if you understood this and broadened your experience, then your desire would change.
- due to lack of imagination. You desire to be a doctor. But if you imagined the life of a doctor more vividly and accurately, then your desire would change.
- due to emotional displacement. You desire to harm a certain group as an outlet for anger and hostility caused by other sources. But if you cleared up your personal problems, then your desire would change.

A desire might be irrational for various reasons.

My favorite example of an irrational desire used to be my father's desire not to eat yogurt. His desire came from misinformation ("Yogurt contains bad germs"), his association of yogurt with weird people (his children), and his anti-yogurt upbringing. But he recently broadened his knowledge and experience, and changed his desires. Now he eats yogurt regularly.

My current favorite example is my desire not to eat worms. My desire is irrational since I'd lose it if I broadened my knowledge and experience. I know that my society conditioned me to shudder at the very idea of eating worms; and I know that worms can be prepared in healthy and appetizing ways, are easy to farm, and are a delicacy in some cultures. But I lack experience. Some day I may visit a distant land and enjoy a delicious *ver de terre* (earthworm) meat loaf. With an openness to new experiences, I could change my irrational desire not to eat worms.

My anti-worm desire is trivial. But it isn't trivial when people are conditioned to hate people of another group. The fact that socially taught desires can be rationally criticized is important.

These definitions of *rational ethical belief* mirror those given for *rational desire*:

BS   Your *ethical belief* is *rational* (in *how* you believe it) =df
     With respect to your belief, you satisfy to a high degree the
     conditions needed for practical rationality.

BO   Your *ethical belief* that-A-ought-to-be-done-in-situation-S is
     rational (the content of the belief, abstracting from how you
     hold it) =df If you satisfied the conditions needed for practi-
     cal rationality as far as possible, you'd believe that A ought
     to be done in situation S.

BS (the *subjective* sense) has to do with flaws (like inconsistency and ignorance) in *how* you hold your ethical belief. BO (the *objective* sense) is about the *content* of the belief – whether you'd believe this content if you were as rational as possible.[1] If you act against your conscience, then your ethical belief is irrational in *how* you hold it; but it might be rational in its *content*.

These define, not "true" or "acceptable," but "rational." Some-one might satisfy the conditions of practical rationality to a high degree and still have moral beliefs that are incorrect or that we don't want to accept. This wouldn't disprove the definitions.

7.2 Rationality by Recursion

Here's a rough summary of our rationality conditions:

Be consistent in your beliefs and in coordinating ends and means.
Keep your ethical beliefs in harmony with how you live. Make
similar evaluations about similar cases. Treat others only in ways
that you're willing to be treated. Be informed on the facts – and
represent these facts vividly in your imagination. Feel free to
develop your ideas, have a broad experience of life, and have
feelings of concern for yourself and for others.

---

[1] As before, "in situation S" in BO is important. Without it, "I ought to be more rational" would be irrational, since I wouldn't hold it if I were as rational as possi-ble. But I'd then hold that *in the present situation* (where I'm only partly rational) I ought to be more rational.

Most of these aren't very controversial (although their precise statement might be). If you drew up your own rationality conditions, you'd probably include a few things that I didn't think of, and you'd likely arrange and word things differently. But I'd be surprised if we disagreed about the main points.

Why should we follow this list and not some other one? How can we *justify* a set of rationality conditions for ethical beliefs?

To find additional conditions that we overlooked, we'd first try to satisfy the current ones reasonably well (which includes finding out what other people think); then we'd ask what further things we'd want people to do when they form their ethical beliefs. This is a good way to generate *additional* conditions; but it's also a good way to generate our *current* conditions. Suppose that we have a preliminary partial set S_1 of conditions for rational ethical beliefs. We ask, "Insofar as we tried to satisfy set S_1, what additions and refinements would we want to make, to reflect how we want people to form their ethical beliefs?" We'd make the changes and produce an improved set S_2 of conditions. We'd repeat the process with set S_2, and so on, until we couldn't come up with further changes:

$$S_1 \rightarrow S_2 \rightarrow ... \rightarrow S_n$$

The last set S_n would be our best current view of the conditions for ethical rationality. So we'd generate the rationality conditions by repeatedly applying S_1 and its successors. Over time, our rationality ideal would be progressively refined and developed; a partial wisdom would evolve into an ever fuller wisdom.[1]

Rationality conditions are prima-facie *ought* judgments (though I phrase them loosely as imperatives). They say: "When you deliberate on how to act, you ought (ideally) other-things-being-equal to do such and such." At any given stage i, the conditions in S_i give us our best current view of how to reach *ought* judgments. Now further rationality conditions are themselves *ought* judgments. So at any given stage i, the conditions in S_i give us our best current view of how to reach further rationality conditions.

---

[1] It would be rash to think that our present account of moral rationality is the last word on the subject and that future reflection won't bring refinements and clarifications. Ideal observer theories that try to give a complete specification of "ideal observer" ignore the fact that an ideal observer who satisfied *our* criteria could probably produce *better* criteria.

I suggest that we start with "Be consistent and informed" as S_1 (where consistency is understood in terms of the theorems of formal ethics) – and add an explicit growth clause G:

S_1 When you deliberate on how to act, you ought (ideally) other-things-being-equal to be *consistent* and *informed*.

G   Insofar as you satisfy the current conditions fairly well, feel free to refine and add to them, to accord with how you want people (ideally) to deliberate – and then repeat this process.[1]

If we don't put "Be informed" into S_1, it will get into S_2. Since we demand that others try to be informed when they deliberate about how to act toward us, we will, if consistent, demand this of ourselves too – and hold that people *ought* to be so informed. Further stages would develop toward a set of conditions something like those we gave in the previous section.

Various starting points will likely produce much the same ending point. I suggest that we start with "Be consistent and informed." We might instead start with our current views on how people ought to deliberate. Some might want to start with "Promote self-interest" (viewing this as the basic rationality requirement); we provided for this in previous chapters when we showed how to defend our formal consistency principles from self-interest. Any starting points that can justify our formal principles will tend to converge a few steps down the road. While most conditions aren't very controversial, there may be disputes about details.

Since our rationality conditions are *ought* judgments, their status is a metaethical issue. Are they objective irreducible truths about how we ought to do our ethical thinking? Are they demands of society, of ideal observers, or of God? Are they prescriptions or expressions of emotion, instead of truths? People will disagree on the *status* of the rationality conditions; but they may still largely agree on their *content*. Indeed, I think that the most plausible content is much the same regardless of our metaethical views.

---

[1] These work like the recursive definitions of logic and mathematics. You can define "natural number" by two clauses: (a) 0 is a natural number, and (b) if n is a natural number then so is n+1. Similarly, you can (roughly) generate the conditions of practical rationality by: (a) "Be consistent" and "Be informed" are conditions of practical rationality, and (b) if you fairly well satisfy the conditions of practical rationality generated so far and you want to add more conditions, then these further ones are also conditions of practical rationality. The parallel is rough because later stages also can *qualify* earlier conditions; they could, for example, refine our "Be informed" requirement or qualification QF that's an implicit part of "Be consistent" (see Section 2.3).

7.3 Racism and Rationality

Applying our view of moral rationality to racism will show concretely how the view works. As before, I'll imagine that we're arguing with Ima Racist (see Sections 2.2 and 4.2 Q9), who defends extreme racist policies like Southern slavery or segregation, South African apartheid, or Nazism. I'll give two strategies.

If Ima gives an argument, we can use this attack-principle strategy (which stresses logicality and conscientiousness):

(1) Formulate an argument that expresses Ima's reasoning. The premises must be clearly stated, and the conclusion must clearly follow from the premises.

(2) If needed, criticize the factual premises.

(3) Test Ima's consistency by applying his ethical principle to actual or hypothetical cases – especially those involving his own race.

If Ima changes his argument, then go back to step 1 and work on the new argument. If he keeps his argument obscure, point this out and show how his argument is implausible if expressed clearly.

Step 1 is to formulate a clear argument. Suppose that Ima says, "We ought to treat blacks poorly – because they're inferior." We shouldn't let him get away with being so vague. What does he mean by *inferior*? Is it a matter of IQ, education, wealth, physical strength, or some combination of these? Unless we know what he means, we won't understand his principle. Let's suppose that Ima by *inferior* means *of low IQ* (less than 80). Since he's claiming that *all* blacks ought to be treated poorly, he has to hold that *all* blacks have an IQ of less than 80. Then his argument goes:

Ima Racist's argument:
All blacks have an IQ of less than 80.
All who have an IQ of less than 80 ought to be treated poorly.
∴ All blacks ought to be treated poorly.

Here the premises are fairly clear[1] and the conclusion follows using a recognized system of logic.

---

[1] I'm ignoring the problem of how to define the oppressed group. What makes a person "black" or "Jewish"? One might be *black* by skin color, racial features, culture, or descent. One might be *Jewish* by religion, racial features, culture, or descent. These elements can exist in various combinations, degrees, and mixtures.

Racist policies generally require giving precise boundaries to something by nature vague. The Nazis in 1935, for example, resorted to arbitrary stipulations for deciding in borderline cases who goes to the concentration camp (see Haas 1988: 62–5 and 133–5). Traditional American racism arbitrarily stipulated that *any* black

Step 2 is to criticize the factual premises, if needed. Here the factual premise is clearly false and easy to criticize empirically. Ima can't get around this by changing what he means by *inferior*. No plausible meaning will separate the races cleanly, so that all blacks will be on one side and all whites on the other.

Step 3 tests Ima's consistency. By logicality, Ima has to believe that all *whites* who have an IQ of less than 80 ought to be treated poorly (as he treats blacks). By conscientiousness, he has to *want* these whites to be treated poorly. As a racist who favors whites, he won't accept these. And so he'll be inconsistent.[1]

We might also appeal to hypothetical cases where some whites (such as his daughter) have an IQ of less than 80. (This works regardless of whether any whites in fact have this IQ.) Ima has to believe that his daughter ought to be treated poorly if she had this IQ. And he has to *desire* that his daughter be treated poorly in this case. Again, I don't expect Ima to be consistent.[2]

Ima might try another principle – for example:

AV *Everyone* in a race ought to be treated poorly if the *average* genetic IQ of that race is lower than that of some other race.

While AV involves questionable factual premises,[3] it's clearer to challenge Ima's consistency. Have him imagine a case where he and his family are geniuses, even though some other race has a higher average IQ than his. Ought he and his family (all geniuses)

---

ancestor makes you *black* – even if you are white according to your culture and physical features (see Zack 1993, who herself had ancestors of three different races); this would make Ima's first premise mean "All who have at least one black ancestor (no matter how far back) have an IQ of less than 80."

[1] If he says these whites ought to be treated poorly (as blacks are treated), then he's given up racism in favor of elitism. Here I'm only concerned with racism.

[2] These challenges about hypothetical cases assume that Ima takes his principle to give the *reason* why these people ought to be treated poorly, and thus to support counterfactuals. If his principle doesn't do this, we can push him for the more basic principle behind it that does. Concerning counterfactuals, see Sections 3.8 (response to #17) and 5.4 (Q11).

[3] It's unwise to spend much time debating about the *average* genetic IQ of various races. First, there are problems about the value and cultural neutrality of the IQ test. Second, it's difficult to separate genetic from environmental factors; an oppressed group can be *expected* to perform less well, simply because they're oppressed (see Silberman 1964). Third, the moral relevance of average IQ is unclear. Suppose that we prove that one group has a lower *average* genetic IQ; why should we conclude that *all* members of the group ought to be treated poorly – even those with a high IQ? To link a claim about *average* IQ to a policy of discrimination against *all* members of the group requires a premise like AV – a premise that's seldom mentioned and hard to hold consistently.

then to be treated poorly? I don't expect Ima to be consistent. Or have him imagine that blondes are proved to have a lower average genetic IQ.[1] Ought *all* blondes then to be treated poorly – even those who have a high IQ? Does he desire that if his daughter were a blond genius then she be treated poorly – just because blondes in general have a lower genetic IQ?

Or Ima might appeal to this principle:

> BW All blacks ought to be treated poorly – just because they have black skin. And all whites ought to be treated well – just because they have white skin.

But Section 4.2 Q9 showed that BW has bizarre implications that Ima wouldn't accept. Or Ima might appeal to race as the relevant factor (instead of skin color):

> NC All of the Negro race ought to be treated poorly – just because they're Negroes. And all of the Caucasian race ought to be treated well – just because they're Caucasians.

He then has to desire that he and his family would be treated poorly if they were Negro. Ask Ima to repeat these words slowly – and see if he can mean them (see Q11 of Section 5.4): "I really desire that if I were Negro then I'd be treated poorly." Ima is unlikely to have such desires; so I don't expect him to be consistent.[2]

Few people support principles like BW and NC; they sound too racist even for a racist. Most would use some variation on the "inferior" argument. We ought to treat people of another group poorly because they're less intelligent (or perhaps less moral). But these arguments, once we spell them out clearly, have premises that the racist won't consistently accept.

The weakness in our attack-principle strategy is that it only attacks specific arguments. Ima could respond:

> I don't know how to defend my racist policies. But so what? Can you liberals defend your views any better? You suggest liberal theories, and others demolish them. But you don't give up your liberal views. So why should I give up my racist views just because I don't yet have a coherent theory to defend them?

---

[1] Blondes are often alleged (foolishly) to be of less than average intelligence. Witness all the jokes about "dumb blondes." Why then are people of black skin discriminated against, but not people of blond hair?

[2] However, Ima might dislike Negroes so much that he *does* desire that he and his family be treated poorly if they were Negroes (or if they were found out to have Negro ancestry). We'll deal with such desires later.

Ima exaggerates, but he has a point. It isn't enough to attack arguments supporting racism. We must also attack racist actions and judgments directly. That's what the GR strategy does.

Our GR strategy has four steps:

(1) Get Ima to understand the facts. Be sure to have him understand the situation of the other person – including how the other person is affected by the action.

(2) Get Ima to imagine himself, vividly and accurately, in the place of the other person on the receiving end of the action.

(3) If needed, try to make Ima's desires (about how he be treated in the other person's place) as rational as possible.

(4) If Ima acts in a given way toward another, and yet doesn't consent to himself being treated that way in such circumstances, then he's inconsistent and violating the golden rule.

We shouldn't appeal to the golden rule (step 4) too quickly. GR depends on understanding, imagination, and desires – which may be flawed. After dealing with these other factors, we can apply GR more rationally and effectively.

Step 1 is to get Ima to understand the facts. This involves knowing circumstances, alternatives, consequences on people, pros and cons. When Kennedy applied GR to racism (see Section 5.1), he first tried to get whites to understand what segregation was doing to black people. Blacks were treated as second class citizens because of skin color; they couldn't vote, go to the best public schools, eat at most public restaurants, or sit in the front of the bus. These facts brought further poverty, frustration, and a decreased sense of self-worth. We learn about the situation of others mainly by observation, personal experience, and testimony. So we might have Ima *observe* blacks – how they live and how segregation affects them. We might have him reflect on any *personal experience* where he was treated as a second class citizen – and how this affected him. And we might have him listen to the *testimony* of blacks on how they are treated.

Step 2 tries to get Ima to realize the *human significance* of the facts. He needs a vivid and accurate awareness of the situation of blacks, and what it's like to be in that situation. Accordingly, he might read a novel or watch a movie that portrays their lives. Or he might listen to blacks who vividly describe their experiences, or might, in a role-playing exercise, play a black person who is discriminated against. Or he might recall cases in his own life where he was treated poorly because of his race or ethnic background or religion.[1] Or he might just reflect quietly on what it would be like to be in their shoes.

Step 4 involves applying the golden rule. If we sense that steps 1 and 2 have prepared Ima sufficiently, we might ask him:

> Now you better understand the situation of blacks and can vividly imagine what it would be like to be treated as a second class citizen in their place. Do you consent to the idea of yourself and your family being treated this way in their place?

Ima likely won't consent to this; so he'll likely be inconsistent and violate GR. However, let's suppose that he does satisfy GR and does consent to the idea of himself being treated as a second class citizen in their place. This could only happen if he has a disinterested hatred for blacks and thus desires that all blacks suffer – including himself and his family if they were black (or found to have black ancestry).[2]

Step 3 is needed if GR is blocked by Ima's intense hatred of blacks. Then we have to criticize his desires by appealing to consistency, factual data, imagination, and personal qualities. Ima's hateful desires might be:

- based on *current* false beliefs. He might think that Aryans are superior and racially pure. We can criticize this on factual grounds.

- due to *previous* false beliefs. He might hate blacks because of previous false beliefs (about blacks or about race). He's given up the false beliefs; his hatred of blacks, however, remains.

- based on social conditioning. Ima may hate blacks because he was taught this as a child. Perhaps the people he respected hated blacks and called them names, he was given anti-black propaganda (distortions and biased selections of facts), and he encountered only a few atypically nasty blacks. Presumably if Ima understood how his hatred originated in his past history and he broadened his experience and knowledge of blacks in an open way, his hateful desires would diminish.

Ima's desires against blacks reminds me of my irrational desire not to eat worms (even when prepared in healthy and appetizing

---

[1] Exodus 23:9 suggests this approach: "You shall not oppress an alien; you well know how it feels to be an alien, since you were once aliens yourselves in the land of Egypt." (See also Leviticus 19:34.)

[2] There's a story about a Nazi who hated Jews and put them in concentration camps. One day he discovered that he had Jewish ancestry. Since he hated Jews in a disinterested way, he came to hate himself and his family. So he had himself and his family put into concentration camps and killed. This Nazi was consistent.

ways). Both desires came from false beliefs or social conditioning. Both would diminish with greater knowledge (including about how the desire originated) and a wider experience (if we're open to this). Both are hard to change. Both are irrational.

We also might have Ima consider other socially taught prejudices.[1] All over the world, people in one group are taught to dislike people in another group. We teach young children:

> Be suspicious of *those other people*. They're of a different race (or religion, or ethnic background, or sexual preference, or caste). They aren't our kind. They have strange customs, and do strange things. They're evil and inferior.

When we broaden our knowledge and experience, we conclude, "They're people too, in many ways like us, with many of the same virtues and vices."

The hatreds that are programmed into us from our youth might never disappear; but a wider knowledge and experience will reduce them. This is all that GR needs. Only a very strong hatred of blacks can make Ima desire to be treated as a second class citizen if he were black. Only with such a hatred can Ima repeat these words and mean them: "I really desire that if I were black then I'd be treated as a second class citizen." And we can criticize such desires on rational grounds.

So I conclude that Ima won't be a consistent racist if he understands the situation of blacks, vividly and accurately imagines what it would be like to be treated as a second class citizen in their place, and has his desires rationalized by a wider knowledge and experience. In short: racism is irrational.

This leads to a further question: Why would otherwise normal and rational people commit atrocious acts against other races? Haas 1988 has a complicated historical explanation of how ordinary people were led to embrace Nazi racial policies. It talks about the gradual escalation of ancient racial animosities – about nationalism, charismatic leaders, powerful organizations, social pressures – about fear, greed, hatred, blind obedience – about lies,

---

[1] I have a friend in India (a fellow Jesuit named Tony Raj) who did a doctorate in the United States. In India, he's regarded as an outcast – an untouchable – the lowest of the low. I have a hard time understanding this. He's of the same race, color, language, and so forth as those of higher castes, and he's intelligent and educated; yet he's treated as dirt. The prejudices of another culture often don't make sense to us. As we grow in our understanding and experience, the prejudices of our own society make less and less sense to us too.

stereotypes, ignorance, and uncriticalness – and about how you get used to killing when the people around you find it acceptable. In addition, the Nazis compartmentalized their thinking. They were highly "rational" in a narrow sense (involving the choice of means to ends), but not in a wider sense that involved the rational appraisal of ends. They applied empathy and the golden rule to their own families, but not to Jews; to apply them to Jews would show a despicable weakness. This combination of forces was powerful and overcame the weak voice of reason.

The scientist Charles Darwin was surprised at how ordinary people can be blinded to the inhumanity of their actions:

> While staying at this estate, I was very nearly ... an eye-witness to one of those atrocious acts which can only take place in a slave country. Owing to a quarrel and a lawsuit, the owner was on the point of taking all the women and children from the male slaves, and selling them separately at the public auction at Rio.... I do not believe the inhumanity of separating thirty families, who had lived together for many years, even occurred to the owner. Yet I will pledge myself, that in humanity and good feeling he was superior to the common run of men. It may be said there exists no limit to the blindness of interest and selfish habit.

> (Darwin 1839: 35)

He traces much of this blindness, in people who professed to love their neighbor as themselves and to try to do God's will, to a lack of empathetic imagination:

> Those who look tenderly at the slave owner, and with a cold heart at the slave, never seem to put themselves into the position of the latter; ... picture to yourself the chance, ever hanging over you, of your wife and your little children ... being torn from you and sold like beasts to the first bidder!

> (Darwin 1839: 526–7)

As the scientist Darwin stresses empathetic imagination, so this dialogue from *Uncle Tom's Cabin* stresses factual accuracy:

A: "The most dreadful part of slavery, to my mind, is its outrages on the feelings and affections – the separating of families, for example."

B: "That is a bad thing, certainly," said the other lady...; "but then, I fancy, it don't occur often."

A: "O, it does," said the first lady, eagerly; "I've lived many years in Kentucky and Virginia both, and I've seen enough to make any one's heart sick. Suppose, ma'am, your two children, there, should be taken from you, and sold?"

B: "We can't reason from our feelings to those of this class of
      persons," said the other lady.

(Stowe 1852: 125)

So black slaves don't feel the pain that whites would feel? To
rebut this idea, the novel later describes how a young slave
woman, whose young son was taken from her and sold, was heart-
broken and drowned herself.

To guard against racist atrocities, we need knowledge (instead
of ignorance and lies), empathetic imagination (instead of insensitivity), and the golden rule (instead of treating others simply as a
means to our own ends).

7.4 Teaching Moral Rationality

We understand views of moral rationality better when we see how
they apply to practical problems like racism and moral education.
Accordingly, I'll now apply my view to moral education. I won't
talk about how to teach specific moral rules, although this is
important; rather, I'll focus on moral rationality. I'll imagine that
we're trying to teach a child, call her *Ima Daughter*, to be more
rational in her choices and ethical beliefs.

My view sees moral rationality as involving many different
elements (like logicality, ends–means consistency, conscientiousness, impartiality, the golden rule, factual data, imagination, and
personal qualities). Adults can teach these elements both by
example and by promoting the corresponding skills and attitudes.

Logicality requires that we be consistent in our beliefs. Accordingly, adults should be consistent in dealing with children and
should exemplify logical thinking. Ima should be given clear,
stable rules that are well thought out and don't have absurd implications. And she should be encouraged to develop her logical
skills – to reason things out for herself, to raise objections to
proposed rules, and to be consistent in her beliefs.

Ends–means consistency requires that we coordinate our ends
and means, and that we keep to possible ends. Adults should
exemplify such rationality. A father gives a poor example if he has
a goal (for example, to control his drinking) but doesn't carry out
the means. Adults should bring children into family plans about
ends and means. And children should be encouraged to be clear on

their goals, to pick realistic and compatible goals, to decide on proper means, and to carry out the means.

Conscientiousness requires that we keep our ethical beliefs in harmony with how we live. Accordingly, adults should take moral judgments seriously and put them into practice in their lives – lest Ima be taught by example to say, "Yes, it's wrong, but I don't care." Similarly, Ima should be encouraged to take moral beliefs seriously and to follow them conscientiously.

Impartiality requires that we make similar evaluations about similar cases. Adults should stress that the same standards apply to everyone and give reasons for differences in treatment. When Ima (appealing to universalizability) asks "Mom, why can Jimmy do this but not me?" she deserves a better answer than "Just shut up and do what Mom says!" Similarly, Ima should be encouraged to think through moral issues and to propose principles or reasons (applicable to everyone alike) why actions are right or wrong. Ima will be stunted in her moral growth if she's always just told what she ought to do and is never encouraged to think things out for herself and to search for principles or reasons.

The golden rule requires that we treat others only in ways that we're willing to be treated. Adults should be models of GR thinking, especially in dealing with children. So Ima's parents should find out how their actions affect their daughter, imagine themselves in her place, and treat her only as they're willing to be treated in such circumstances. Similarly, Ima should be encouraged to live in accord with the golden rule. When she does something rude or vicious, she should be challenged, "Ima, how would you like it if someone did that to you?"[1]

The factual data condition tells us to be informed on the facts. Adults should try to get the information they need for making decisions. So Ima's parents must get to know their daughter (and how things affect her) when making decisions that concern her. Similarly, Ima should be encouraged to gain the information needed to make her own decisions. As she deliberates about what to do, her parents should encourage her to ask questions like: "What are my alternatives?" – "What effect would this have on myself and on others?" – "What are the pros and cons here?"

---

[1] Schulman and Mekler 1994 have useful suggestions for teaching the golden rule (90–117) and empathetic imagination (52–89) to children. Their approach to moral education is very much in harmony with my approach.

The imagination condition has us represent the facts vividly in our imagination – and picture ourselves in the place of another person (or in our own future situation). Accordingly, Ima's parents should listen sympathetically to their daughter's views and problems, and try to imagine what her life is like; this will teach by example how important it is to understand the perspective of another person. And Ima can be encouraged to listen sympathetically to others, to read novels or watch movies that portray the lives and struggles of people in a realistic way, and to experience different kinds of people. She can be encouraged to share her reactions with others and to understand their reactions and points of view ("How would Jimmy feel if such and such happened?"). She also can be encouraged to imagine the future consequences of her actions.

The personal qualities condition requires various things – for example, that we seek to find out how we ought to live, feel free to develop our own ideas (and not think that we have to follow the crowd), and respect the views of those who are wiser than we are. It's particularly important to have genuine feelings of concern for ourselves and for others. Again, adults would try to follow these in their own lives and encourage them in children.

When Ima grows up and reaches sufficient intellectual maturity, she should be encouraged to carry her moral education further by seeking the rational foundations of morality – in the discipline known as "philosophy."

In these ways and others that I haven't mentioned, children can be taught to make choices and moral judgments more rationally. This teaching is difficult – but there are many concrete ways to do it. Judging from the low state of moral thinking in the world around us, it's a task of great importance.

7.5 Aiding Other Theories

I've sketched how my principles might be defended from various approaches to ethics. Now I'll go further and sketch how my principles can *help* these other approaches.

Most obviously, formal ethics can give useful tools for moral thinking. We elaborated a set of formal and semiformal rationality conditions. We can generate the set by applying these two principles (which use "consistent" in the wide sense of "satisfying the demands of formal ethics"):

S_1 When you deliberate on how to act, you ought (ideally) other-things-being-equal to be *consistent* and *informed*.

G   Insofar as you satisfy the current conditions fairly well, feel free to refine and add to them, to accord with how you want people (ideally) to deliberate – and then repeat this process.

Let's call the other conditions that we'd arrive at "derivative conditions" (keeping in mind that these can grow with further reflection). So S_1 and G require that in deliberating we be consistent, be informed, and satisfy derivative conditions.

Section 2.6 discussed various *ideal* theories. The ideal observer theory gives a definition of "ought":

"We ought to do A" means "A person who was ideally consistent, informed, impartial, etc. would desire that we do A."

Ideal nonnaturalism, emotivism, and prescriptivism give a similar definition of "reasonable ethical belief":

Your ethical beliefs are reasonable if and only if you're consistent, informed, impartial, etc. about them.

These views face two major questions:

(1)   What do these qualities mean? What does it mean, for example, to say that a person is "impartial" or "consistent"?

(2)   Why pick this list of ideal qualities and not another? What higher-order principle specifies how to fill out the "etc."?

Without answers to these questions, the *ideal* theories seem to give an arbitrary and incomplete list of vague qualities.

Formal ethics can help with both questions. (1) It gives formal principles that clarify notions like "impartial" and "consistent." (2) It gives defensible higher-order principles (S_1 and G) for picking the list of ideal qualities. Using the notion of "derivative conditions" explained above, we can reformulate the ideal observer theory this way:

"We ought to do A" means "A person who ideally satisfied the conditions of practical rationality (to be consistent and informed, plus derivative conditions) would desire that we do A."[1]

---

[1] How far should this view idealize the requirement to be informed? Do IOs (ideal observers) know *everything*? Then we humans couldn't be IOs and perhaps can't even ask what we'd believe if we were IOs. Or do IOs know all the *relevant* facts? There are technical problems about which facts are *relevant*. (See Brandt 1955; Carson 1984: 48–97, 175–9; Firth 1952, 1955; Harrison 1956.) I suggest that an IO must know enough to make a clear judgment on the case. More

And we can define "reasonable ethical belief" as follows:

> Your ethical belief is reasonable if and only if you highly satisfy the conditions needed for practical rationality (to be consistent and informed, plus derivative conditions) with respect to the belief.

So formal ethics can aid views that appeal to ideal moral thinking.

Formal ethics also can aid views that have meager accounts of moral rationality. Such views tend to evolve toward richer accounts of rationality; formal ethics can help this process along.

Consider nonnaturalism. Extreme forms say that we have a direct grasp of self-evident ethical truths. But this leads to an early stalemate on ethical issues; we can't argue with racists if they have basic moral intuitions that differ from ours. A more moderate view says that we can use one intuition to criticize another; we look for views that are maximally consistent with all our intuitions. This leads to a slightly later stalemate with a racist who has absorbed from his society a whole system of racist intuitions. One response is to say that the racist only has prejudices and not genuine intuitions. But how do we distinguish between the two? Formal ethics can help here, since it has powerful tools to criticize moral beliefs; these tools can help us to distinguish between genuine moral intuitions and mere prejudices (like those of the racist).

Consider emotivism. Extreme forms say that ethical feelings and beliefs aren't subject to rational criticism – so there's no way to rationally criticize those who were brought up to have racist feelings and no way to teach children to make reasonable moral judgments. A more sensible view says that ethical beliefs to be reasonable have to be consistent and informed. Formal ethics shows how to extend these two requirements into a powerful way of reasoning about ethics. Being consistent could include making similar evaluations about similar cases, and keeping our actions and desires in harmony with our moral beliefs. Being informed could include knowing the origin of our beliefs and feelings, and imagining the facts in a vivid and accurate way. And the way we hold our moral views (whether we're creative, or believe out of habit or social pressure) could influence the belief's reasonable-

---

precisely, if an IO is judging an act then there must be some conjunction of properties F such that (1) the IO knows that the act is F and (2) the IO would have the same reaction to every actual or hypothetical act that is F (demanding that it be done, or that it not be done, or being indifferent to it).

ness. Formal ethics can thus encourage emotivism to grow toward a richer view of moral rationality.

Cultural relativism doesn't seem to provide for much moral rationality. If society supports racism, then racism is right – even if society is inconsistent and ignorant. And teaching children to do what's right is teaching them to conform. Yet cultural relativism could embrace a rich view of moral rationality. We've shown how social conventions might justify our formal axioms; and many societies teach that people should try to change unreasonable norms. So an enlightened cultural relativism might criticize current social norms on the basis of rationality standards that it takes to be ultimately rooted in social conventions.

Formal ethics can serve supernaturalism by helping us to understand the golden rule (which most religions teach) and practical reason (whose ideals of perfect knowledge, consistency, empathy, and concern are perfectly realized only in God). The goal of trying to become more rational in our policies and ethical judgments ultimately coincides with the goal of trying to become more God-like in these policies and judgments.

Formal ethics can help utilitarianism by clarifying and systematizing socially useful ideas – like the golden rule and moral rationality. It can help Ross's theory by giving rational ways to reason about ethical beliefs when prima facie duties conflict, so we have more to appeal to than just bare intuition. It can help universal prescriptivism to become more internally consistent (see Section 6.5) and to further clarify some of its core ideas (like universalizability and rationality).

Formal ethics also can help the view that ethical terms are radically ambiguous. On this view, five people using "ought" might mean five different things by it (as reflected in five different metaethical theories). This ambiguity view raises two questions:

(1) How can we then agree or disagree (more than just verbally) on moral issues?

(2) How can we then reason with each other on moral issues?

The parties in an ethical discussion will normally be practically committed (for their own diverse reasons) to the axioms of formal ethics. This means that the parties try to

- keep their beliefs consistent,
- keep their means in harmony with their ends,

- keep their actions, resolutions, and desires in harmony with their ethical beliefs, and

- make similar evaluations about cases that are exactly or relevantly similar in their universal properties.

Then a verbal (dis)agreement between the parties will typically go with a (dis)agreement of will; this is more than just a verbal matter. And our formal and semiformal principles give ways to reason and argue on moral issues, ways that don't assume that the various parties mean the same thing by "ought." Our approaches to racism and to moral education (Sections 7.3 and 7.4) work just as well if "ought" has no widely-shared common meaning.

7.6 Concluding Questions

(Q1) So do you really think that you've eliminated all the nonrational aspects of our ethical thinking?

No, that wasn't my intention. It's obvious that there are many cultural and emotional influences on our ethical thinking. It isn't quite so obvious how we can reason and argue on moral issues. I'm content to clarify some ways that we can do this – but without denying the cultural and emotional influences.

When people ask how "reason" fits into ethics, they're often asking how thinking (as opposed to feeling and desiring) can contribute. This isn't my question. Instead, I'm asking how we *ought* to make ethical judgments. I'm convinced that we need to integrate various elements – including logical and quasi-logical principles, empirical knowledge, imagination, desires, and feelings. So my moral rationality conditions include all these things.

Reason and morality are often weak forces in us; they need powerful allies like habits, feelings, and social approval. We'll have a difficult time following the golden rule, for example, unless we develop strong habits and feelings about fairness and concern for others, and have these reinforced by the society around us.

(Q2) If we completely satisfied all the conditions of practical rationality, would we then agree on all our ethical judgments?

If we idealize these conditions (requiring perfect knowledge and imagination), then it's causally impossible for us to satisfy the conditions completely. Then the question, as a causal counterfactual, would have no answer.[1]

Would we all agree if we satisfied the conditions as well as we could? The answer seems to be no. Humans trying to be as rational as possible often disagree on the facts or weigh factors differently, and thus disagree ethically. Scientists and mathematicians who try to be as rational as possible also disagree. We humans are limited in how rational we can be; and many issues, moral or otherwise, are complex and difficult to resolve. It can be good that we disagree on such issues, since this can lead to fruitful discussions and to combining complementary insights. Should we hope for eventual rational agreement on ethics? Or should we not care about agreement, but just try to live consistently with our own beliefs? Formal ethics is compatible with either attitude.

We could take the question theologically. Would quasi-human deities who satisfied the conditions of practical rationality completely agree on all their ethical judgments? I suspect that they might weigh factors differently. But I'm not sure; polytheistic psychology isn't a highly developed science.

As we speculate on the ideal limits of rationality in ethics, we should recall that our concept of moral rationality is still growing. The last few years have seen major advances, due to thinkers like Brandt, Hare, and Rawls. The future may bring further advances.

(Q3) Hare 1981 claims that rational universal prescribers must be utilitarians. Do you agree?

No. Let me roughly sketch Hare's argument. Suppose that I'm a rational universal prescriber deliberating about my duty. When I put myself in the place of the parties affected by the act, (1) I take on their desires about the act. Then (2) my total desire about the act is positive or negative, depending on whether the total of these desires is positive or negative. Thus I desire to do what maximizes the total desire-satisfaction of the parties involved. While a full treatment of Hare's argument would take many pages, let me just say that I have doubts about (1) and (2).

Suppose that act A maximizes the total desire-satisfaction but badly harms one person. When I put myself in the place of the

---

[1] Just as a self-contradiction P logically implies any statement Q (since "~◇P" entails "□(P ⊃ Q)"), so too a causally impossible statement P causally implies any statement Q (since "~◈P" entails "⊡(P ⊃ Q)").

parties, I may be more impressed by the great harm to the one than the slight benefits to the many. Thus I may universally prescribe the nonutilitarian belief that I *ought not* to do A. I can't see why consistency forces the utilitarian belief that I *ought* to do A.[1]

(Q4) What about Hare's fanaticism problem? Does this affect your theory too?

Hare's fanaticism problem is that GR can hit a snag when used against one who holds obnoxious views – if the person is content to be treated in an obnoxious way.[2] The classic example is a racist who desires that he be treated poorly if he were in the place of the blacks. Why would a racist desire this?

> His grounds are ... simply a horror of the very idea of a black man mating with a white woman. This cannot be touched by any scientific or factual argument of the sort described. And it may well be true that, if miscegenation is to be prevented, it is necessary to have a rigid colour bar; and that if this is enforced ... we shall have the whole apparatus of racial repression. If this is true, then it will be hard for us to argue with this man. He detests miscegenation so much that he is prepared to live in a police state in order to avoid it.
>
> (Hare 1963: 220)

Hare thought that, while GR usually works against racism, it won't work against fanatics who don't care if they or others are badly harmed in the pursuit of racist goals.

In accord with our custom, let's call the man *Ima Racist*. Ima is supposed to have a horror of the idea of a black man mating with a white woman. So he strongly desires that this never happen. But this desire could be criticized as irrational, in ways that we previously discussed (Sections 7.1 and 7.3).[3]

I'd be surprised if Ima really desired this. White slaveowners often mated with black slave women. Presumably, white women sometimes mated with black slave men. Slaves were seen as possessions to be used for your own purposes. I don't see how Ima

---

[1] Seanor and Fotion 1988 has valuable discussions on Hare's argument (which is more subtle than my rough sketch brings out).

[2] Hare 1981 (171–3) claims to have solved the problem: rational moral thinking leads to utilitarianism (Q3), which conquers the fanatic and leads to complete agreement among ideal observers (Q2).

[3] This involves Brandt's method of criticizing desires using facts and logic. Hare supports this method (see 1981: 101 and Seanor and Fotion 1988: 217–18); but the method came out somewhat after Hare 1963.

could have a horror about interracial mating, since it was an accepted part of the slaveowner mentality.

I suspect that Ima is horrified rather at the idea of love and marriage between whites and blacks. He strongly desires that this *not* happen. But this desire comes from social conditioning. We'd attack it, as before, by having Ima understand why he has this desire and broaden his experience and knowledge.

I'm reminded of a story from my father. In 1940, he announced to his German-Irish family his intention to marry my mother. His family opposed the idea because my mother was of Polish background. Such a woman was obviously *not good enough* for my father! His family had been taught when they were young:

> Be suspicious of *those other people*. They're of a different ethnic background. They're not our kind. They have strange customs, and do strange things. They're not as good as us.

My father likes to repeat this story because it seems so incredible now. Once the two sides of the family got to know each other, the barriers fell. The divisions came from ignorance.

So I think that the GR argument is decisive against at least the grosser forms of racism – if we include methods to criticize irrational desires. However, GR might run into snags on other topics (including subtle forms of racism), and not do as much as we want. But I'm not worried about this.

The golden rule is a tool of argumentation. If it's useful much of the time, that's fine. If it sometimes doesn't help, that's all right. Maybe we need another tool – or maybe no tool will do the job that we want. As long as GR is useful much of the time, that's enough to justify keeping it in our ethical toolbox.

(Q5) Besides Hare and Kant, have others emphasized formal considerations in ethics?

Yes. Others with a formal stress include Bond 1968; Broad 1950; Edgley 1969; Gewirth 1978b; Habermas 1990; O.A. Johnson 1969; Kohlberg 1973, 1979, 1986; Kohlberg *et al.* 1983, 1990; Lewis 1955, 1957, 1969; G. Mead 1934 (379–89); Nagel 1970; Nelson 1956; Piaget 1948; Pollock 1973, 1976; Sartre 1957; and M. Singer 1955, 1971. I've learned a lot from these thinkers. Of these, Broad and Lewis are the closest to my orientation.

(Q6) You give the same rationality conditions for deciding *what to do* and deciding *what we ought to do*. Are these the same?

They are closely related. I can't rationally decide that I *ought* to do something (in the strong all-things-considered evaluative sense) and yet not decide to do it. On the other hand, I might conclude that there's no *ought* in a given situation – that doing A and not doing A are both permissible. Then I might rationally decide to do A without accepting any *ought* judgment about A.

(Q7) Gauthier distinguishes between two conceptions of practical reason: the maximizing and the universalistic. Which do you accept?

Gauthier 1986 (6–7) explains his distinction this way:

- Maximizing conception: Rational persons always seek the greatest satisfaction of their own preferences.
- Universalistic conception: When the interests of others aren't affected, rational persons always seek the greatest satisfaction of their own preferences. When the interests of others are affected, rational persons always seek to satisfy all preferences.

Each is a family of approaches; for "preferences" we can substitute terms like *interests*, *advantages*, *benefits*, or *satisfactions*. These needn't be taken in a self-interested way; "my advantage" covers the good of my children if I have concern for them.

Gauthier favors the maximizing conception, which he sees as more widely accepted in economics and other social sciences (except presumably among psychologists like Erikson, Kohlberg, and Piaget). He associates the universalistic conception with Kantian views (including Hare). Gauthier argues that the maximizing conception will justify moral impartiality (which the universalistic conception takes for granted).

Formal ethics is compatible with taking either of these as the basic conception of rationality, so long as its principles can be at least a derived conception. Gauthier gives valuable ideas that can be used to justify formal ethics from a maximizing approach. My own view (which I haven't incorporated into formal ethics as such) is that the most basic conception of rationality is *consistency*; our first duty as rational beings is to be consistent in thought and action.

I find both of Gauthier's conceptions puzzling. Let's assume that act A doesn't involve the interests of others. Then both conceptions would agree to this:

> If you're rational about how you act, you'll seek the greatest satisfaction of your own preferences.

Suppose that there's no conflict of preferences. Then we can avoid the obscure notion of *greatest satisfaction*[1] and put the principle this way:

> If you're rational, then if you want to do E and believe that your doing M is causally necessary for you to do E, then you'll do M.

This can be interpreted two ways, depending on whether we take it as a *don't-combine* or as an *if–then*:

(a) It isn't rational to combine (1) wanting to do E, (2) believing that your doing M now is causally necessary for you to do E, and (3) not acting to do M.

(b) If you want to do E and believe that your doing M is causally necessary for you to do E, then it's rational for you to do M.

The *don't-combine* version (a) is true; it becomes theorem **Ed1** (the descriptive format of theorem **E1**) if we replace "rational" with "consistent." The *if–then* version (b) is false; your end and means might both be irrational (because inconsistent, impossible to realize, or based on ignorance – see the objections in Section 3.3 to **E1a**). But Gauthier later (21–6) makes clear that he's talking about *rational* (informed and coherent) preferences. This would lead us to rephrase (b) as follows:

(c) If you *rationally* want to do E and *rationally* believe that your doing M now is causally necessary for you to do E, then it's rational for you to do M.

This is a fine principle.

---

[1] I sometimes make decisions by reflecting on the various factors and then considering what I most desire. If this is what "maximizing" amounts to, then it makes sense. But I have problems if it assumes a numerical approach – which seems meaningful only in special circumstances (as in Las Vegas gambling). For most cases, it's difficult to see how we could assign meaningful numbers to degrees-of-desire and then pick the alternative with the highest number.

Could we assign numerical weights to desires by asking survey questions? You might give me a questionnaire asking millions of things like, "Which would you bet on, if you could pick between a 2/3 chance of getting vanilla ice cream (instead of nothing) and a 1/3 chance of getting rocky road ice cream (instead of nothing)?" But I couldn't answer most of these questions; even the one about ice cream baffles me. A.I. Goldman 1993 (349) mentions studies that seem to show that people don't have well-defined preference orderings. As Kant stressed (1785: 417–18), we have no determinate total concept of what we really want.

To be plausible, the maximizing view has to support (a) or (c). Both recognize the prior claims of consistency. This accords with my view that the most basic form of rationality is consistency.

Gauthier's universalistic conception says: "When the interests of others are affected, rational persons always seek to satisfy all preferences." "Satisfy all preferences" is a vague way to state various views (utilitarian, Kantian, Rawlsian, and so forth) that give weight to the interests or preferences of others. I'd support a clearer principle. Rationality requires that we not give a certain weight to the preferences of others without also consenting to others in similar cases giving this weight to *our* preferences. This follows from our theorems, which are about consistency.

The fact that we appeal to consistency in dealing with skeptics suggests that it's the most basic form of rationality. We ask whether skeptics live consistently with their theories; if they don't, then they're violating rationality. When all other forms of reason fail us, we appeal to consistency.

(Q8) How do you deal with someone who says "Yes, I'm inconsistent and irrational; but I don't care about consistency and rationality"?

It's likely that people who say this don't understand what they're saying (see Section 2.3) – or that they accept in their lives what they deny in their theories (see Section 2.7). I've heard people speak this way who are very consistent and reasonable people.

Some who say this may indeed not care about consistency and rationality. It's hard to imagine such people living a normal life. You can't *argue* with them (at least if they're consistent about their inconsistency principle) – since they reject reasoning and argument from the start. You may be able to deal with them in some other way, if you can figure out what's causing the problem.

(Q9) How could evolution have produced the kind of rational moral thinking that you describe?

Darwin 1871 (253–330) sketched how rational moral thinking could arise through evolutionary mechanisms. With social animals – like ants, bees, buffaloes, and humans – evolution encourages variations that benefit the group.[1] So humans have evolved built-in

---

[1] A fuller story would be more complicated and would answer questions like: "Wouldn't individual altruistic ants and humans be weeded out because of their

tendencies toward sympathy and concern for others. Over time, these basic instincts are channeled by socialization, deepened by religious feelings, and refined by intellectual powers (including observation, imagination, inductive reasoning, ends–means reasoning, and abstract thinking). While present in lower animals in a rudimentary way, these elements in humans lead to ever more sophisticated moral thinking; thus we move from a self-interested concern for fellow tribal members to a purer inherent concern for everyone. Darwin sums up his view as follows:

> The moral sense perhaps affords the best and highest distinction between man and the lower animals; but ... I have ... endeavoured to shew that the social instincts ... with the aid of active intellectual powers and the effects of habit, naturally lead to the golden rule, "As ye would that men should do to you, do ye to them likewise"; and this lies at the foundation of morality.
>
> (Darwin 1871: 317)

Darwin didn't support a dog-eat-dog "social Darwinism." Instead, he puts GR thinking at the heart of morality.

While I basically agree with Darwin's explanation, I'd like to strengthen our "intellectual powers" to include our formal and semiformal rationality elements. These elements are part of *objectification* – the process whereby we generate the concepts that we use to talk about the world. I'd explain the origin of morality in part by positing an evolving world where humans have:

- instinctive desires (for food and water, health and safety, love and companionship, knowledge and achievement, and so on), and
- an increasing capacity to construct allegedly objective concepts (like "red object" and "good action") from subjective experiences (like red images and desired objects) and to submit these concepts to the demands of an impartial, intersubjective reason.

Both elements (desires and objectification) have an evolutionary explanation.[1] A fuller account of morality's evolutionary origin

---

reduced tendency to survive and reproduce?," "What is the unit of evolutionary selection: the individual, the group, or the gene?," and "How do we explain the complex human mix of altruism and selfishness?" See Badcock 1986, Ridley and Dawkins 1981, and Trivers 1971 and 1981.

[1] What mechanisms bring about objectification? Has evolution hard-wired into us certain innate, *a priori*, universal structures about language, logic, and ethics (Stent 1976)? Or are formal logical and ethical norms neither innate nor taught – but rather rationally constructed in social contexts (Piaget 1948)? What role does cognitive dissonance play? Formal ethics is compatible with various explanations.

would bring in the other elements that Darwin mentions: socialization, religion, and benevolent instincts.

Our attraction to GR reflects its multifaceted origins. When I treat others as I don't want to be treated, I may sense that I violate consistency, internalized social norms, my relationship to a loving God, and deep sympathetic instincts. I've focused on consistency; but the other dimensions are also important.

(Q10) Could you say more about these "dimensions"?

Approaches that make morality depend on just one thing (such as feeling, thinking, empirical knowledge, or religion) oversimplify. Morality ideally involves various "parts" of the self working together; but it can function amazingly well even if a few parts are weak or missing. Let me propose a metaphor inspired by St Paul (see 1 Corinthians 12:12–13:13). Morality is ideally like a body (or a person) with many parts that work together:

heart	↔	desires (especially altruism)
eyes	↔	empirical knowledge
right brain	↔	imagination (especially empathy)
ears and mouth	↔	dialogue with others
soul	↔	religious motivation
hands and feet	↔	moral action
left brain	↔	consistency (especially GR)

You have desires (for food, rest, companionship, and so on) – and you have the desire to do good and not harm to others. You have a keen empirical knowledge of the world. You can vividly imagine yourself in the place of another. You dialogue with other people – and they challenge your ethical thinking. You sense the higher purpose of morality in religious or quasi-religious terms. You act morally. You process your thinking and willing for inconsistencies of various sorts – and especially for GR violations; formal ethics focuses on this appeal to consistency.

GR is especially important, because we tend to be self-centered. It has a criticizing function, telling us when our *action* (toward another) conflicts with our *desires* (about how we be treated). GR filters out inconsistencies. For the output of the filter to be of high value, the inputs (knowledge, imagination, desires) have to be of high value; otherwise, we have "junk in and junk out."

(Q11) How does your theory relate to Kant's?

Kant's ethical theory can be interpreted in various ways. I read Kant for inspiration, without concern for what historians of philosophy think that he actually meant. So I'd prefer not to make claims about what Kant meant.

However, formal ethics has many Kantian ideas: formal principles, consistency, *ought*-implies-*can*, hypothetical imperatives, the formula of universal law, rationality, and so forth. A Kantian interpretation of formal ethics might make these claims:

- Moral realism is true, in the sense that there are objective truths about how we *ought* to live that we can know and discover.

- True *ought* judgments (categorical imperatives) are truths that logically entail imperatives. Hence *ought* judgments have a rational authority. If you accept that you ought to do A now, then you'll act to do A – or else you're inconsistent.

- The basic axioms of ethics are formal *a priori* truths that are accessible to and bind any rational being (not just humans). The axioms include ends–means and prescriptivity (both analytic), plus universalizability and rationality (both synthetic).

- The formal part of ethics can be organized as a deductive system. The formula of universal law is an important theorem. Roughly the same idea can be expressed in the golden rule and in the rule about treating people as ends and not just means.

- Ethical rationality involves formal and semiformal conditions, with the latter ultimately depending on the former. We arrive at material ethical knowledge, not by following our moral intuitions, but rather by seeing what it is rational to will.

- The highest moral motivation is to do the right thing because it's rational and right and shows concern and respect for the inherent dignity of each person.

I think Kant would be happy with this view. I think it's the right view. Defending this Kantian moral realism is a future project – but a different project from what I'm doing here. The goal of this present book, rather, is to explain and defend some formal tools of moral reasoning (especially the golden rule) that can supplement and enhance virtually any approach to ethics.

Chapter 8

Symbolic Logic

Ethics raises difficult formal issues. If I've put some order and clarity into this area, much of the credit is due to the tools of symbolic logic. This chapter explains the main tools. The chapter is optional: you don't have to know about the tools that went into constructing the edifice. But you might want to know, and knowing may help you to understand the edifice better.

I'll presume some basic knowledge of logic. If you're puzzled about how I use imperative or deontic logic in earlier chapters, you might look at Sections 8.1 and 8.2 as you read these chapters. I'll take an intuitive approach here. Don't look for technical rules for well-formed formulas or proofs. A more casual tone fits this present book. I handled the technical details in my *Symbolic Logic* (Gensler 1990).[1]

8.1 Imperative Logic

I'll use these symbols in a standard way:

- Symbols for *not*, *and*, *or*, *if–then*, and *if-and-only-if*: ~, ·, ∨, ⊃, ≡
- Parenthesis for grouping: ( )
- Quantifiers for *all* and *some*: (x), (∃x)
- Modal operators for *necessary* and *possible*: □, ◇
- Letters for statements, predicates, and relations: A, B, C, …
- Letters for individual constants: a, b, c, …
- Letters for individual variables: x, y, z, …

Presume appropriate rules for well-formed formulas and proofs.

---

[1] Chapters 1–6 of *Symbolic Logic* cover propositional, quantificational, and modal logic. Chapter 7 deals with imperative and deontic logic. Chapter 8 is about belief logic as a system of consistency imperatives. Chapter 9 gives a formalized version of formal ethics – ending with a long formal proof of the golden rule.

I'll follow Castañeda's approach (1960a, 1960b, 1967, 1970) to imperative and deontic logic. This is the best approach to the subject and the only one adequate to the demands of formal ethics. It makes imperative logic simple and intuitive.

We'll form an imperative by underlining:

- S = "You're smiling" (indicative).
- $\underline{S}$ = "Smile" (imperative).

Here are some further examples:

- $\sim\underline{S}$ = Don't smile.
- $(\underline{S} \vee \underline{L})$ = Smile or laugh.
- $\sim(\underline{S} \vee \underline{L})$ = Don't either smile or laugh.
- $\sim(\underline{S} \cdot \underline{L})$ = Don't both smile and laugh = Don't combine smiling with laughing.

We'll underline imperative parts but not factual parts:

- $(S \cdot L)$ = You're smiling and laughing.
- $(S \cdot \underline{L})$ = You're smiling, but laugh.
- $(\underline{S} \cdot \underline{L})$ = Smile and laugh.
- $(S \supset L)$ = If you smile, then you laugh.
- $(S \supset \underline{L})$ = If you smile, then laugh.
- $(\underline{S} \supset L)$ = Smile, only if you laugh.

English doesn't permit an imperative after "if"; so we can't read "$(\underline{S} \supset L)$" as "If smile, then you laugh." But we can read it as the equivalent "Smile, only if you laugh." This means the same as "$(\sim L \supset \sim \underline{S})$" – "If you aren't laughing, then don't smile."[1]

Regarding which arguments are valid, imperatives work much like indicatives. We need no new inference rules. But we must treat "S" and "$\underline{S}$" as different wffs – as if the two were different letters. So "$(S \cdot \sim\underline{S})$" isn't a contradiction; it's consistent to say, "You're smiling, but don't smile."[2]

---

[1] Our system permits constructions that English doesn't – like "$(\underline{S} \supset \underline{L})$." English can't say "If smile, then laugh." But we can always find an equivalent formula that goes into English. Here the equivalent "$\sim(\underline{S} \cdot \sim\underline{L})$" translates as "Don't combine smiling with not laughing."

[2] "Don't smile" tells you not to smile in the immediate future. So my example means "You're smiling now, but don't smile in the immediate future" and shifts tense. But both of these are also consistent:

(1) You're smiling now, but would that you weren't smiling now.
(2) You'll smile in the immediate future, but would that you not smile in the immediate future.

Neither can tell someone to do something; but both can put into words a consistent combination of believing and willing (see Section 3.1).

Consider this valid imperative argument (see Section 3.2):

> If the cocoa is boiling, remove it from the heat.   (B ⊃ R̲)
> The cocoa is boiling.   B
> ∴ Remove it from the heat.   ∴ R̲

"Valid" here doesn't mean that it's impossible to have true premises and a false conclusion – for imperatives aren't true or false. We'll use a definition that avoids "true" and "false":

> A *valid* argument is one in which the conjunction of the premises with the contradictory of the conclusion is inconsistent.

So to say that our cocoa argument is "valid" means that this combination is inconsistent:

> If the cocoa is boiling, remove it from the heat. The cocoa is boiling. But don't remove it from the heat.

This is inconsistent. So our argument is *valid* in this new sense.

I call this invalid argument *the diet fallacy*:

> If you don't eat cake, give yourself a gold star.   (~E ⊃ G̲)
> Don't eat cake.   ~E̲
> ∴ Give yourself a gold star.   ∴ G̲

Imagine that your diet book tells you to follow both premises – and you immediately give yourself a gold star (thus following the conclusion). This is premature, since you might yield to your temptation to eat cake. It's consistent to conjoin the premises with the following (which denies the conclusion): "You're eating cake – don't give yourself a gold star." So the argument is invalid.

I call this invalid argument *the bicycle fallacy*:

> Don't combine accelerating and braking.   ~(A̲ · B̲)
> You're accelerating.   A
> ∴ Don't brake.   ∴ ~B̲[1]

The first premise is sensible; you waste energy and wear down your brakes if you accelerate and brake together. You may in fact

---

[1] If the schema "~(A̲ · B̲), A → ~B̲" were valid, we could prove "A ↔ A̲" (where the arrows represent entailment and mutual entailment). This would collapse the distinction between the indicative "You do A" and the imperative "Do A" – an absurd result. My proof goes as follows:

   ~(A̲ · B̲), A → ~B̲ {Proposed schema.}
∴ ~(A̲ · ~A̲), A → ~~A̲ {Instance of prior step, substituting "~A" for "B."}
∴ A → A̲ {Simplified form of prior step, eliminating the analytic premise "~(A̲ · ~A̲)" and the double negation.}
∴ ~A → ~A̲ {From the prior step (which would hold for every value of "A"), substituting "~A" for "A."}
∴ A ↔ A̲ {X is logically equivalent to Y if X entails Y and ~X entails ~Y.}

be accelerating (making the second premise true). But maybe you need to stop quickly – and thus to brake and stop accelerating. The argument is invalid, since it's consistent to conjoin the premises with the following (which denies the conclusion): "Brake and stop accelerating."[1] The argument would be valid if the first premise had the *if–then* form "(A ⊃ ~B̲)."

In formal ethics, the difference between the *if–then* and *don't-combine* forms is crucial; consistency principles require the latter. In symbols, the difference is this:

- (A ⊃ ~B̲) = If you're doing A, then don't do B.
- ~(A̲ · B̲) = Don't combine doing A with doing B.

Underlining distinguishes the two.[2] The *if–then* form says that if A is true, then you aren't to do B. The *don't-combine* form just forbids a combination – doing A and B together. If you're doing A, it doesn't follow that you aren't to do B. Maybe instead you're to do B and stop doing A.

Logicians debate what it means to call an imperative argument "valid." The popular satisfaction (obedience) view[3] says that an imperative argument is *valid* if the imperative conclusion would be followed whenever the imperative premises are followed and the indicative premises are true. If you check it out, you'll see that this would make our diet and bicycle fallacies valid – and make the *don't-combine* and *if–then* forms logically equivalent. Both results are absurd. So the satisfaction view is wrong.

The threat view takes "Do A" to mean "Either you'll do A or else S will happen" – where sanction "S" is some unspecified bad thing. This view tests for validity by substituting "(A ∨ S)" for each imperative "A̲" and then checking the resulting argument.

---

[1] One might object that the invalidity comes from using a future conclusion: "Don't brake (in the future)." But the example also works if we are careful about tenses. Suppose that we accept the premise "For no time t are you to combine accelerating at time t with braking at time t." If we add "You're accelerating now" we can't infer "Would that you not brake now" – since we could add instead "Would that you were braking now and not accelerating."

[2] The second form is equivalent to "(A̲ ⊃ ~B̲)"; but English can't say "If do A, then don't do B." Here's a point to ponder. *Don't-combine* imperatives are important for human rationality. But computer programs and languages, while they use *if–then* imperatives extensively, never use *don't-combine* imperatives – and the idea of their using such imperatives doesn't seem to make sense. Does this mark an important difference between humans and computers? If so, then what is it about humans that forms the basis for the difference?

[3] Hare 1972d (25–43, 59–73) accepts this view.

But this view too would make our diet and bicycle fallacies valid – and would make the *don't-combine* and *if–then* forms logically equivalent. Both results are absurd. So the threat view is wrong.

The satisfaction and threat views both stumble on examples mixing imperative and indicative elements. These examples show that it's better to analyze "valid" using "inconsistent."

Logicians also debate about how to form the contradictory of an imperative. There are two views:

- Modal view: The contradictory of "Do A" is "You may omit doing A."
- Anti-modal view: The contradictory of "Do A" is "Don't do A."[1]

What does "contradictory" mean here? Since imperatives aren't true or false, we can't use the standard definition – that P and Q are contradictories if it's logically necessary that exactly one is true. I propose this broader definition:

P and Q are *contradictories* if (1) P is inconsistent with Q, and (2) no consistent R is inconsistent both with P and with Q.[2]

One could then attack the anti-modal view as follows:

"You may do A and you may omit doing A" is consistent, but is inconsistent both with "Do A" and with "Don't do A."
∴ "Do A" and "Don't do A" aren't contradictories. {This follows using our definition of *contradictories*.}

The anti-modal view has to reject the premise; so it must claim that "Do A" is consistent with "You may omit doing A." Then it follows that "Do A" doesn't entail "You may not omit doing A"; the former is weaker than the latter.

I take both views to be correct; each view fits a different sense of "Do A." Imperatives can express either *demands* or *preferences*. A *demand imperative* is more clearly expressed as "You may not omit doing A"; this fits legal contexts and the modal view. A *pref-*

---

[1] In surveying the literature, I once found 10 people taking the modal view and 8 people taking the anti-modal view. Hare takes the anti-modal view. But his doctrine violates the principle that, if P is inconsistent with R, and R is the contradictory of Q, then P entails Q. On his view, "You may omit doing A" is inconsistent with "Do A," and "Do A" is the contradictory of "Don't do A" – and yet "You may omit doing A" doesn't entail "Don't do A." See Hare 1972d (26–7, 37–41).

[2] To avoid "contradictory" in our definition of "valid," we can define a *valid* argument as one in which anything that's consistent with the premises is also consistent with the conclusion.

erence imperative is more clearly expressed as "As-first-choice do A"; this fits personal advice contexts and the anti-modal view.

You tell your child "Have some desert" and "Finish your vegetables." The first might express a preference (consistent with permitting the opposite), while the second expresses a demand; the tone of voice might signal the difference. You might say more explicitly, "Preferably have some desert – but I'm not requiring that you do this – you may (if you wish) omit desert – but you *are* required to finish your vegetables."

I'll use "Do A" ("<u>A</u>") for preference imperatives; its contradictory is "Don't do A" ("~<u>A</u>"). When I say "imperative" without qualification, I'll mean "preference imperative." I'll use "You may not omit doing A" ("~M~<u>A</u>") for demands; its contradictory is "You may omit doing A" ("M~<u>A</u>").[1]

I'll also form quantificational imperatives by underlining (using the letter for the agent if this is expressed):

- Hu = "You're hiking" (indicative).
- H<u>u</u> = "Hike" (imperative).
- Sux = "You're stealing from X" (indicative).
- S<u>u</u>x = "Steal from X" (imperative).

These examples use quantifiers:

- (x)Ax = Everyone does A.
- (x)A<u>x</u> = Let everyone do A.
- (∃x)A<u>x</u> = Let someone do A.
- (x)(Ax ⊃ B<u>x</u>) = Let everyone who (in fact) is doing A do B.
- (∃x)(Ax · B<u>x</u>) = Let someone who (in fact) is doing A do B.
- (∃x)(A<u>x</u> · B<u>x</u>) = Let someone do both A and B.

Notice which letters are underlined.

8.2 Deontic Logic

Deontic logic adds two new operators: "O" for "ought" and "R" for "all right." These work much like the modal "□" and "◇."

---

[1] Hare takes "You may do A" to be like "I don't tell you not to do A" or "I hereby withhold the command or request that not A" (1972d: 38, 1989b: 25). I think rather that "You may do A" withholds the *demand* (but not necessarily the preference or request) not to do A. I might consistently say "Give me rocky road ice cream instead of chocolate chip. This is my request and preference, but I don't care that much about it. You *may* give me chocolate chip instead."

Deontic operators attach to imperative wffs, as modal operators attach to indicative wffs.

Here are the basic forms:

- O$\underline{A}$ = Act A ought to be done.
- R$\underline{A}$ = Act A is all right (permissible).

These are slightly more complicated:

- ~R$\underline{A}$ = O~$\underline{A}$ = Act A is wrong.
- (R$\underline{A}$ · R~$\underline{A}$) = (~O$\underline{A}$ · ~O~$\underline{A}$) = Act A is neutral.
- (O$\underline{A}$ ∨ O$\underline{B}$) = Either A ought to be done or B ought to be done.
- O($\underline{A}$ ∨ $\underline{B}$) = It ought to be that A or B be done.

These are the deontic *if–then* and *don't-combine* forms:

- (A ⊃ O~$\underline{B}$) = If you do A, then you ought not to do B.
- O~($\underline{A}$ · $\underline{B}$) = You ought not to combine doing A with doing B.

The second is equivalent to "O($\underline{A}$ ⊃ ~$\underline{B}$)"; but this is harder to translate into English.[1]

Here are some basic quantificational examples:

- OA$\underline{x}$ = X ought to do A.
- OA$\underline{x}$$\underline{y}$ = X ought to do A to Y.

These examples use quantifiers:

- O(x)A$\underline{x}$ = It's obligatory that everyone do A.
- ~O(x)A$\underline{x}$ = It isn't obligatory that everyone do A.
- O~(x)A$\underline{x}$ = It's obligatory that not everyone do A.
- O(x)~A$\underline{x}$ = It's obligatory that everyone not do A.

Order can make a difference. Compare these two:

- O(∃x)A$\underline{x}$ = It's obligatory that someone or other answer the phone.
- (∃x)OA$\underline{x}$ = There's someone (some specific person) who has an obligation to answer the phone.

The first might hold without the second. These also differ:

- (x)RS$\underline{x}$ = It's all right for anyone to stay home.
- R(x)S$\underline{x}$ = It's all right for everyone to stay home.

Again, the first might hold without the second; maybe it's all right for any specific person to stay home from work today – and yet it would be disastrous if everyone did it.

---

[1] The distinction between the deontic *if–then* and *don't-combine* forms is some-what like the modal distinction between "(A ⊃ □B)" and "□(A ⊃ B)." In both cases, it's important whether we put the operator inside or outside the parentheses – and it's difficult to express the difference clearly in ordinary language.

The popular indicative-operator approach attaches "O" to indicative formulas – using "OA" instead of "O<u>A</u>." While this is simpler, it destroys some important distinctions. Consider these formulas:

- O(∃x)(Kx · R<u>x</u>) = It's obligatory that some who kill repent.
- O(∃x)(K<u>x</u> · Rx) = It's obligatory that some kill who repent.
- O(∃x)(K<u>x</u> · R<u>x</u>) = It's obligatory that some both kill and repent.

The three differ greatly. Underlining shows what parts are obligatory: repenting, or killing, or killing-and-repenting. If we attached "O" to indicatives, then all three would translate the same way, as "O(∃x)(Kx · Rx)." Such examples show that we need to attach "O" to imperative wffs.[1]

Here are similar examples using "R":

- R(x)(~Hx ⊃ T<u>x</u>) = It's permissible that everyone who isn't hateful be thankful.
- R(x)(~Tx ⊃ H<u>x</u>) = It's permissible that everyone who isn't thankful be hateful.
- R(x)(T<u>x</u> ∨ H<u>x</u>) = It's permissible that everyone be either thankful or hateful.

Again, the three differ greatly; underlining indicates the permissible parts. The indicative-operator approach would make the formulas logically equivalent.

The indicative-operator approach also leads to the good Samaritan paradox. Consider this argument:

It's obligatory that Al help someone or other that Bob beats up.
∴ It's obligatory that Bob beat up someone.

The indicative-operator approach wrongly makes this valid:

O(∃x)(Bbx · Hax)   VALID
∴ O(∃x)Bbx

The symbolic premise doesn't say which part is obligatory – the beating or the helping.[2] Our symbolization goes this way:

---

[1] We couldn't distinguish these as "(∃x)(Kx · ORx)," "(∃x)(OKx · Rx)," and "(∃x)O(Kx · Rx)," since putting "(∃x)" outside the "O" changes the meaning; see the example about "O(∃x)A<u>x</u>." Besides Castañeda, Fisher 1962 and Hare 1981 (23) also take the imperative-operator approach.

[2] The problem isn't about the temporal sequence; there are similar examples where the evil deed happens *after* the good deed. It might be obligatory that Al warn someone or other that Bob *will* try to beat up. This doesn't entail that Bob ought to try to beat up someone. Again, we can't solve the problem by moving the "(∃x)" and "Bbx" outside the "O" since this changes the meaning.

$O(\exists x)(Bbx \cdot H\underline{a}x)$ INVALID
∴ $O(\exists x)Bb\underline{x}$

The underlining in the premise says that *helping* is obligatory; *beating* is descriptive and just picks out the one to be helped.

8.3 Belief Logic

Now we'll add the symbol ":" for constructing belief formulas. Here are some simple examples:

- u:A = You believe A = You accept (endorse, assent to) A.
- u:~A = You believe not-A.
- ~u:A = You don't believe A.

The last one might be true because you believe that A is false or because you take no position on A. Here are further examples:

- (~u:A · ~u:~A) = You take no position on A.
- (u:A ⊃ ~u:B) = If you believe A, then you don't believe B.
- u:(x)OA$\underline{x}$ = You believe that everyone ought to do A.

These are all indicatives. To construct imperative belief formulas, we'll underline the small letter before ":"; for example:

- $\underline{u}$:A = Believe A.
- (~$\underline{u}$:A · ~$\underline{u}$:~A) = Take no position on A.
- ~($\underline{u}$:A · $\underline{u}$:B) = Don't combine believing A with believing B.

Logic in the ordinary sense is about valid inferences – what logically follows from what; belief logic would then study what belief formulas validly follow from what other belief formulas. But, given that someone believes A, we can deduce little or nothing about what else the person believes. People can be confused and illogical; students and politicians can assert A and assert not-A almost in the same breath. So this approach won't work.

A belief logic is possible in an extended sense of "logic." It might study how people would believe if they were consistent.[1] Or it might generate consistency requirements that hold if we assume that one ought to be consistent. I take the latter approach, since it gives a basic framework for formal ethics. By adding to this

---

[1] Hintikka 1962 used roughly this approach; his work was an important influence on my formal ethics. (See also Fisher 1964.) Quine 1986 (79) objects that "believes" is too *colorful* to be a logical particle on par with *austere* notions like "not" and "some." But our austere world needs a little color; and I'm only talking about "logic" in an extended sense.

framework, we can bring in ends–means, conscientiousness, impartiality, the golden rule, and the formula of universal law.

Given the symbols that we've introduced, we can symbolize the logicality principles of Chapter 2. Our main theorems go this way:

L1   If A and B are inconsistent, then you ought not to combine accepting A with accepting B.

= $\sim\!\Diamond(A \cdot B) \supset O\!\sim\!(\underline{u}{:}A \cdot \underline{u}{:}B)$

L2   If A entails B, then you ought not to combine accepting A with not accepting B.

= $\Box(A \supset B) \supset O\!\sim\!(\underline{u}{:}A \cdot \sim\!\underline{u}{:}B)$

These *either–or* forms are equivalent by an imperative version of De Morgan's equivalences:

L1* If A and B are inconsistent, then you ought to either not accept A or not accept B.

= $\sim\!\Diamond(A \cdot B) \supset O(\sim\!\underline{u}{:}A \vee \sim\!\underline{u}{:}B)$

L2* If A entails B, then you ought to either accept B or not accept A.

= $\Box(A \supset B) \supset O(\underline{u}{:}B \vee \sim\!\underline{u}{:}A)$

Here are the corresponding *if–then* nontheorems:

L1a $\sim\!\Diamond(A \cdot B) \supset (\underline{u}{:}A \supset O\!\sim\!\underline{u}{:}B)$

L2a $\Box(A \supset B) \supset (\underline{u}{:}A \supset O\underline{u}{:}B)$

Our other logicality theorems go this way (for $n \geq 1$):

L3 $\sim\!\Diamond(A_1 \cdot \ldots \cdot A_n) \supset O\!\sim\!(\underline{u}{:}A_1 \cdot \ldots \cdot \underline{u}{:}A_n)$

L4 $\Box((A_1 \cdot \ldots \cdot A_n) \supset B) \supset O\!\sim\!(\underline{u}{:}A_1 \cdot \ldots \cdot \underline{u}{:}A_n \cdot \sim\!\underline{u}{:}B)$

L5 $O\!\sim\!((\underline{u}{:}A \cdot \underline{u}{:}B) \cdot \sim\!\underline{u}{:}(A \cdot B))$

The first two are schemas for producing specific formulas.

8.4 Symbolizing Formal Ethics

This last section of the book puts the finishing touches on our logical machinery. Thus we can complete the symbolization of our formal ethical principles.

First, we need to expand our interpretation of ":" to cover willing as well as believing (see Section 3.1). We'll now interpret ":" generically to mean "accepts." To *believe* is to accept a statement, while to *will* is to accept an imperative:

- $\underline{u}{:}A$ = You accept (endorse, assent to, say in your heart) "A is true" = You believe A.

- u:<u>A</u> = You accept (endorse, assent to, say in your heart) "Let act A be done" = You will that act A be done.

In translating "u:<u>A</u>," we'll often use terms more specific than "wills." We'll use words like "acts," "resolves," or "desires."[1] Which of these fits depends on whether the imperative is past, present, or future – and whether it applies to oneself or to another. Here are three examples:

- u:A<u>u</u> (if the act is present) = You accept the imperative for you to do A now = You act (in order) to do A.
- u:A<u>u</u> (if the act is future) = You accept the imperative for you to do A in the future = You're resolved to do A.
- u:A<u>x</u> = You accept the imperative for X to do A = You desire that X do A = You want X to do A.

As before, "You act (in order) to do A" ("u:A<u>u</u>") is about what you try or intend to do, while "You do A" ("Au") is about what you actually do (perhaps accidentally).

Consider these formulas:

- u:(∃x)(Kx · R<u>x</u>) = You desire that some who kill repent = You say in your heart "Would that some who kill repent."
- u:(∃x)(K<u>x</u> · Rx) = You desire that some kill who repent = You say in your heart "Would that some kill who repent."
- u:(∃x)(K<u>x</u> · R<u>x</u>) = You desire that some both kill and repent = You say in your heart "Would that some both kill and repent."

These differ greatly. Underlining shows the desired parts: repenting, or killing, or killing-and-repenting. If we attached "desire" to indicative formulas, all would translate the same:

You desire that (∃x)(Kx · Rx) = You desire it to be the case that there's someone who both kills and repents.

This destroys important distinctions. So it's better to symbolize "desire" as accepting an imperative.[2]

These formulas tell someone to will something:

---

[1] There's some looseness in translations involving tense, since we can't tell from "A<u>u</u>" whether it's past, present, or future.

[2] Thus analyzing *willing* as accepting an imperative (see Section 3.1) has some advantages besides theoretical neatness; the popular view of *desiring* as an attitude toward a state of affairs doesn't let us make important distinctions.

Our repenting-argument is much like the one we used in Section 8.2 to show that "O" should attach to imperative formulas. As before, we can't get around the problem by putting "(∃x)" outside the "u:" since this changes the meaning. "u:(∃x)A<u>x</u>" says that you want someone or other to do A, while "(∃x)u:A<u>x</u>" says that there's some specific person that you want to do A.

- u:A<u>u</u> (if the act is present) = Accept the imperative for you to do A now = Act (in order) to do A.
- u:A<u>u</u> (if the act is future) = Accept the imperative for you to do A in the future = Resolve to do A.
- u:A<u>x</u> = Accept the imperative for X to do A = Desire that X do A = Want X to do A.

Underlining can be confusing. This chart shows the basic cases:

Indicatives	*Imperatives*
u:A = You believe A.	<u>u</u>:A = Believe A.
u:<u>A</u> = You will A.	<u>u</u>:<u>A</u> = Will A.

Underlining the letter before ":" makes the formula an imperative (instead of an indicative). Putting an imperative after ":" makes the formula about willing (instead of believing).

We need five new symbols. "M" ("may") is for permissives and demands; it works much like the deontic operator "R." "⊡" and "⟐" are for causal necessity and possibility;[1] these work much like "□" and "◇." "■" ("in every actual or hypothetical case") is used in deontic and prescriptive counterfactuals; this works much like "□." Finally, "*" is used in representing the complete description of an act in universal terms. Here are examples:

- M<u>A</u> = Act A may be done.
- ⊡A = It's causally necessary that A.
- ⟐A = It's causally possible that A.
- ■O<u>A</u> = In every actual or hypothetical case, A ought to be done.
- F*<u>A</u> = F is the complete description of act A in universal terms.

In addition, we need three new kinds of variable:[2]

- Universal property variables: F, G, H, ...
- Action variables: <u>X</u>, <u>Y</u>, <u>Z</u>, ...
- Time variables: t, t′, t″, ...

Universal property variables attach to imperative wffs: "F<u>A</u>" means "Act A has universal property F" – and "(∃F)F<u>A</u>" means "For some universal property F, act A has F." We'll use action

---

[1] My use of "⊡" and causal logic is adapted from Burks 1977 (337–478).

[2] The function of capital letters depends on context. "F" in "((F · Fa) ⊃ (Fbc · F<u>A</u>))" is used first for a statement, then for a property of an individual entity, then for a relation between individual entities, and finally for a universal property of an action. The meaning of "F" in each case is distinct; for the sake of clarity, we'd normally use different capital letters. Note that "F<u>A</u>" translates as "Act A is F" – not as "The imperative 'Do A' is F."

variables to quantify over individual actions: "$(\underline{X})(F\underline{X} \supset O\underline{X})$" means "For every act X, if act X has universal property F then act X ought to be done" ("All acts that are F ought to be done").

We can now symbolize the remaining axioms and theorems. Our rationality axiom (Section 3.2) symbolizes this way:

R   If A_1, ..., A_n, either by themselves or conjoined with other axioms of formal ethics, form an inconsistent set, then you ought not to combine accepting A_1, ..., and accepting A_n.

= $\sim\Diamond(A_1 \cdot \ldots \cdot A_n \cdot C) \supset O\sim(\underline{u}{:}A_1 \cdot \ldots \cdot \underline{u}{:}A_n)$

If A_1, ..., A_n, either by themselves or conjoined with other axioms of formal ethics, entail B, then you ought not to combine accepting A_1, ..., accepting A_n, and not accepting B.

= $\Box((A_1 \cdot \ldots \cdot A_n \cdot C) \supset B) \supset O\sim(\underline{u}{:}A_1 \cdot \ldots \cdot \underline{u}{:}A_n \cdot \sim\underline{u}{:}B)$

These (which hold for n≥1) are schemas for producing specific formulas; here "C" can represent any conjunction of instances of the other axioms (E, P, U). R is the *ought* format Ro; the imperative format Ri is similar, but without "O." I didn't add logical machinery for the virtue, descriptive, and hypothetical imperative formats (Rv, Rd, and Rh).

Our ends–means axiom (Section 3.3) symbolizes this way:

E   "Do end E" entails "If your doing means M is causally necessary for you to do end E, then do means M."

= $\Box(\underline{E} \supset (\boxdot(\sim M \supset \sim E) \supset \underline{M}))$

This is our main ends–means theorem:

E1   You ought not to combine wanting to do E, believing that your doing M now is causally necessary for you to do E, and not acting to do M.

= $O\sim(\underline{u}{:}E\underline{u} \cdot \underline{u}{:}\boxdot(\sim Mu \supset \sim Eu) \cdot \sim\underline{u}{:}M\underline{u})$

This is the traditional hypothetical imperative form:

E1a $(u{:}E\underline{u} \cdot u{:}\boxdot(\sim Mu \supset \sim Eu)) \supset O\underline{u}{:}Mu$

Here are the other ends–means theorems:

E2 $\Box(O\underline{A} \supset \Diamond A)$

E3 $\Box(O\underline{E} \supset (\boxdot(\sim M \supset \sim E) \supset O\underline{M}))$

E4 $\Box(O\sim\underline{M} \supset (\boxdot(\sim M \supset \sim E) \supset O\sim\underline{E}))$

E5 $\Box(\underline{A} \supset \Diamond A)$

E6 $\Box(R\underline{A} \supset \Diamond A)$

E7 $\Box(\sim\Diamond A \supset \sim O\underline{A})$

E8 $\Box(\sim\Diamond(A \cdot B) \supset (\sim O\underline{A} \lor \sim O\underline{B}))$

E9 $\Box((O(\underline{A} \lor \underline{B}) \cdot \sim\Diamond A) \supset O\underline{B})$

E10 $\sim$($\underline{u}$:$\sim$◈A$\underline{u}$ · $\underline{u}$:A$\underline{u}$)

We stated the prescriptivity axiom this way (Section 3.5), but specified that it also covers counterfactuals:

P   If you ought to do A, then do A.
       If it's all right for you to do A, then you may do A.

=   (OA̲ ⊃ A̲)
       (RA̲ ⊃ MA̲)

This formulation makes the counterfactual application explicit:

P   ■(OA̲ ⊃ A̲)
       ■(RA̲ ⊃ MA̲)

Strong prescriptivity is a logical entailment:

SP   □(OA̲ ⊃ A̲)
       □(RA̲ ⊃ MA̲)

Now that we have demand imperatives (Section 8.1), we could strengthen "A̲" to "$\sim$M$\sim$A̲" in the first line of these formulas;[1] but none of our theorems depend on this. Unlike the permissive minister who spoke of the "Ten Suggestions," we should hold that an *ought* commits us to a *demand* (not just a *preference*), and thus commits us to not consenting to the opposite.

Our main conscientiousness theorem goes this way:

C1   Don't combine believing that you ought to do A now with not acting to do A.

=   Don't believe that something is your duty without acting to do it.

= $\sim$($\underline{u}$:OA$\underline{u}$ · $\sim$$\underline{u}$:A$\underline{u}$)

This is the *if–then* nontheorem:

C1a (u:OA$\underline{u}$ ⊃ OA$\underline{u}$)

Here are the other theorems:

C2 $\sim$($\underline{u}$:O$\sim$A$\underline{u}$ · $\underline{u}$:A$\underline{u}$)
C3 $\sim$($\underline{u}$:RA$\underline{u}$ · $\sim$$\underline{u}$:MA$\underline{u}$)
C4 $\sim$($\underline{u}$:(x)OA$\underline{x}$ · $\sim$$\underline{u}$:A$\underline{u}$)
C5 $\sim$($\underline{u}$:(x)OA$\underline{x}$ · $\sim$$\underline{u}$:(x)A$\underline{x}$)
P1   □((A̲ · P) ⊃ RA̲)
C6 $\sim$($\underline{u}$:A$\underline{u}$ · $\sim$$\underline{u}$:RA$\underline{u}$)

---

[1] Following Torrance 1981, the biconditionals would then also hold. Here's how to derive the converse of "(RA̲ ⊃ MA̲)":

     (O$\sim$A̲ ⊃ $\sim$M$\sim$$\sim$A̲) {From the strengthened P, substituting "$\sim$A̲" for "A̲."}
∴   (M$\sim$$\sim$A̲ ⊃ $\sim$O$\sim$A̲) {Contrapositive.}
∴   (MA̲ ⊃ RA̲) {Substituting equivalents.}

Our pacifism example (Section 3.6) was about the principle that one ought in no conceivable case to kill. This translates as "■(x)O~K$\underline{x}$" – "In every actual or hypothetical case, for all x, x ought not to kill." This committed my pacifist friend Jim to resolving that he not kill if he were to come home and find a madman about to kill his family. This involves accepting the imperative "■(S ⊃ ~K$\underline{i}$)" – "In every actual or hypothetical case, if situation S were to take place (about the madman) then would that I not kill."[1] The theorem behind the example goes this way:

C7   Don't combine believing that one ought in no conceivable case to do A with not being resolved to refrain from doing A if situation S took place.

=   ~($\underline{u}$:■(x)O~A$\underline{x}$ · ~$\underline{u}$:■(S ⊃ ~A$\underline{u}$))

Here's our universalizability axiom (Section 4.1):

U   If act A ought to be done, then there is some conjunction F of universal properties such that (1) act A is F and (2) in any actual or hypothetical case every act that is F ought to be done.

=   O$\underline{A}$ ⊃ (∃F)(F$\underline{A}$ · ■($\underline{X}$)(F$\underline{X}$ ⊃ O$\underline{X}$))

The *all right* part would translate in a similar way.

Section 4.1 defined *exactly* and *relevantly* similar. We'll use "E" and "S" for these notions, and define them as follows:

- E($\underline{A}$, $\underline{B}$) = Act B is *exactly similar* to act A (in its universal properties) = Acts A and B have the exact same universal properties =df (F)(F$\underline{A}$ ≡ F$\underline{B}$)

- S($\underline{A}$, $\underline{B}$) = Acts A and B are *relevantly similar* in their universal properties =df There's some conjunction of universal properties F such that: (1) acts A and B are both F, and (2) for any act that is F it is morally irrelevant what further universal properties it has (in the sense that if the act's complete description in universal terms would make it obligatory (wrong, neutral) then so would F) = (∃F)(F$\underline{A}$ · F$\underline{B}$ · ■($\underline{C}$)(G)((F$\underline{C}$ · G*$\underline{C}$) ⊃ ((■($\underline{D}$)(G$\underline{D}$ ⊃ O$\underline{D}$) ⊃ ■($\underline{D}$)(F$\underline{D}$ ⊃ O$\underline{D}$)) · (■($\underline{D}$)(G$\underline{D}$ ⊃ O~$\underline{D}$) ⊃ ■($\underline{D}$)(F$\underline{D}$ ⊃ O~$\underline{D}$)) · (■($\underline{D}$)(G$\underline{D}$ ⊃ (~O$\underline{D}$ · ~O~$\underline{D}$)) ⊃ ■($\underline{D}$)(F$\underline{D}$ ⊃ (~O$\underline{D}$ · ~O~$\underline{D}$))))))

These definitions apply only when we're talking about actions in *actual* situations. When we talk about actions in *hypothetical* (counterfactual) situations, we'll use a different analysis.

---

[1] "(S ⊃ ~K$\underline{i}$)," since it's trivially entailed by "~S," is too weak to express this imperative about a hypothetical case. "□(S ⊃ ~K$\underline{i}$)" is too strong, since it's false – and accepting it doesn't involve resolving not to kill in a hypothetical situation. We need a notion like "■" to express such imperatives.

"F*$\underline{A}$" means that F is the complete description of act A in universal terms. We can define this as follows:

F*$\underline{A}$ = F is a description of act A in universal terms that includes all the universal properties of act A = Act A is F, and, for every universal property G that A has, it's logically necessary that every act that's F is G =df F$\underline{A}$ · (G)(G$\underline{A}$ ⊃ □($\underline{X}$)(F$\underline{X}$ ⊃ G$\underline{X}$))

We use this idea for the following theorem (Section 4.2):

U1   If it would be all right for you to do A to X, then in an exactly reversed situation it would be all right for X to do A to you.

=   RA$\underline{u}$x ⊃ (∃F)(F*A$\underline{u}$x · ■(FA$\underline{x}$u ⊃ RA$\underline{x}$u))

This says: "If it's all right for you to do A to X, then, for some universal property F, F is the complete description of your-doing-A-to-X in universal terms, and, in any actual or hypothetical case, if X-doing-A-to-you is F then it would be all right for X to do A to you." We'd omit "*" for a *relevantly* reversed situation. Here are some related theorems:

I1   ~($\underline{u}$:RA$\underline{u}$x · ~$\underline{u}$:(∃F)(F*A$\underline{u}$x · ■(FA$\underline{x}$u ⊃ RA$\underline{x}$u)))
U2   RA$\underline{u}$x ⊃ (∃F)(F*A$\underline{u}$x · ■(x)(FA$\underline{x}$u ⊃ RA$\underline{x}$u))
U3   (O~$\underline{A}$ · S($\underline{B}$, $\underline{A}$)) ⊃ O~$\underline{B}$
U4   (OA$\underline{u}$ · O~A$\underline{x}$) ⊃ ~S(A$\underline{u}$, A$\underline{x}$)

This is our main golden rule theorem (Section 5.1):

G1   Don't combine acting to do A to X with not consenting to the idea of A being done to you in an exactly similar situation.

=   Treat others only in ways that you're willing to be treated in the same situation.

=   ~($\underline{u}$:A$\underline{u}$x · ~$\underline{u}$:(∃F)(F*A$\underline{u}$x · ■(x)(FA$\underline{x}$u ⊃ MA$\underline{x}$u)))

This says: "Don't accept the imperative to do A to X without also accepting the permissive 'Act A may be done to me in an exactly similar situation.'" The permissive is analyzed as "For some universal property F, F is the complete description in universal terms of my doing A to X, and, in any actual or hypothetical situation, if someone's doing A to me is F, then this person may do A to me."

Our GR nontheorems (Section 5.2) go this way:

G1a $\underline{u}$:A$\underline{x}$u ⊃ A$\underline{u}$x
G1c (∃F)(F*A$\underline{u}$x · ■(x)(FA$\underline{x}$u ⊃ $\underline{u}$:A$\underline{x}$u)) ⊃ A$\underline{u}$x
G1d $\underline{u}$:(∃F)(F*A$\underline{u}$x · ■(x)(FA$\underline{x}$u ⊃ A$\underline{x}$u)) ⊃ A$\underline{u}$x

The English version of **G1b** is ambiguous between **G1c** and **G1d**. I won't symbolize GR variations **G2** to **G13** (Section 5.3).[1]

This is our main universal law theorem (Section 6.2):

O4 Don't act to do A without also consenting to the idea that any exactly similar act may be done.

= Act only as you're willing for anyone to act in exactly similar circumstances.

= $\sim(\underline{u}{:}A\underline{u} \cdot \sim\underline{u}{:}(\exists F)(F^*A\underline{u} \cdot \blacksquare(\underline{X})(F\underline{X} \supset M\underline{X})))$

This says: "Don't accept the imperative to do A without also accepting the permissive 'Any exactly similar act may be done in any actual or hypothetical situation.'" The permissive is analyzed as "For some universal property F, F is the complete description in universal terms of my doing A, and, in any actual or hypothetical situation, any act that's F may be done."

Our UL nontheorems go this way:

O4a $RA\underline{u} \supset u{:}(x)Ax$

O4b $RA\underline{u} \supset u{:}(\exists F)(F^*A\underline{u} \cdot \blacksquare(\underline{X})(F\underline{X} \supset M\underline{X}))$

These are the other UL theorems (Section 6.1):

O1 $\sim(\underline{u}{:}A\underline{u} \cdot \sim\underline{u}{:}(\exists F)(FA\underline{u} \cdot \blacksquare(FA\underline{x} \supset MA\underline{x})))$

O2 $\sim(\underline{u}{:}A\underline{u}t \cdot \sim\underline{u}{:}(\exists F)(FA\underline{u}t \cdot \blacksquare(FA\underline{u}t' \supset MA\underline{u}t')))$

O3 $\sim(\underline{u}{:}A\underline{u}xt \cdot \sim\underline{u}{:}(\exists F)(FA\underline{u}xt \cdot \blacksquare(FA\underline{x}ut' \supset MA\underline{x}ut')))$

O2 and **O3** require variables for times.

If we were doing formal ethics as a rigorous formal system, we'd give a proof mechanism and then prove our main theorems. If you want to see what this is like, look at the end of my *Symbolic Logic* book (Gensler 1990).

---

[1] To be provable, G13 and G14 need the proviso that it's logically possible for you to be in X's exact place on the receiving end of the action. (If "A" in "Axy" contains an indexical reference, this might not be so.) So **G14** translates as "$\sim(\underline{u}{:}(\exists F)(F^*A\underline{u}x \cdot \blacksquare(x)(FA\underline{x}u \supset \sim M\sim A\underline{x}u) \cdot \Diamond(\exists x)FA\underline{x}u) \cdot \sim\underline{u}{:}A\underline{u}x)$."

Bibliography

Abrahams, I. (1967) *Studies in Pharisaism and the Gospels*, New York: Ktav Publishing House.

Allinson, R.E. (1992) "The golden rule as the core value in Confucianism and Christianity," *Asian Philosophy* 2: 173–85.

Aristotle. *Aristotle's Metaphysics*, trans. H.G. Apostle, London and Bloomington: Indiana University Press, 1973.

Aronson, E. (1969) "The theory of cognitive dissonance: a current perspective," in L. Berkowitz (ed.) *Advances in Experimental Social Psychology*, vol. 4, London and New York: Academic Press, 1–34.

Atkinson, D.A. (1982) "The golden rule," *The Expository Times* 93: 336–8.

Audi, R. (1989) *Practical Reasoning*, London and New York: Routledge.

Augustine (400) *The Lord's Sermon on the Mount*, trans. J.J. Jepson, Westminister, MD: Newman Press, 1948.

Ayer, A.J. (1946) *Language, Truth, and Logic*, New York: Dover.

Bachmeyer, T.J. (1973) "The golden rule and developing moral judgment," *Religious Education* 68: 348–66.

Badcock, C.R. (1986) *The Problem of Altruism,* Oxford: Basil Blackwell.

Barry, B. (1973) *The Liberal Theory of Justice*, Oxford: Clarendon Press.

Becker, L.C. (1986) *Reciprocity*, London and New York: Routledge & Kegan Paul.

Blackburn, S. (1993) *Essays in Quasi-Realism*, Oxford: Oxford University Press.

Blackstone, W.T. (1965) "The golden rule: A defense," *Southern Journal of Philosophy* 3: 172–7.

Bond, E.J. (1968) "The supreme principle of morality," *Dialogue* 7: 167–79.

Boyd, R.N. (1988) "How to be a moral realist," in G. Sayre-McCord (ed.) *Essays on Moral Realism*, London and Ithaca, NY: Cornell University Press, 181–228.

Brandt, R.B. (1955) "The definition of an 'ideal observer' theory in ethics" and "Some comments on Professor Firth's reply," *Philosophy and Phenomenological Research* 15: 407–13 and 422–3.

—— (1959) *Ethical Theory*, Englewood Cliffs, NJ: Prentice-Hall.

—— (1970) "Rational desires," *Proceedings and Addresses of the American Philosophical Association* 43: 43–64.

—— (1972) "Rationality, egoism, and morality," *Journal of Philosophy* 69: 681–97.

—— (1976) "The psychology of benevolence and its implications for philosophy," *Journal of Philosophy* 73: 429–53.

—— (1983) "The concept of rational action," *Social Theory and Practice* 9: 143–65.

—— (1989) "Hare on abortion," *Social Theory and Practice* 15: 15–24.

Brink, D.O. (1989) *Moral Realism and the Foundations of Ethics*, New York and Cambridge: Cambridge University Press.

Broad, C.D. (1950) "Imperatives, categorical and hypothetical," *Philosopher* 2: 62–75.

Brook, R. (1987) "Justice and the golden rule: A commentary on some recent work of Lawrence Kohlberg," *Ethics* 97: 363–73.

Browne, L. (1946) *The World's Great Scriptures*, New York: Macmillan.

Bruce, D. (1995) *The Thru-Hiker's Handbook*, Hot Springs, NC: Center for Appalachian Trail Studies.

Brussel, E.E. (ed.) (1970) *Dictionary of Quotable Definitions*, Englewood Cliffs, NJ: Prentice-Hall.

Burks, A. (1977) *Chance, Cause, Reason*, Chicago: University of Chicago Press.

Butler, J. (1726) *Sermons*, London: W. Botham.

Cadoux, A.T. (1912) "The implications of the golden rule," *Ethics* 22: 272–87.

Carnap, R. (1945) "On inductive logic," *Philosophy of Science* 12: 72–97.

Carson, T.L. (1984) *The Status of Morality,* Dordrecht: D. Reidel.

Castañeda, H.N. (1960a) "Imperative reasonings," *Philosophy and Phenomenological Research* 21: 21–49.

—— (1960b) "Outline of a theory on the general logical structure of the language of action," *Theoria* 26: 151–82.

—— (1967) "Actions, imperatives, and obligations," *Proceedings of the Aristotelian Society* 68 (1967–8): 25–48.

—— (1970) "On the semantics of the ought-to-do," *Synthese* 21: 448–68.

Chan, W.T. (1955) "The evolution of the Confucian concept Jên," *Philosophy East and West* 4: 295–319.

—— (1963) *A Source Book in Chinese Philosophy*, Princeton, NJ: Princeton University Press.

Clarke, S. (1706) *A Discourse Concerning the Unchangeable Obligations of Natural Religions*, London: W. Botham.

Cohen, B. (1977) "Three ethical fallacies," *Mind* 86: 78–87.

Cohen, J.L. (1989) "Belief and acceptance," *Mind* 98: 367–89.

Crombie, I.M. (1966) "Moral principles," in I.T. Ramsey (ed.) *Christian Ethics and Contemporary Philosophy*, London: SCM, 234–61.

Dancy, J. (1977) "The logical conscience," *Analysis* 37: 81–4.

—— (1993) *Moral Reasons*, Oxford: Blackwell.

Daniels, N. (1979) "Wide reflective equilibrium and theory acceptance in ethics," *Journal of Philosophy* 76: 256–82.

Darwall, S.P. (1983) *Impartial Reason*, London and Ithaca, NY: Cornell University Press.

Darwin, C. (1839) *The Voyage of the Beagle*, New York: P.F. Collier, 1909.

—— (1871) *The Descent of Man*, Chicago: Encyclopedia Britannica, 1952.

Derksen, A.A. (1978) "The alleged lottery paradox resolved," *American Philosophical Quarterly* 15: 67–74.

Dickens, C. (1854) in G. Ford and S. Monod (eds) *Hard Times*, New York: W.W. Norton, 1966.

Donagan, A. (1984) "Consistency in rationalist moral systems," *Journal of Philosophy* 81: 281–309.

Dreier, J. (1990) "Internal and speaker relativism," *Ethics* 101: 6–26.

Dudman, V.H. (1992) "Probability and assertion," *Analysis* 53: 204–11.

Eckhoff, M. (1994) "Talking with animals: The rule that's golden," in *Best Friends*. This is available on the internet World Wide Web (at http://www.enews.com/magazines/best_friends/archive/120194.4.html).

Edgley, R. (1969) *Reason in Theory and Practice*, London: Hutchinson.

Eisler, R. (1947) "Religion for the age of reason," *Hibbert Journal* 45: 334–41.

Emerson, R.W. (1841) "Self-reliance," in J. Slater, A.R. Ferguson, and J.F. Carr (eds) *The Collected Works of Ralph Waldo Emerson*, vol. 2, Cambridge: Harvard University Press, 1979, 25–51.

Epictetus (90) *The Golden Sayings of Epictetus*, trans. H. Crossley, London: Macmillan, 1935.

Erikson, E.H. (1964) "The golden rule in the light of new insight," in *Insight and Responsibility*, New York: W.W. Norton, 217–43.

Ewing, A.C. (1965) *Ethics*, New York: The Free Press.

Festinger, L. (1957) *A Theory of Cognitive Dissonance*, Stanford, CA: Stanford University Press.

Firth, R. (1952) "Ethical absolutism and the ideal observer," *Philosophy and Phenomenological Research* 12: 317–45.

—— (1955) "Reply to Professor Brandt," *Philosophy and Phenomenological Research* 15: 414–21.

Fisher, M. (1962) "A system of deontic-alethic modal logic," *Mind* 71: 231–6.

—— (1964) "Remarks on a logical theory of belief statements," *Philosophical Quarterly* 14: 165–9.

Flynn, W.J. (1990) "The Williamsburg Charter: A golden rule for preserving religious freedom," *Journal of Law and Religion* 8: 221–22.

Fodor, J.A. (1984) "Fodor's guide to mental representation," *Mind* 93: 76–100.

Foley, R. (1979) "Justified inconsistent beliefs," *American Philosophical Quarterly* 16: 247–57.

—— (1992) "The epistemology of belief and the epistemology of degrees of belief," *American Philosophical Quarterly* 29: 111–24.

—— (1993) "Rationality and perspective," *Analysis* 53: 65–8.

Frankena, W.K. (1954) "Obligation and motivation in recent moral philosophy," in A.I. Melden (ed.) *Essays in Moral Philosophy*, London and Seattle: University of Washington Press, 40–81.

—— (1966) "Two concepts of morality," *Journal of Philosophy* 63: 688–96.

—— (1970) "Love and principle in Christian ethics," in K. Pahel and M. Schiller (eds) *Readings in Contemporary Ethical Theory*, Englewood Cliffs, NJ: Prentice-Hall, 540–60.

—— (1973) *Ethics*, Englewood Cliffs, NJ: Prentice-Hall, second edition.

Friedman, M. (1989) "The impracticality of impartiality," *Journal of Philosophy* 86: 645–56.

Gauthier, D.P. (1968) "Hare's debtors," *Mind* 77: 400–5.

—— (1986) *Morals by Agreement*, Oxford: Oxford University Press.

Gensler, H.J. (1976) "The prescriptivism incompleteness theorem," *Mind* 85: 589–96.

—— (1983) "Acting commits one to ethical beliefs," *Analysis* 43: 40–3.

—— (1984) "How incomplete is prescriptivism?" *Mind* 93: 103–7.

—— (1985) "Ethical consistency principles," *Philosophical Quarterly* 35: 157–70.

—— (1986a) "A Kantian argument against abortion," *Philosophical Studies* 49: 83–98.

—— (1986b) "Ethics is based on rationality," *Journal of Value Inquiry* 20: 251–64.

—— (1989) *Logic: Analyzing and Appraising Arguments*, Englewood Cliffs, NJ: Prentice-Hall.

—— (1990) *Symbolic Logic: Classical and Advanced Systems*, Englewood Cliffs, NJ: Prentice-Hall.

Gerhardsson, B. (1987) "Agape and imitation of Christ," in E.P. Sanders (ed.) *Jesus, the Gospels, and the Church*, Macon, GA: Mercer University Press.

Gert, B. (1990) "Rationality, human nature, and lists," *Ethics* 100: 279–300.

Gewirth, A. (1978a) "The golden rule rationalized," *Midwest Studies in Philosophy* 3: 133–47.

—— (1978b) *Reason and Morality*, Chicago: Chicago.

Gilligan, C. (1982) *In a Different Voice*, Cambridge: Harvard University Press.

Goldman, A.I. (1993) "Ethics and cognitive science," *Ethics* 103: 337–60.

Goodman, J. (1688) *The Golden Rule*, London: Samuel Roycroft.

Govier, T.R. (1972) "Is conscientiousness always – or ever – a virtue?" *Dialogue* 11: 241–51.

Haas, P.J. (1988) *Morality after Auschwitz*, Philadelphia: Fortress Press.

Habermas, J. (1990) *Moral Consciousness and Communicative Action*, Cambridge: MIT Press.

Hale, M. (1805) "Of doing as we would be done unto," in *Works*, vol. 1, London: R. Wilks, 378–416.

Handlin, H.C. (1992) "The company built upon the golden rule: Lincoln Electric," *Journal of Organizational Behavior Management* 12: 151–63.

Hare, R.M. (1952) *The Language of Morals*, Oxford: Clarendon Press.

—— (1955) "Have I a duty to my country as such?" *Listener* 44: 651–2.

—— (1963) *Freedom and Reason*, Oxford: Clarendon Press.

—— (1964) "The promising game," *Revue Internationale de Philosophie* 18: 389–412.

—— (1972a) *Applications of Moral Philosophy*, Berkeley: University of California.

—— (1972b) *Essays on the Moral Concepts*, Berkeley: University of California.

—— (1972c) *Essays on Philosophical Method*, Berkeley: University of California.

—— (1972d) *Practical Inferences*, Berkeley: University of California.

—— (1973) "Rawls' theory of justice," *Philosophical Quarterly* 23: 144–55 and 241–52.

—— (1977) "Geach on murder and sodomy," *Philosophy* 52: 467–72.

—— (1978) "Relevance," in A.I. Goldman and J. Kim (eds) *Values and Morals*, Dordrecht: D. Reidel, 73–90.

—— (1979a) "Universal and past-tense prescriptions: A reply to Mr Ibberson" *Analysis* 39: 1b61–5.

—— (1979b) "What makes choices rational?" *Review of Metaphysics* 32: 623–37.

—— (1981) *Moral Thinking,* Oxford: Clarendon Press.

—— (1984) "Some reasoning about preferences: A response to essays by Persson, Feldman, and Schueler," *Ethics* 95: 81–5.

—— (1989a) "Brandt on fairness to happiness," *Social Theory and Practice* 15: 59–65.

—— (1989b) "A Kantian approach to abortion" and "Reply to Brandt," *Social Theory and Practice* 15: 1–14 and 25–32.

—— (1989c) "Some sub-atomic particles of logic," *Mind* 98: 23–37.

—— (1993) *Essays on Bioethics*, Oxford: Clarendon Press.

Harman, G. (1986) *Change in View*, Cambridge: MIT Press.

Harrison, J. (1956) "Some comments on Professor Firth's ideal observer theory," *Philosophy and Phenomenological Research* 17: 256–62.

Harsanyi, J.C. (1958) "Ethics in terms of hypothetical imperatives," *Mind* 67: 305–16.

Heifetz, M. (1991) "A concept of ethics," in L. Meier (ed.) *Jewish Values in Health and Medicine*, Lanham, MD: University Press of America, 73–9.

Henry, M. (1827) *An Exposition of the Old and New Testament*, New York: Robert Carter and Brothers.

Hertzler, J.O. (1934) "On golden rules," *Ethics* 44: 418–36.

Hintikka, J. (1962) *Knowledge and Belief*, Ithaca, NY: Cornell University Press.

Hobbes, T. (1651) *Leviathan*, Oxford: Basil Blackwell, 1947.

Hoche, H.U. (1982) "The golden rule: New aspects of an old principle," trans. J.C. Evans, in D.E. Christensen (ed.) *Contemporary German Philosophy*, London and University Park, PA: Pennsylvania State University Press, 69–90.

—— (1990) "Prescriptivity of 'ought'-sentences: Logical entailment of imperatives, or pragmatic implication of 'I intend'-sentences." This paper was given at a symposium near Saarbrücken, Germany in June 1990.

Hoffman, M.L. (1981) "The development of empathy," in Rushton and Sorrentino 1981, 41–63.

Holoviak, S.J. (1993) *Golden Rule Management*, Reading, MA: Addison-Wesley.

Hume, D. (1751) *An Enquiry Concerning the Principles of Morals*.

Hume, R.E. (1959) *The World's Living Religions*, New York: Charles Scribner's Sons.

Ibberson, J. (1979) "A doubt about universal prescriptivism," *Analysis* 39: 153–8.

Interpreter's Bible (1951) "Golden rule," Nashville: Parthenon 7: 329–30.

Jennings, R.E. (1974) "Pseudo-subjectivism in ethics," *Dialogue* 13: 515–18.

Jewish Encyclopedia (1962) "Golden rule," New York: Ktav 6: 21–2.

Johnson, D.M. (1987) "The Greek origins of belief," *American Philosophical Quarterly* 24: 319–27.

Johnson, O.A. (1969) *The Moral Life*, London: George Allen & Unwin.

Kalin, J. (1970) "In defense of egoism," in D.P. Gauthier (ed.) *Morality and Rational Self-Interest*, Englewood Cliffs, NJ: Prentice-Hall, 64–87.

Kant, I. (1785) *Groundwork of the Metaphysics of Morals*, trans. H.J. Paton, New York: Harper & Row, 1964.

—— (1787) *Critique of Pure Reason*, trans. N.K. Smith, New York: St Martin's Press, 1965.

—— (1788) *Critique of Practical Reason*, trans. L.W. Beck, New York: Library of Liberal Arts, 1956.

—— (1797) *The Doctrine of Virtue*, trans. M.J. Gregor, New York, Harper & Row, 1964.

—— (1924) *Lectures on Ethics*, trans. L. Infield, New York, Harper & Row, 1963. (P. Menzer edited this from student notes in 1924.)

Kaplan, M. (1981) "A Bayesian theory of rational acceptance," *Journal of Philosophy* 78: 305–30.

Katz, R.L. (1963) *Empathy: Its Nature and Uses*, London: Collier-Macmillan.

Kaufman, W. (1963) *The Faith of a Heretic*, New York: Doubleday.

Kennedy, J.F. (1963) Speech at the University of Alabama, in the *New York Times* (June 12), 20.

King, G.B. (1928) "The 'negative' golden rule," *Journal of Religion* (1928) 8: 268–79 and (1935) 15: 59–62.

Kitcher, P. (1990) "The division of cognitive labor," *Journal of Philosophy* 87: 5–22.

Kohlberg, L. (1973) "The claim to moral adequacy of the highest stage of moral judgment," *Journal of Philosophy* 70: 630–48.

—— (1979) "Justice as reversibility," in P. Laslett and J. Fishkin (eds) *Philosophy, Politics and Society*, fifth series, New Haven, CT: Yale University Press, 257–72.

—— (1986) "A current statement on some theoretical issues," in S. and C. Modgil (eds) *Lawrence Kohlberg: Consensus and Controversy*, Philadelphia: Falmer, 485–546.

Kohlberg, L., Levine, C., and Hewer, A. (1983) *Moral Stages: A Current Formulation and a Response to Critics*, Basel: Karger.

Kohlberg, L., Boyd, D.R., and Levine, C. (1990) "The return of stage 6: Its principle and moral point of view," in T.E. Wren (ed.) *The Moral Domain*, London and Cambridge, MA: MIT Press, 151–81.

Krebs, D. (1982) "Psychological approaches to altruism: An evaluation," *Ethics* 92: 447–58.

Laertius, D. (1925) *Lives of Eminent Philosophers*, trans. R.D. Hicks, Cambridge: Harvard University Press.

Levin, M.E. (1979) "The universalizability of moral judgments revisited," *Mind* 88: 115–19.

Lewis, C.I. (1946) *An Analysis of Knowledge and Valuation*, La Salle, IL: Open Court.

—— (1955) *The Ground and Nature of the Right*, New York: Columbia.

—— (1957) *Our Social Inheritance*, Bloomington, IN: Indiana University Press.

—— (1969) *Values and Imperatives*, Stanford, CA: Stanford University Press.

Lincoln, A. (1854) *Abraham Lincoln: Speeches and Writings*, New York: Library of America, 1989.

Little, D., and Twiss, S.B. (1978) *Comparative Religious Ethics*, San Francisco: Harper and Row.

Locke, D. (1968) "The trivializability of universalizability," *Philosophical Review* 77: 25–44.

Locke, J. (1706) *An Essay Concerning Human Understanding*, London: Dent, 1967.

London, J. (1903) *The People of the Abyss*, New York: Garrett Press, 1970.

McArthur, H.K. (1967) "Golden rule," in J. Macquarrie (ed.) *Dictionary of Christian Ethics*, Philadelphia: Westminster Press, 136–7.

McCann, H.J. (1991) "Settled objectives and rational constraints," *American Philosophical Quarterly* 28: 25–36.

MacKay, A.F. (1986) "Extended sympathy and interpersonal utility comparisons," *Journal of Philosophy* 86: 305–22.

McKenzie, J.L. (1968) Comments in R.E. Brown, J.A. Fitzmyer, and R.E. Murphy (eds) *The Jerome Biblical Commentary*, Englewood Cliffs, NJ: Prentice-Hall, 2: 75 and 136.

Mackie, J.L. (1977) *Ethics: Inventing Right and Wrong,* London: Penguin.

Management (anonymous) (1985) "The golden rule leads to success at Robinson's," *Management Review* 74: 10.

Mead, F.S. (ed.) (1965) *The Encyclopedia of Religious Quotations*, Westwood, NJ: Flemming H. Revell.

Mead, G.H. (1934) *Mind, Self, and Society*, Chicago and London: University of Chicago Press.

Mill, J.S. (1861) *Utilitarianism*, New York: Library of Liberal Arts, 1957.

Monroe, K.R., Barton, M.C., and Klingemann, U. (1990) "Altruism and the theory of rational action: Rescuers of Jews in Nazi Europe," *Ethics* 101: 103–22.

Moore, G.E. (1912) *Ethics*, Oxford: Oxford University Press.

Mulholland, L.A. (1988) "Autonomy, extended sympathy, and the golden rule," in S.H. Lee (ed.) *Inquiries into Values*, Lewiston, NY: Edwin Mellen Press, 89–98.

Nagel, T. (1970) *The Possibility of Altruism*, Oxford: Clarendon Press.

Nash, A. (1923) *The Golden Rule in Business*, New York: Fleming H. Revell.

Nelson, L. (1956) *System of Ethics*, trans. Norman Guterman, New Haven, CT: Yale University Press.

New American Bible (1992) New York: Catholic Book Pub. Co.

Outka, G. (1972) *Agape: An Ethical Analysis*, New Haven, CT: Yale University Press.

Phipps, W.E. (1982) "The glittering rule," *Theology Today* 39: 194–8.

Piaget, J. (1948) *The Moral Judgment of the Child*, trans. Marjorie Gabain, Glencoe, IL: Free Press.

Plantinga, A. (1974) *The Nature of Necessity*, Oxford: Oxford University Press.

—— (1993a) *Warrant: The Current Debate*, New York: Oxford University Press.

—— (1993b) *Warrant and Proper Function*, New York: Oxford University Press.

Plato. *Republic*.

Pollock, L. (1973) "Freedom and universalizability," *Mind* 82: 234–48.

—— (1976) "The freedom principle," *Ethics* 86: 332–42.

Postow, B.C. (1991) "Gert's definition of irrationality," *Ethics* 102: 103–9.

Quine, W.V. (1986) *Philosophy of Logic*, Cambridge: Harvard University Press.

Rawls, J. (1971) *A Theory of Justice*, Cambridge: Harvard University Press.

—— (1980) "Kantian constructivism in moral theory," *Journal of Philosophy* 77: 515–72.

Ricoeur, P. (1990) "The golden rule," *New Testament Studies* 36: 392–7.

—— (1992) *Oneself as Another*, trans. Kathleen Blamey, Chicago: University of Chicago Press.

Ridley, M., and Dawkins, R. (1981) "The natural selection of altruism," in Rushton and Sorrentino 1981, 19–39.

Rieser, M. (1958) "An outline of intellectualistic ethics," *Journal of Philosophy* 55: 367–75.

Rimland, B. (1982) "The altruism paradox," *Psychological Reports* 51: 221–2.

Robinson, J.M. (1966) Review of A. Dihle's *Die Goldene Regel*, *Journal of the History of Philosophy* 4: 84–7.

Rogers, C.R. (1959) "A theory of therapy, personality, and interpersonal relationships as developed in the client-centered framework," in S. Koch (ed.) *Psychology: A Study of a Science*, New York: McGraw-Hill, 3: 184–256.

Romig, R.E. (1984) *Reasonable Religion: A Commonsense Approach*, Buffalo, NY: Prometheus Books.

Rønnow-Rasmussen, T. (1993) *Logic, Facts and Representation: An Examination of R.M. Hare's Moral Philosophy*, Lund, Sweden: Lund University Press.

Ross, D. (1930) *The Right and the Good*, Oxford: Clarendon Press.

Rost, H.T.D. (1986) *The Golden Rule*, Oxford: G. Ronald.

Rowley, H.H. (1940) "The Chinese sages and the golden rule," *Bulletin of the John Rylands Library* 24: 321–52.

Royce, J. (1886) *The Religious Aspects of Philosophy*, Boston: Houghton, Mifflin and Company.

Runes, D.D. (1959) *Pictorial History of Philosophy*, New York: Philosophical Library.

Rushton, J.P. (1982) "Altruism and society: A social learning perspective," *Ethics* 92 (1982): 425–46.

Rushton, J.P., and Sorrentino, R.M. (eds) (1981) *Altruism and Helping Behavior*, Hillsdale, NY: Lawrence Erlbaum.

Sapontzis, S.F. (1979) "The obligation to be rational," *Journal of Value Inquiry* 13: 294–8.

Sartre, J.P. (1957) *Existentialism and Human Emotions*, New York: Wisdom Library.

Schueler, G.F. (1984) "Some reasoning about preferences," *Ethics* 95: 78–80.

Schulman, M., and Mekler, E. (1994) *Bringing Up a Moral Child*, New York: Doubleday.

Seanor, D., and Fotion, N. (eds) (1988) *Hare and Critics*, Oxford: Oxford University Press.

Sedgwick, C.J. (1993) "The golden rule," *Expository Times* 104: 273–4.

Sharp, F.C. (1928) *Ethics*, New York: Century.

Shaw, B. (1903) "Maxims for revolutionists," in *Man and Superman*, New York: Wm. H. Wise & Company, 217–29.

Sher, G. (1977) "Hare, abortion, and the golden rule," *Philosophy and Public Affairs* 6: 185–90.

Sheridan, J.H. (1991) "Managing by the golden rule," *Industry Week* 240: 24.

Sidgwick, H. (1901) *The Methods of Ethics*, New York: Dover, 1966.

Silberman, C.E. (1964) *Crisis in Black and White*, New York: Random House.

Singer, M.G. (1955) "Generalization in ethics," *Mind* 64: 361–75.

—— (1963) "The golden rule," *Philosophy* 38 (1963): 293–314.

—— (1967) "The golden rule," in P. Edwards (ed.) *Encyclopedia of Philosophy*, vol. 3, London and New York: Macmillan and the Free Press, 365–7.

—— (1971) *Generalization in Ethics*, New York: Atheneum.

Singer, P. (1988) "Reasoning toward utilitarianism," in Seanor and Fotion 1988, 147–59.

Smiley, T., and Priest, G. (1993) "Can contradictions be true?" *Proceedings of the Aristotelian Society*, supplement 67: 17–54.

Stent, G.S. (1976) "The poverty of scientism and the promise of structuralist ethics," *Hastings Center Report* 6: 32–40.

Stotland, E. (1969) "Exploratory investigations of empathy," in L. Berkowitz (ed.) *Advances in Experimental Social Psychology*, vol. 4, London and New York: Academic Press, 271–314.

Stowe, H.B. (1852) *Uncle Tom's Cabin*, New York: Harper & Row, 1965.

Tasker, J.G. (1906) "Golden rule," in J. Hastings (ed.) *A Dictionary of Christ and the Gospels*, vol. 1, Edinburgh: T. & T. Clark, 653–5.

Thornton, M.T. (1971) "Hare's view of morality," *Mind* 80: 617–19.

Torrance, S.B. (1981) "Prescriptivism and incompleteness," *Mind* 90: 580–5.

Training (anonymous) (1992) "Sales techniques meet the golden rule," *Training* 29: 16.

Trivers, R.L. (1971) "The evolution of reciprocal altruism," *Quarterly Review of Biology* 46: 35–57.

—— (1981) "Sociology and politics," in E. White (ed.) *Sociobiology and Human Politics*, Lexington, MA: Lexington Books.

Twain, M. (1884) *The Adventures of Huckleberry Finn*, Berkeley: University of California Press, 1985.

Urantia Foundation. (1955) "The rule of living," in *The Urantia Book*, Chicago: The Urantia Foundation, 1650–1.

Vickrey, C.V. (1928) *International Golden Rule Sunday*, New York: George H. Doran.

Von Wright, G.H. (1963) *The Varieties of Goodness*, London: Routledge & Kegan Paul.

Votaw, C.W. (1904) "Sermon on the mount," in J. Hastings (ed.) *A Dictionary of the Bible*, New York: Charles Scribner's Sons, 5: 40–3.

Wattles, J. (1987) "Levels of meaning in the golden rule," *Journal of Religious Ethics* 15: 106–29.

—— (1993) "Plato's brush with the golden rule," *Journal of Religious Ethics* 21: 69–85.

—— (1996) *The Golden Rule and Human Kinship*, New York: Oxford University Press.

Weiss, P. (1941) "The golden rule," *Journal of Philosophy* 3: 421–30.

Westermarck, E. (1912) *The Origin and Development of the Moral Ideas*, London: Macmillan.

Whately, R. (1857) *Lessons on Morality*, Cambridge, MA: John Bartlett.

Williams, B. (1965) "Ethical consistency," *Proceedings of the Aristotelian Society*, supplement 39: 103–24.

Williams, J.N. (1981) "Inconsistency and contradiction," *Mind* 80: 601–2.

Williamson, T. (1982) "Intuitionism disproved?" *Analysis* 42: 203–7.

Wilson, B. (1988) "On a Kantian argument against abortion," *Philosophical Studies* 53: 119–30.

Wiseman, M.B. (1978) "Empathetic identification," *American Philosophical Quarterly* 15: 107–13.

Wulff, H.R. (1994) "Against the four principles: A Nordic view," In R. Gillon (ed.) *Principles of Health Care Ethics*, New York: John Wiley & Sons, 278–86.

Zack, N. (1993) *Race and Mixed Race*, Philadelphia: Temple University Press.

Zimmerman, M. (1962) "The 'is–ought': An unnecessary dualism," *Mind* 71: 53–61.

Index

abortion 61, 64, 140, 144, 147
Abrahams, I. 108, 110
Allinson, R.E. 108
animals, treatment of 81f, 117f
Aquinas 9
Aristotle 9, 21, 36, 39, 49, 105
Aronson, E. 31, 86
Atkinson, D.A. 108
Audi, R. 42
Augustine 105, 110f
autonomy 124, 152
axioms 44–6, 52f, 69f, 131, 180,
    193–5
Ayer, A.J. 58, 85

Bachmeyer, T.J. 116
Badcock, C.R. 178
Barcan formulas 3
Barry, B. 131
Becker, L.C. 116
beneficence and nonmaleficence
    108f, 126–8, 134
Bible 12, 16, 32f, 72, 76, 87, 89,
    105, 108f, 116, 127, 145, 147, 162,
    179
Blackburn, S. 56
Blackstone, W.T. 93
BO and BS (rationality of moral
    beliefs) 155
Bond, E.J. 174
Boyd, R.N. 34
Brandt, R.B. 59, 68, 79, 86, 132,
    140, 153, 168, 172f
Brink, D.O. 34
Broad, C.D. 93, 174
Brook, R. 131
Browne, L. 105
Bruce, D. 148
Brussel, E.E. 105

Bunch, A. 138
Burks, A. 70, 74, 192
Butler, J. 105

C-principles (consciousness) 25,
    53–5, 67, 92, 194f
Cadoux, A.T. 93
Carnap, R. 74
Carson, T.L. viii, 153, 168
Castañeda, H.N. 38, 182, 188
causality 46–52, 61, 66f, 88, 113,
    171f, 192f
Chan, W.T. 108f
Christianity 32, 105, 108f, 120, 125,
    134
Clarke, S. 72, 105
Cohen, J.L. 28
Cohen, B. 45
Confucius 12, 105f, 109
conjunctivity 23–5
consistency, concept of 15–25,
    29–40, 44–6, 69, 94–5, 121–3,
    149, 183, 189
conscientiousness 27, 40, 52–68,
    94f, 124, 134, 152, 158f, 165f, 194
contradictitis 30f, 56
counterfactuals 53, 65, 70, 113f,
    153, 159, 172, 192–6
Crombie, I.M. 125
cultural relativism 30, 32, 35, 58, 85,
    170

Dancy, J. 54, 71
Daniels, N. 34
Darwall, S.P. 44
Darwin, C. 105, 164, 177–9
De Morgan equivalence 190
deontic logic 10, 14, 38, 48–51,
    137–41, 181f, 186–8

Derksen, A.A. 23f
desires, rationality of 153–5
determinism 51f
Dewey, J. 9
Dickens, C. 102
Didrikson, B. 77
dissonance, cognitive 31, 59, 86,
    132, 178
DO and DS (rationality of desires)
    153– 5
Donagan, A. 50
don't-combine form 16–19, 44, 47f,
    53f, 76, 95, 99f, 104, 123, 143,
    176, 184f, 187
Dr Evil 20, 108
Dreier, J. 58
Dudman, V.H. 24

E-principles (ends–means) 46–52,
    65–7, 123, 134, 193f
Eckhoff, M. 118
Edgley, R. 174
Eisler, R. 108
Emerson, R.W. 35f
emotivism 11f, 30, 34, 58, 60, 85,
    87, 134, 143, 168–70
ends and means 5, 46–52, 56, 120,
    122f, 134, 145, 152f, 165f, 193
Epictetus 105, 147
Erikson, E.H. 116, 129, 132, 175
Ewing, A.C. 54

Festinger, L. 31, 86
Firth, R. 168
Fisher, M. 188f
Flynn, W.J. 119
Fodor, J.A. 28
Foley, R. 24, 152
formal ethical principles 1, 5–11,
    13f, 19–21, 35
formal ethics, concept of 1, 5f, 9–13,
    78, 174
formal logical principles 1–5, 8–9,
    21–3
formats for consistency principles
    25–27, 46, 101, 133f, 193

Frankena, W.K. 26, 28, 34, 52, 58,
    66, 125
Frege, G. 9, 16
Friedman, M. 152
future-regard formula 122f, 130

G-principles (golden rule) 13, 25,
    76, 93–120, 123f, 128, 136, 143,
    196f
Gauthier, D.P. 64, 175–7
Gensler, H.J. 2f, 14, 55, 67, 138,
    147, 181, 197
Gerhardsson, B. 125
Gert, B. 152
Gewirth, A. 93, 174
Gilligan, C. 122
God 1, 4, 9, 12, 32f, 60, 85–7, 120,
    125, 132–4, 145, 147, 152, 170,
    179
golden rule (GR): analogues
    125–31; Augustinian form 110f;
    central formulation 93–5; different
    from impartiality 75f; evolution
    177–9; formula of universal law
    121–3; literal version 13, 95f;
    misformulations 95–101, 143–8;
    moral education 165f; positive and
    negative 108–10; racism 93–4,
    147, 161–5, 173–4; symbolization
    196f; universal prescriptivism
    135–43; variations 101–4; various
    issues 104–20; why follow 131–4
Goldman, A.I. 176
Goodman, J. 93
Govier, T.R. 54

Haas, P.J. 158, 163f
Habermas, J. 87, 106, 129, 174
Hale, M. 98, 108
Handlin, H.C. 147
Hare, R.M. vii, viii, 11, 34, 41, 58,
    67, 71, 80, 85f, 91, 93, 97, 112,
    114f, 118, 131, 135–43, 150f,
    172–4, 184–6
Harman, G. 20, 24
Harrison, J. 168
Harsanyi, J.C. 26

Hartshorne, C. 3
Hegel, G.W.F. 36f
Heifetz, M. 105
Henry, M. 108f
Hertzler, J.O. 105
Hillel 12, 104
Hinduism 105
Hintikka, J. 189
Hitler, A. 4
Hobbes, T. 59, 68, 86, 105, 132
Hoche, H.U. 58, 97, 146
Hoffman, M.L. 132, 151
Holoviak, S.J. 147
Homer 106
Hume, D. 85; Hume's Law 66f;
  Humean rationality 48
Hume, R.E. 105
Husserl, E. 9
hypothetical imperatives 26, 31,
  46–9, 63, 100f, 124, 133, 145, 193

I-principles (impartiality) 74, 76,
  196
Ibberson, J. 41
ideal observer theory 9, 12, 30, 32,
  58, 60, 85–7, 134, 156, 168f
ideal rationality theories 30, 33–5,
  87, 134, 149–57, 168–72
idealistic desires 30, 59, 86, 131f
Ima: Absolutist 7, 54; Daughter 165;
  Hater 127f; Law-Student 124;
  Lazy 48, 51, 152; Masochist 99,
  107, 124; Racist 12, 17, 38, 79f,
  158–63, 173f; Robber 124; Student
  15f, 31; Terrorist 53
imagination 72–5, 82, 93f, 111–4,
  123, 128f, 150f, 153f, 161f, 164–7,
  179
impartiality 69–95, 124, 129f, 152,
  166
imperatives: accepting 40–4, 67,
  113f, 190–2; format for consistency principles 26; logic of 14,
  44–7, 50, 57–9, 181–6; moral judgments 34, 52–5, 57–9, 135–43;
  wide sense 41f

internalism 58
intuitions 6f, 11f, 29f, 33f, 60, 87,
  134, 169
Islam 105, 109
Isocrates 105

Jainism 105
Jennings, R.E. 54
Jesus 12, 33, 89, 105, 109
Johnson, D.M. 15
Johnson, O.A. 174
Judaism 12, 105, 109f, 132, 158,
  162–4

Kalin, J. 63
Kant, I. vii, viii, 3, 11, 68, 124f,
  128f, 146f; Kant's Law 49–52,
  67f; Kantian moral realism 180
Kaplan, M. 25
Katz, R.L. 151
Kaufman, W. 108
Kennedy, J.F. 93f, 111, 113, 161
King, G.B. 109
Kitcher, P. 24
Kohlberg, L. 109, 116, 127, 131f,
  152, 174f
Krebs, D. 132

L-principles (logicality) 16–20,
  23–6, 44f, 190
Laertius, D. 105
Levin, M.E. 85
Lewis, C.I. 35, 44, 93, 129, 174
Lincoln, A. 81, 147
Little, D. 117, 125
Locke, D. 71
Locke, J. 105
logicality (consistency in beliefs)
  15–40, 158–60, 165, 190
logicians 3, 8f, 16, 21–3, 27, 36, 38f,
  50, 137, 184f
London, J. 102
lottery paradox 24f
love commandments 89, 125–8, 164

McArthur, H.K. 105
McCann, H.J. 65

MacKay, A.F. 112
McKenzie, J.L. 109
Mackie, J.L. 28, 93, 122, 131
Maimonides, M. 105, 109
Mead, F.S. 105
Mead, G.H. 150, 174
Mekler, E.132, 166
metaethics 6, 9–11, 29–35, 83, 157,
    167–71
Mill, J.S. 9, 12, 66, 105, 134
modal logic 2–4, 8, 29, 112, 181,
    186f
modus tollens 5
Monroe, K.R. 132
Moore, G.E. 87
moral education 165–7
Mulholland, L.A. 82

Nagel, T. 174
Nash, A. 147
Nazis 132, 158, 162–4
Nelson, L. 129, 174
noncontradiction, law of 3, 21f, 36f
nonnaturalism 30, 33–5, 58, 60, 83,
    85, 87, 134, 143, 168f

O-principles (omniperspective,
    universal law, UL) 121–5, 130f,
    134, 142, 197
omni-perspective 45, 121
ought-implies-*can* 49–52, 67f, 180
Outka, G. 125

P-principles (prescriptivity): 52–9,
    62–5, 67, 94, 110, 117, 123f, 142,
    147, 194f
pacifism 55f, 97, 114, 195
Paine, T. 105
PB (probability and beliefs) 24f
permissives ("You may do A") 43f,
    52, 54, 57, 63f, 125, 135–43, 192,
    194
personal qualities for moral rational-
    ity 149, 151–5
Philo 105
Phipps, W.E. 147
Piaget, J. 116, 132, 174f, 178

Plantinga, A. 3, 19, 24f, 29, 152
Plato 16, 41, 45, 62
Pollock, L. 174
Postow, B.C. 152
PP (practice what you preach) 6f, 9f
prescriptivism 30, 33–5, 57f, 84f,
    135–43, 168, 170
prescriptivity principle 52–60, 135,
    139, 143, 180, 194
Priest, G. 3
promote-desire justifications 30f, 59,
    85f, 131–4
psychologistic view of logic 8, 29,
    62

QF (qualifications for formal ethics)
    20f, 25, 27f, 44, 65, 108, 117, 157
QL (qualifications for logic) 23
Quakers 147
Quine, W.V. 8, 29, 39, 189

R (rationality axiom) 44–7, 53f, 64,
    74, 94, 108, 117, 123, 131, 134,
    146f, 193
racism 12, 17f, 38, 61, 68, 79–81,
    111–3, 158–65, 169f, 173f
Raj, T. 163
Ramsey, F. 9
rationality 1, 13, 33–5, 44, 48, 58,
    107, 110f, 114f, 122f, 127f,
    149–80, 184, 193
Rawls, J. 18, 34, 130, 172
realism 3, 9, 35, 180
Reid, T. 105
relevantly similar cases 70f, 75–9,
    101f, 114, 124, 195f
retaliation (*lex talionis*) 89f, 115f,
    145
reversed situations 72–5, 93–102,
    196
Ricoeur, P. 93, 120, 125, 127, 145
Ridley, M. 178
Rieser, M. 108
Rimland, B. 133
Robinson, J.M. 145
Rogers, C.R. 127, 151

Romig, R.E. 120
Rønnow-Rasmussen, T. 115
Ross, D. 31f, 60, 87, 126, 134, 170
Rost, H.T.D. 106
Rowley, H.H. 109
Royce, J. 128
Runes, D.D. 105
Rushton, J.P. 132
Russell, B. 16, 36

Samaritan 72–5, 78f, 188
Sapontzis, S.F. 44, 152
Sartre, J.P. 28, 85, 129, 174
Schueler, G.F. 115
Schulman, M. 132, 166
Seanor, D. 112, 115, 118, 173
Sedgwick, C.J. 108
self-interest 30f, 59, 62f, 68, 86,
    121–3, 132f
self-regard principles 121–3
semiformal principles 11, 13, 149
Seneca 105
Severus 105
Sharp, F.C. 109
Shaw, B. 119
Sher, G. 82
Sheridan, J.H. 147
Sidgwick, H. 75, 100
Sikhism 105, 109
Silberman, C.E. 159
Singer, M.G. 109, 174
Singer, P. 86
Smiley, T. 3
Socrates 15
SP (strong prescriptivity) 57f, 84,
    135, 139, 142f, 194
Spinoza, B. 105
Stent, G.S. 178
Stevenson, C.L. 87
Stotland, E. 151
Stowe, H.B. 147, 165
SU (strong universalizability) 84f,
    135, 141–3
supernaturalism 12, 30, 32f, 58, 60,
    85–7, 170

Taoism 105, 109
Tasker, J.G. 108
Thales 105
Thornton, M.T. 64
tin rule 145
Torrance, S.B. 194
Trivers, R.L. 132, 178
Twain, M. 54
Twiss, S.B. 117, 125

U *see* universalizability
universal law (UL) 5, 13, 45, 103,
    116, 121, 123–5, 129–31, 134,
    146, 197
universal property 69–71, 82f, 192
universalizability 7f, 11, 69–92, 94,
    114, 117f, 123, 134f, 141–3, 166,
    180, 195f
Urantianism 105, 116
utilitarianism 12, 30f, 60, 71, 86,
    115, 126, 130, 134, 170, 172f

Vietnam 55
virtue 26f, 46, 68, 101
Vickrey, C.V. 146
Von Wright, G.H. 109
Votaw, C.W. 108

Wattles, J. viii, 93, 106, 116, 120,
    146
Weiss, P. 93
Westermarck, E. 106
Whately, R. 53, 93
Williams, B. 50
Williams, J.N. 25
Williamson, T. 4
Wilson, B. 64
Wiseman, M.B. 112
Wittgenstein, L. 9
Wulff, H.R. 119

Zack, N. 159
Zaharias, B. 77
Zimmerman, M. 26
Zoroaster 105

DATE DUE

JAN 0 2 2003			
			Printed in USA

HIGHSMITH #45230

Formal Ethics

Inspired by the ethical theories of Kant and Hare, and modeled on formal logic, formal ethics is the study of formal ethical principles. More broadly, it studies rational patterns in our ethical thinking.

Formal ethics focuses on the golden rule: "Treat others as you want to be treated." It also deals with a family of related formal ethical principles, which include:

- Follow your conscience.
- Practice what you preach.
- Be logically consistent in your beliefs.

These principles are important and useful. But each leads to absurdities if taken literally. Formal ethics formulates these principles more clearly and adequately, organizes them into a defensible system, and shows how they can help us to think more rationally about morality.

Formal ethics supplements, but does not replace, traditional ethical theories. It does not promote any particular foundational position, but explains and defends a number of formal tools for moral reasoning that can enhance virtually any approach to ethical questions.

While intended mainly for specialists in ethics and moral philosophy, *Formal Ethics* is written in simple and direct language. It will appeal not only to professionals, but also to graduates and advanced undergraduates studying moral philosophy, ethics, and applied logic.

Harry J. Gensler, S.J., is Associate Professor of Philosophy at the University of Scranton. He is the author of *Gödel's Theorem Simplified*, *Logic: Analyzing and Appraising Arguments*, and *Symbolic Logic: Classical and Advanced Systems*. He has also written *LogiCola*, a logic instructional program.